D1114196

CHANGING LITERACIES

CHANGING EDUCATION

Series Editors:
Professor Andy Hargreaves, Ontario Institute for Studies in Education
Professor Ivor Goodson, University of Western Ontario

This authoritative series addresses the key issues raised by the unprecedented levels of educational change now facing schools and societies throughout the world.

The different directions of change can seem conflicting and are often contested. Decentralized systems of school self-management are accompanied by centralized systems of curriculum and assessment control. Moves to develop more authentic assessments are paralleled by the tightened imposition of standardized tests. Curriculum integration is being advocated in some places, more specialization and subject departmentalization in other.

These complex and contradictory cross-currents pose real challenges to theoretical and practical interpretation in many fields of education and constitute an important and intriguing agenda for educational change. *Changing Education* brings together leading international scholars who address these vital issues with authority and accessibility in areas where they are noted specialists. The series will commission books from all parts of the world in an attempt to cover the global and interlinked nature of current changes.

Forthcoming titles

John Elliott: *Changing Curriculum*
Colin Lankshear: *Changing Literacies*
Kenneth Leithwood: *Changing Leadership for Changing Schools*
Shirley Steinberg and Joe Kincheloe: *Changing Multiculturalism*

CHANGING
LITERACIES

COLIN LANKSHEAR
with James Paul Gee,
Michele Knobel and Chris Searle

OPEN UNIVERSITY PRESS
Buckingham · Philadelphia

LC 149
.L 255
1997

Open University Press
Celtic Court
22 Ballmoor
Buckingham
MK18 1XW

and 1900 Frost Road, Suite 101
Bristol, PA 19007, USA

First published 1997

Copyright © Colin Lankshear 1997

All rights reserved. Except for the quotation of short passages for the purposes of criticism and review, no part of this publication may be reproduced, stored in a retrieval system, or transmitted, in any form or by any means, electronic, mechanical, photocopying, recording or otherwise, without prior permission of the publisher or a licence from the Copyright Licensing Agency Limited. Details of such licences (for reprographic reproduction) may be obtained from the Copyright Licensing Agency Ltd of 90 Tottenham Court Road, London, W1P 9HE.

A catalogue record of this book is available from the British Library

ISBN   0 335 19636 5 (pbk)   0 335 19637 3 (hbk)

Library of Congress Cataloging-in-Publication Data
Lankshear, Colin.
    Changing literacies / Colin Lankshear with James Paul Gee . . . [*et al.*].
        p.   cm. — (Changing education)
    Includes bibliographical references and index.
    ISBN 0-335-19637-3 (hbk)   ISBN 0-335-19636-5 (pbk)
    1. Literacy—Social aspects.   2. Sociolinguistics.   3. Critical
pedagogy.   4. Educational innovations.   5. Educational change.
I. Title.   II. Series.
LC149.L255   1997   96-38317
                                                              CIP

Typeset by Type Study, Scarborough
Printed in Great Britain by St Edmundsbury Press, Bury St Edmunds, Suffolk

for
peter, jen, richard, anna, michael, rima and pat
keeping the faith

y para
mi familia en San José, Monte Fresco
mi cariño, siempre
adelante

CONTENTS

SERIES EDITORS' PREFACE

Around the world, schools, and the societies of which they are a part, are confronting the most profound changes – changes the like of which have not been seen since the last great global movement of economic and educational restructuring more than a century ago. The fundamental forms of public education that were designed for an age of heavy manufacturing and mechanical industry are under challenge and fading fast as we move into a world of high technology, flexible workforces, more diverse school populations, downsized administrations and declining resources.

What is to follow is uncertain and unclear. The different directions of change can seem conflicting and are often contested. Decentralized systems of school self-management are accompanied by centralized systems of curriculum and assessment control. Moves to develop more authentic assessments are paralleled by the tightened imposition of standardized tests. Curriculum integration is being advocated in some places, more specialization and subject departmentalization in others.

These complex and contradictory cross-currents pose real challenges to theoretical and practical interpretation in many fields of education, and constitute an important and intriguing agenda for educational change – and for this series, which is intended to meet a deep-seated need among researchers and practitioners. International, social and technological changes require a profound and rapid response from the educational community. By establishing and interpreting the nature and scope of educational change, *Changing Literacies* will make a signification' contribution to meeting this challenge.

We are delighted that Colin Lankshear has provided this series with a provocative and critical account of *Changing Literacies*. So much of the work

on educational change and restructuring is silent as to matters of empowerment and social justice. Hence Lankshear's long-standing commitment to the
exploration of these issues was attractive to us in first commissioning this
volume for the series. Ivor Goodson had worked with Colin in conceptualizing and commissioning a previous book, *Literacy, Schooling and Revolution*.
This volume became a prize-winning text which pioneered some of the
investigation of the interface between literacies and social change.

Following on from this pioneering text, Lankshear explores through a
critical and culturalist perspective the debates and discourses which surround
literacy. In the initial chapters in the book he lays out his value position with
regard to patterns of literacy, language and social process. It is a powerful and
attractive statement of morality and values in a field which is not always
driven to state or explore such perspectives.

In the central part of the book he relates this value position to an
exploration of the emergent 'new work order'. So much of the new division of
labour is emergent that exploratory discourses of this sort are incredibly
important. Lankshear's tentative but powerful cognitive maps are generative
not least because they begin to explore the parameters of the new work order
but also because he applies this to the Third World, which is likely to benefit
least from these new structures. By placing this analysis of social structure at
the centre of the text, readers are allowed to interrogate versions of literacy
and patterns of changing literacy with a clear handle on how this interacts
with the global division of labour.

From this cleverly worked platform of statements of morality linked to
analysis of social structure, Lankshear goes on to investigate the perils and
potentials of new technologies. His work in this regard is highly innovative,
focusing as it does on the student's social practices and the differential impact
on different social groups of new technological innovations.

We have long been an admirer of Lankshear's work on literacies and hope
that readers of this volume will agree that his work takes literacy studies to
new and exciting thresholds. Certainly those involved in 'Changing Education' would be wise to read and digest the messages contained in this book.

ACKNOWLEDGEMENTS

To Jim Gee, Michele Knobel and Chris Searle – my esteem and thanks, always, for being who and what you are: educators and comrades, true to the end of the road, as honest as the day is long, and as wise as we need to be. In your own ways you make it all make sense. I hope I'm not too old to learn.

To Pedro and Salvadora, Isabel and Santiago, Cándida, Luisa, Mamá, Noél, all your family, and to Padre José – thank you for the education of a lifetime, and for creating such joy out of dust. Had Uncle Sam *known* you, maybe he wouldn't have done it. Maybe.

To Cathie Wallace – thank you for so many ideas and so much grace.

To Michael and Rima Apple, fellow travellers – my thanks, always, for seeing me safely started on a difficult but necessary journey, for being staunch throughout, and for helping so much with the map.

To Ivor Goodson, Shona Mullen, Pat Lee, Sue Hadden, Anita West and the rest of the team at Open University Press – thank you for the chance to put this book together, and for all your work in seeing it to completion.

To Ivan Snook – thank you for an exemplary undergraduate and postgraduate education, and for your superb mentoring. I'll esteem your contributions to my life always.

To the Faculty of Education, Queensland University of Technology my appreciation for research funding and moral support, without which this work could not have been undertaken.

I wish to acknowledge also the goodwill of the following organizations and journals for granting permission to republish modified versions of previously published work and invited addresses: *Critical Forum* (for much of Chapter 1); the Australian Curriculum Studies Association (who originally commissioned and published a position paper on critical literacy, upon which

Chapter 2 is based); *Discourse* (whose editors invited and published the original version of Chapter 4); the Australian Reading Association (for inviting a 1995 conference keynote address, which has become Chapter 6 here).

FOREWORD: A DISCOURSE APPROACH TO LANGUAGE AND LITERACY

James Paul Gee

What's Colin Lankshear up to in this book? From my perspective, he's up to what anyone adopting a sociocultural approach to language and literacy ought to be. I want to try, very briefly, to say just what this is. We can start with our imaginations.

Imagine yourself interacting with: an ebullient toddler; a stodgy old boss; your closest friend; an exciting new lover. Imagine yourself in these places: cheering from the stands for the home-town team; in church at the funeral of a relative; at a bar after a long hard day; in your bedroom all by yourself. Imagine yourself holding: a cute little kitten (you just want to cuddle it); a taut bongo drum (you just want to bang it); a highly sensitive photo in a plain brown wrapper (you just want to peek); a 2000-year-old precious relic (you just don't want to drop it). Imagine yourself saying these sorts of words: declaiming a moving poem; reading aloud the gruesome details of a shocking murder; telling a dirty joke; asking for something in a foreign language; announcing the death of a loved one. Imagine yourself in: a $2000 'power suit'; a clown costume, red nose and all; a skimpy swimsuit; your underwear; fancy wedding garments.

Different people, different places and activities, different objects and tools, different words, different clothes, all of these bring out — we might even say 'recruit' — different aspects of ourselves. In relationship to and with different people, places, objects, tools, words and clothes we feel like, act like, and look like *different people*. We are different *situated selves*. As we imagine the scenarios above, we can feel identity changes at work in our bodies.

The scenarios above suggest a way of looking at identity, a way that stresses what I will call 'coordinations'. Coordinations are made up of different elements, some of which are people and some of which are other sorts of things. Each element in a coordination, whether human or not, simultaneously plays two roles: it actively *coordinates* the other elements ('in its own interests') and it passively *gets coordinated by* the other elements in the coordination (Latour 1987; Knorr Cetina 1992). The elements in a coordination are (among others): people – as well as their ways of thinking, feeling, valuing, acting, interacting, dressing, gesturing, moving, and being – places, activities, institutions, objects, tools, language, and other symbols. Each element gets and is got 'in sync', 'in step', 'with it'. Within such coordinations we humans become *recognizable* to ourselves and to others and *recognize* ourselves, other people, and things as meaningful in distinctive ways.

Speaking of coordinations highlights not just human actors, but the role of non-human things, as well, whether these are characteristic ways of talking, thinking, or valuing, or objects, tools, or places. Non-human things, too, can play an active role as coordinators of the other elements, and not just a passive role as getting coordinated. Hammers, classrooms and textbooks have certain affordances that 'invite' certain uses and resist other ones. Latour (1994), in making this same point, refers to a speed bump as a 'concrete policeman' which controls human drivers in certain ways, and which solidifies, in concrete, certain 'interests' (albeit ultimately human ones). Of course, the affordances and resistances of non-human elements in coordinations can be overridden, but so, too, can human affordances, intentions and resistances.

What makes us humans multiple beings, then (as, too, what makes non-human things like texts, dwellings or cars multiple beings), is our entry into multiple coordinations, each of which has the capacity to tease out of us a different situated self. Me holding a pennant and shouting cheers in the stands with the home-town crowd is a different me than the me holding lecture notes at a podium in a graduate class in linguistics. Each of these coordinations involves, too, different ways of thinking, feeling, acting, interacting, gesturing, dressing, and so on and so forth. But, if this is what makes each of us multiple, then what makes each of us also one? After all, most of us are not schizophrenics or victims of 'multiple personality' disorder.

Well, of course, we each have but one body. But what is important about this body is the coordinations it has been part of. Your body (and mind) has its own unique history, it has moved through a unique *trajectory* of coordinations. However, it is important at once to note that your trajectory through a myriad of such coordinations – real as it is (the world is *not* 'just discourse') – is meaningless unless and until it has been *narrativized* by yourself and others. Your own trajectory constrains what narratives you or others can tell about it; but different narratives render your trajectory meaningful in quite different ways. Narratives, of course, are themselves elements in coordinations, with their own trajectories – but, for now, we are discussing the human and will return only later to the non-human.

Ironically, then, your trajectory through highly multiple coordinations makes you unique and individual – it is your very multiplicity that renders you an individual. This perspective – people as variably narrativizable trajectories through multiple coordinations that render different identities recognizable – greatly attenuates several standard social science dichotomies. The dichotomy between the individual (in our terms, the trajectory) and the social (in our terms, the coordinations that constitute the trajectory) is muted. The dichotomy between people as active subjects (coordinating others) and as passive recipients (getting coordinated) is also muted: people are active and passive at one and the same time, since coordinating-and-getting-coordinated is the glue that holds the coordination together in the first place.

Another dichotomy that is muted is that between 'culture' and 'nature'. The social and cultural do *not* precede and 'determine' coordinations; rather, the social and the cultural and the elements of coordinations (human and non-human) come into existence simultaneously. They codetermine each other. To see this rather obtuse point more clearly, consider this: not just any random throwing together of humans and non-humans *works* as a coordination in the sense of giving rise to recognizable situated identities for each of the elements in the coordination. Randomly throwing people and objects into a classroom won't get you a working coordination. To work in this sense, the coordination itself has to be recognized as a recurrent one, the sort of configuration that has occurred before – not exactly, of course, but as a recognizable pattern.

This recognizability as a pattern makes the coordination a constituent of what I will call a 'Discourse' (with a big 'D', as opposed to 'discourse', which means just stretches of language, see Gee 1992, 1990/1996). A Discourse is a way of 'being together in the world' for humans, their ways of thinking and feeling (etc.), and for non-human things, as well, such that coordinations of elements, and the elements themselves, take on recognizable identities. 'Discourse' names the patterning of coordinations, their recognizability, as well as that of their elements.

For example: in this coordination, here and now, that person is recognizable to himself, others in his Discourse, and to some others outside his Discourse, as a Los Angeles African-American gang member (of a certain sort) and that street as a 'hang out' and those clothes as insignia and that car as a . . . (you see, I have run out of the ability to name the elements, because I am not in the Discourse, and, it is clear, I am not able to coordinate its elements and get coordinated by them, which is just a way to repeat that I am not in the Discourse).

There are, of course, innumerable Discourses (e.g. gangs, academic disciplines, bar gatherings, ethnic groups, friendship networks, types of men, women, gays, children, students, classrooms, workers, workplaces, etc. and etc.). Discourses, by their very nature, cannot have discrete boundaries – after all, they are made up of coordinations which are 'enough alike' to count as the 'same', coordinations which are always changing and moving through history (and whose elements are always being contested by other Discourses). But the key thing to note here is that *at one and the same time* the Discourse (the recognizability of the coordination and its elements) is what gives the elements meaning (identity) *and* the elements having meaning (identity) is what constitutes the Discourse. Gender, class, ethnicity, culture, social group: these are just words by which academics and non-academics alike seek to carve up the world of ever-changing, transforming, and emerging Discourses, which is far vaster than any such labels can capture.

Thus far, I have stressed, for the most part, the human elements of coordinations, and, of course, we humans do have pride of place as the ultimate narrativizers and recognizers. One type of element of coordinations that is of particular interest to those of us who work on language and literacy are, of course, texts (whether oral or written). Of course, we can say about texts just what we have said about people. Imagine a particular book on theoretical biology. Now imagine it in the hands of a biologist, a stylistics professor in the English department, a historian of science, a critic of jargon and rationalism, an ardent creationist, an undergraduate needing to plagiarize something – anything – at the last minute, a parent looking to read some nonsense to her toddler, an actor trying to sound erudite or a comedian looking for parody. Imagine the 'biology' book left out on the coffee table to impress guests, sitting in the library to impress an accreditation committee, in a lab with a stack of reference books, on reserve in the library for the highly motivated student, in the physicist's office with the new mail. As the text coordinates and is coordinated (remember it has its affordances, you can't do just anything with it, at least not easily), it takes on different situated identities, has different meanings. Apart from some coordination – which must be in some Discourse if the coordination itself is to have meaning – the text has no recognizability, no meaning, no identity.

Just as in the human case, we can ask: if the text is multiple, what makes it also one? And, again, the answer is the same: the text has an actual historical trajectory through multiple coordinations, though one that stands always in need of narrativization. We call it a 'biology book' to privilege its affordances and the Discourse which has most determined its trajectory (thus far).

For those of us who work in the area of sociocultural (really, Discourse) approaches to language and literacy, there is some bite to this perspective on humans and texts. The bite is this: it makes absolutely no sense to take the text out of the coordinations it is in, its trajectory through 'coordination space', and the Discourses which render all this meaningful. Outside these it is, quite literally, meaningless, unrecognizable, nothing (the same is true also, of course, not just for texts, but, for instance, for various tools and technologies, as well). In this sense, there is *no other* approach to texts, language, and literacy than a sociocultural one. The decontextualized approach typical of traditional work in reading and literacy is, for the most part, incoherent. What coherence it has it gains through quietly and indirectly smuggling context and Discourses back in, often by tacitly assuming mainstream, school-based, middle-class, or dominant Discourses as the only 'real' ones.

Sociocultural approaches to language and literacy are committed not only to situating people and texts in coordinations, trajectories, and Discourses, but to a certain sort of what we might call, in an unfortunately vexed and ambiguous phrase, 'critical literacy'. For me, critical literacy arises from the very nature of elements-in-coordinations-in-Discourses. Any element is meaningful only within a recognizable coordination, that is, a coordination that is part of a Discourse. But, as we have repeatedly said, elements are differentially meaningful in different coordinations within and across Discourses. In fact, Discourses contest with each other for the 'right' to 'name' ('recognize') specific elements. It is here that we gain an edge for critical literacy, in the sense in which I want to use that term.

Let me give a concrete example of how an element changes significance as it switches between Discourses which are competing over it. Roger Lewontin, in his book *Biology as Ideology* (1991), points out that, from the point of view of medical science, it is a truism that the cause of tuberculosis is the tubercle bacillus. Tuberculosis, tubercle bacillus, a certain way of thinking and valuing, as well as various practices in various biological and medical sites coordinate, in various recognizable ways, across time and space, so as to make this statement an inevitable truth.

However, Lewontin points out that tuberculosis was a very common disease in the sweatshops and factories of the nineteenth century, whereas it was much less common among country people and in the upper classes. So, why don't we conclude that *the* cause of tuberculosis is unregulated industrial capitalism? In fact, in light of the history of health and disease in modern Europe, that explanation makes good sense. Lewontin argues that an examination of records first systematically recorded in the 1830s in Britain and a bit later in North America show that most people did, indeed, die of infectious diseases. But as the nineteenth century progressed, the death rate from all these diseases continuously decreased, with no obvious cause, and certainly not any strictly medical cause. For instance, by the time a chemical therapy was introduced for tuberculosis in the early twentieth century, more than 90 per cent of the decrease in the death rate from this disease had already occurred (pp. 43–4).

It was not modern sanitation or less crowding in cities that led to the progressive reductions in the death rate, since the major killers in the nineteenth century were respiratory and not waterborne, and parts of our cities are as crowded today as they were in the 1850s. More likely, claims Lewontin, the reduction in death from infectious diseases is due to general improvement in nutrition related to an increase in the real wage in 'developed countries': 'In countries like Brazil today, infant mortality rises and falls with decreases and increases in the minimum wage' (p. 44).

Thus, one Discourse (actually a set of biological and medical Discourses) renders the statement 'the tubercle bacillus causes tuberculosis' obviously true. Another Discourse (a sociopolitical one) renders it problematic. One Discourse makes the bacillus a *cause* (and a 'final' one at that), the other makes it but an *agent* of a larger cause, namely unregulated capitalism. The two Discourses compete over the way in which the bacillus is to be coordinated with other human and non-human elements (and the bacillus, of course, offers its own affordances and resistances). Further, we see in this case how one Discourse 'cuts off context' before the other one does, and, in doing so, 'cuts off' meaning before it gets social and political.

Critical literacy, then, is, for me, the ability to juxtapose Discourses, to watch how competing Discourses frame and re-frame various elements. And this is an act that always gives rise immediately to questions and issues about the interests, goals, and power relationships among and within Discourses. Ultimately, critical literacy, however, requires the creation of a new Discourse, with a new community of human elements, that has as its goal the re-framing of elements, human and otherwise, in the name of social justice and more humane treatment for all, human and non-human, as well (Lemke 1995).

This is exactly what Colin Lankshear does in this book. He animates people, texts, objects, technologies, countries, and social settings within their coordinations, trajectories, and Discourses; he exposes how Discourses contest and transform various elements, how they compete to name various trajectories; he continually re-frames elements, coordinations, and Discourses in an emerging critical Discourse passionately committed to fairness, freedom, and social justice – though, true to his roots in philosophy, he interrogates these words as themselves elements with their own trajectories through coordination and Discourse-space.

You will find here a broom produced in a communal factory in a rural village in Nicaragua: is it part of a peasant Discourse, the 'old' capitalism (colonial style), or the new 'quality'-dominated capitalism? A high tech application on the Internet by a 5-year-old: is it exploitation or liberation or both? Are new coordinations here subserving old or new Discourses? Words like 'empowerment', 'flexibility', and 'learning' on the tongues of academics and business people alike: do they mean the same thing? Are Discourses beginning to converge and realign? Poverty and starvation in the Third World and in cities of the 'developed' world: are poor people accidental by-products of global changes, causes of their own degradation, or in need of knowledge about how they have been actively coordinated by dominant social and political forces? Academic and non-academic texts: what sorts of alignments, and in whose favour, do they form across different Discourses? What do they look like when we juxtapose to them the voices of the poor and oppressed speaking out of their own Discourses?

Colin Lankshear roams across these and many other elements within coordinations within Discourses, undeterred by sociological pessimism, hacking away at the underbrush, clearing a path for a new critical-liberatory Discourse. The task is massive, the path just begun. Nonetheless, Lankshear has brought a bit of light into the darkness. It remains to see what strange and wonderful new plants grow in the space he has cleared.

INTRODUCTION

It is by now pretty much a cliché to say that the pace, scope, and impact of changes in the current period are as great as at any previous time in human history – if not greater. Indeed, for some who have caught the current waves of change, and 'surfed' them to the limit in building successful and powerful careers and wielding influence, 'change' hardly seems an appropriate term for the dynamism, speed, and upheaval of New Times. Tom Peters, high-flying architect of 'liberation management' and vortical advocate of 'crazy organizations for crazy times', adopts characteristically high ground here: 'Change? Change! Yes, we've almost all, finally, embraced the notion that "change is the only constant." Well, sorry. Forget change! The word is feeble. Keep saying "revolution"' (Peters 1994: 8).

Yet, while 'change is the only constant' becomes a contemporary commonplace, we are also increasingly reminded from other quarters that *'plus ça change, plus c'est la même chose'*. While change undoubtedly is occurring on many fronts and at many levels, on yet other fronts and at yet other levels it seems to be a case of 'business as usual'. Many things seem indeed to remain the same. As technological and organizational changes bring untold innovations to contemporary work and workplaces on all levels from the most local to the global, we nonetheless find familiar patterns of social advantage and disadvantage, wealth and poverty, control and subordination, continuing to play themselves out – and, if anything, becoming even sharper and more polarized than we had been accustomed to during the long boom of the postwar decades (see Gee *et al.* 1996). Despite changing approaches to and technologies of learning and remediation in classrooms, we continue to find familiar patterns of scholastic achievement and 'underachievement' being reproduced along lines of race-ethnicity, social class, gender, and language background.

This book explores the dynamics of things changing and things remaining the same with respect to literacy. Undeniably, many changes have occurred around literacy during the past two or three decades. For a start, our very *way of talking* about the field of text-mediated practices has changed. Whereas 'literacy' used to refer almost solely to contexts of adult (remedial or compensatory) learning, we now speak routinely of literacy with reference to school-based activities of reading and writing, and learning to do so. In Australia, for example, the Australian Reading Association has recently been renamed the Australian Literacy Educators' Association; its flagship journal, the *Australian Journal of Reading*, was reconstituted as the *Australian Journal of Language and Literacy* some years previously. And the federal government funds a commonwealth research programme of Children's Literacy National Projects. In the United States, President Clinton's February 1996 initiative to ensure that all US children become proficient with new technologies in readiness for the new millennium is called the technology 'literacy' challenge. The change from talking about reading and writing to talking about literacy with respect to children has been somewhat uneven, occurring more commonly in some places than others. As recently as 1992, Chris Searle observed that 'the word *literacy* is not commonly used within the context of British schools', being 'much more widely adopted by adult educators than by schoolteachers' (Searle 1993a: 168). Literacy talk has, however, become more common in Britain subsequently, but probably does still not approximate to its currency in, say, Australia.

This change in literacy's field of reference has been closely associated with significant changes in the ways many theorists have been thinking about text-mediated practices. Many of these changes are captured in Brian Street's (1984, 1993) distinction between the 'autonomous' and 'ideological' models of literacy, and have recently received close attention in the 'multiliteracies' approach of the New London Group (1996). Notions of reading and writing as specific (cognitive) abilities or sets of skills based on an identifiable technology (e.g. alphabetic script) held sway within educational theory and practice, almost to the point of having a monopoly, until the 1970s. Since then greater theoretical space has been usurped by conceptions of reading and writing which stress their inherently *social* character and embeddedness in larger social *practices*. Jim Gee puts the following spin on this change: 'On the traditional view, literacy is seen as a largely psychological ability – something to do with our "heads". We, on the other hand, see literacy as a matter of social practices – something to do with social, institutional, and cultural relationships' (Gee *et al.* 1996: 1).

A burgeoning field of literacy studies has emerged with a strong socio-cultural emphasis. Insofar as traditional psychological emphases have maintained a presence here, they have done so largely around appropriations of work from social cognition, undertaken by people like Jean Lave (Lave 1988; Lave and Wenger 1991), Barbara Rogoff (1990) and Jim Wertsch (1991). 'Literacy studies' privileges meaning over mechanical skills, with 'meaning' seen much more in terms of sociocultural processes than as private internal cognitive states or events. Within this frame, questions of power and the role of literacies as social practices within social productions and distributions of power have often been foregrounded, and 'the politics of literacy' has emerged as a well-subscribed focus of theoretical attention. Changing centres of gravity around functional literacy, cultural literacy, (social) critical literacy and their many 'sub versions' (Wallace 1992; Hamilton *et al.* 1994; Luke and Walton 1994), have been apparent during the past two decades. The once more or less generic field of 'adult literacy' has seen the emergence of 'workplace literacy' as a more specialized sub-domain. And most recently, those who adopt a sociocultural approach to literacy have begun to address in earnest the implications of current developments in electronic technologies, which threaten to move us from print to post-print text cultures. Under the impact of the rapid and broad-based incursion of digital texts into everyday routines, our ways of thinking about text-mediated practices are changing dramatically (New London Group 1996).

The theme of 'changing literacies' can also be approached in terms of changes in broad theoretical orientations toward text-mediated practices that have occurred within sociocultural approaches to literacy. During the past decade a marked shift has occurred within sociocultural studies of literacy, away from a structuralist paradigm toward a post-structuralist paradigm. This is, perhaps, most evident in changing views of meaning: what meanings *are*, where meanings *come from*, how meanings *get fixed*, what *authorizes* particular meanings; and in changing notions of how we treat or handle texts so far as meanings and meaning-making are concerned (Gee 1993b). For example, from a 'critical literacy' perspective we have seen moves from notions of 'ideology critique' based on neo-Marxist positions (such as those developed by members of the Frankfurt School) or, alternatively, derived from the work of Paulo Freire in the 1950s and 1960s, toward distinctively poststructuralist variants such as (textual) deconstruction, discourse analysis, and the like.

At the grassroots educational level of classroom approaches, 'changing literacies' may capture relative shifts in emphasis among 'traditional' approaches (drill and skill, phonics, basic skills, 'look and say', and the like), characteristically 'progressive' approaches (e.g. whole language, process writing, etc.), and 'post-progressivist' approaches (such as 'genre-based' approaches which draw on systemic functional linguistics, 'critical language awareness approaches', 'multiliteracies', etc.).

These are among the many sub-themes of changing literacies that present themselves for investigation if we focus on 'changing' as an adjective. Most of these themes are explored from one angle or another in the chapters which follow. There are, of course, many more potential angles and sub-themes available than can possibly be addressed in a single volume, and I am aware that many have necessarily been passed by here.

'Changing' also functions as a verb. In this case the idea of 'changing literacies' refers to *projects* designed and carried out with a view to transforming our textual practices and the larger social practices with which they are associated. This angle on 'changing literacy' also permeates the book. Chapter 2, for instance, describes an approach to classroom literacy across the curriculum I would like to see more fully present in our children's education and which, in collaboration with others, I have promoted and encouraged in small ways via teacher in-service programmes and like initiatives. At a much more ambitious and influential point on the project scale, we find the grand projects enacted by 'fast capitalist' and 'high tech' advocates. These are projects that are well in train and may seem now to lie beyond critique and political contestation. Both projects are backed by enormous resources of power and influence. Yet we accept these projects uncritically and passively at our peril. They cry out for our active critical engagement in thought and deed. Chapters 4, 5 and 7, in particular, aim to convince us of this and, in doing so, to indicate some of the merits of adopting a critical perspective on textual practices and textual politics (see Lemke 1995) within a broadly sociocultural approach to literacy.

Finally, not even literacy academics remain *completely* static. Some of us certainly change our literacies in theory and practice more slowly than we should, and, when we *do* make changes, cover less new ground than we might. This book hopefully conveys something of my own changing literacies, and to those who seek wider but complementary visions I commend the Foreword and Afterword to this volume and the larger works of their authors.

So much for changes. What remains the same? Quite a lot, it seems. So much, in fact, one may well wonder whether the most effective changes in literacy remain yet at the level of sociocultural literacy *theory*, unrealized to any significant and abiding sense in formal educational practices.

In countries like our own, annual 'league tables of school achievement' continue to reflect long-standing, and by now thoroughly familiar patterns of institutionalized 'success' and 'failure'. Of course, particular 'critical read-ings' of the world suggest we should expect precisely this. Indeed, right now we should expect even more intensified differentials than we have been used to, along both established lines of advantage and disadvantage as well, perhaps, as some new ones. In the context of a new work order (Gee *et al.* 1996: 47), 'the new capitalism is in danger of producing and reproducing an even steeper pyramid than the old capitalism did'. This requires formal education to produce and legitimate even more intense differentials of scholarly success and failure than hitherto, in order that social and economic outcomes continue to present themselves as being tolerably fair and explicable.

As Kevin Harris (1979) stated the problem almost 20 years ago, if all students were 'successfully educated' – if, in other words, 'educational reform' ensured quality schools and quality education for all (Gee *et al.*: 47) – how could we expect all citizens to accept the rules by which a capitalist economic and social order (whether 'new' or 'old') plays? Who would accept unemployment or underemployment sanguinely? Who would willingly choose to be the servants, the 'falling four fifths' of the new work order, as Robert Reich (1992) calls them? Such are the 'non- or low value-adding' routine production workers and in-person service workers, who increasingly constitute a global 'outsourceable' labour market available to multinational enterprises at market rates and without the need to be provided with benefits or even 'good conditions'. To put things another way, if only the relatively small proportion of knowledge workers necessary for modern economies – the value-adding 'symbolic analysts' of the new work order (Gee *et al.* 1996: 177) – actually *need* high order literacies; if, beyond 'demands for basic numeracy and the ability to read', routine production and in-person service work call primarily 'for reliability, loyalty, the capacity to take direction and . . . a pleasant demeanour', why *wouldn't* we expect 'literacies' to mean for most students 'basic competencies', and 'technological literacy' to mean 'keyboarding skills'?

In other words, *'plus ça change, plus c'est la même chose'*. The tendency for formal education to 'broke' differential learning achievement outcomes remains unchanged or, if anything, intensified – new rhetorics of education for capability and competency-based education notwithstanding. Likewise, the underlying need for schools to generate unequal outcomes remains unchanged and, most likely, intensified – given the contours of the new global informational economy, its distinctive new work order (Carnoy *et al.* 1993; see Gee *et al.* 1996) and powerful 'fast capitalist' supporting rhetoric. And the relative absence of a pervasive critical literacy which prioritizes scrutiny of social practices and their embedded textual components remains unchanged. This remains unchanged *despite* apparent changes in awareness of the nature of literacies and their relationship to social practices. How? Why?

When Chris Searle observed that 'literacy' was not widely used in relation to reading and writing within the context of British schools, he suggested a reason why this was so. This was because 'literacy' had often been associated with initiatives that attached high value to 'transforming *consciousness*, and in particular social and political consciousness', in a way that 'reading and writing' do not. Thus, there is 'literacy', which adult students do . . . and 'learning how to read and write', which child students do every day in their schools throughout the 'developed' world. The discomfort that many schoolteachers of language may feel in considering what they do as teaching 'literacy' may well be connected to the implication that whereas 'teaching reading and writing' is simply and mechanically teaching the decontextualized skills to achieve just and only that with a child, *literacy* means going completely against the accepted grain of school life and culture, abandoning curriculum 'neutrality' and 'objectivity' and concerning oneself with the 'adults only' ingredient of . . . consciousness.

(Searle 1993a: 169–70)

While there are good reasons for believing that many school teachers have in fact embraced the notion of literacy, and embraced it in more expansive ways than as a mere synonym for 'the mechanical teaching of decontextualized reading and writing skills', there are equally good reasons for believing that many *more* teachers have taken up the language of 'literacy' *without* meaning by it anything significantly more than 'encoding and decoding print text'. Throughout the period when 'literacy' has come into more common use there have been strong tendencies working to limit and domesticate its signifying range. These include many of the very policies which give voice to 'literacy' in the first place – along with closely related policies to do with economic restructuring and constituting new citizens and citizenship practices, collectively aimed at enhancing the competitive advantage of national economies and securing (or consolidating) privileged places within the new world order.

Hence, for example, in the case of the Australian Language and Literacy Policy (*Australia's Language*, DEET 1991b: 9) we are informed that literacy consists in

the ability to read and use written information and to write appropriately, in a range of contexts. It is used to develop knowledge and understanding, to achieve personal growth and to function effectively in our society. Literacy also includes the recognition of numbers and basic mathematical signs and symbols within text. Literacy involves the integration of speaking, listening, and critical thinking with reading and writing.

Beyond this, the policy states that all Australians need to have 'effective literacy', which is 'intrinsically purposeful, flexible, dynamic and continues to develop throughout an individual's lifetime'. The need for effective literacy is linked not only to the 'personal benefit and welfare' of persons, but also to Australia achieving 'its social and economic goals' (p. 9).

This conception of literacy cuts two ways. It has expansive potential in the association forged between literacy and knowledge, understanding, and critical thinking, and the tacit recognition that literacies are multiple and embedded in diverse social practices. On the other hand, literacy is portrayed as a tool/technology which is 'used to develop knowledge and understanding' – which keeps us close to the notion·of a decontextualized set of skills that await being taken up and applied to various ends. Similarly, and appropriately, literacy and effective literacy are linked to ends that are both personal and 'national' in character. This, of course, is how things are: there is no individual without the society, and no society without individuals. What we need to consider, however, is how these various considerations are weighted and treated in the rest of the policy statement, and in the context of other policy statements and interlocking policy agendas.

Here we find what we should probably expect. Literacy is identified as being crucial to enabling changes in the structure and conduct of Australian industry demanded by global economic forces; to assisting with handling the pace of technological change; and to strengthening the country's drive for innovative employment, education and training practices and reorienting thinking toward international horizons (DEET 1991b: 3–4, 1991a: 1–8). We are told there is a strong and well-demonstrated link between low literacy levels and high levels of unemployment, and other forms of social disadvantage and dysfunctionality. Furthermore, the policy is just one plank in a much larger raft of policies which, collectively, serve to bring education and work domains into much closer alignment. These include policies and guidelines within education that identify key competencies, pull these into national curriculum statements, establish national profiles for key learning areas, and impose a tight regime of diagnostic testing and remedial programmes for those who fall through the testing nets. In this respect, Australia's approach to literacy resonates with those of other Anglo-American nations.

During the past decade in particular, 'literacy' has indeed assumed higher prominence in national education, training, and social-civic agendas and become a keyword in educational discourse. This development has, however, been accompanied throughout by tendencies that keep the 'progress' of literacy tightly constrained within the parameters of larger purposes and agendas. These larger purposes and agendas, despite what may be said about them at 'official' levels, inevitably require a literacy economy in which 'higher order', 'innovative' and (otherwise) 'critical' qualities remain in strictly scarce supply.

In other words, the more that 'literacy things' have changed, the more – in some very important respects – they have remained the same. This belief is woven through this book. It underlies a chapter by chapter search for ways of understanding how, in a world that seems increasingly difficult for many of us to negotiate with a sense of meaningful purpose, and which for more and more of its people is downright hostile to their prospects for dignified and fulfilling lives, we might conceive and build practices and projects of literacy that can serve as 'instruments for better days' (Cardoso 1993: 151).

part 1

CRITICAL AND CULTURAL PERSPECTIVES ON LITERACY

one

LANGUAGE AND CULTURAL PROCESS

Introduction

This chapter outlines an approach to thinking about language and culture, and how they are related, developed from the broad perspective described by James Gee (1996 ch. 6; Gee *et al.* 1996: ch. 1) as a sociocultural approach to literacy studies or, alternatively, as socioliteracy studies. I am going to argue that language is at one and the same time (1) a *necessary precondition* for culture and cultural process and a *consequence* of cultural engagement; (2) a *medium* of culture and cultural process; and (3) a *'broker'* of cultural process.

Culture: some preliminary views

To talk about cultural process requires spelling out what we mean by 'culture'. This is a complex task. 'Culture' has a wide range of everyday and technical uses, conjures up all sorts of images, and has diverse connotations. Consider the following everyday examples:

- culture as artefacts – 'There is a large display of early Aztec culture at the museum';
- culture as ethnic or racial identity – 'There are at least 15 cultures attending this school';
- culture as sophistication or 'class' – 'She's really got culture';
- culture as 'high culture' or 'elite culture' – According to Fiske *et al.* (1987: viii) there is a 'long established . . . criticism bewailing the lack of an Australian culture', based on 'an elitist view of culture' whose advocates

yearn for Australia 'to be seen as the Athens of the south, astounding European visitors with the number of masterpieces of art, music and literature';
● culture as 'otherness', difference, or (especially) 'exotica'. This is the idea that, for example, 'primitive peoples' have culture or have retained their culture, whereas 'modern societies' have lost their culture and no longer have culture.

Such notions of culture tend to divide human beings and societies into those who have culture versus those who do not. They also tend to associate culture with material and objects (artefacts), visible displays (e.g. costumes, dances, ritualistic routines, etc.), or other tangible trappings (such as language or dialect, often in combination with skin colour and the like). In these respects they differ from more technical accounts of culture based on work in anthropology, semiotics, cultural studies, and other social sciences. For example:

● culture 'is all human creation' (Freire 1974: 47);
● culture is 'the active process of generating and circulating meanings and pleasures within a social system' (Fiske 1989a: 23); culture is 'the "way of life" of a people, the constant and complex process by which meanings are made and shared among us' (Fiske *et al.* 1987: ix–x);
● culture 'is the outcome of the capacity for conceptual thought' (Oakley 1954: 27);
● culture is 'the actions and results of humans in society, the way people interact in their communities, and the addition people make to the world they find. Culture is what ordinary people do every day, how they behave, speak, relate, and make things. Everyone has and makes culture, not only aesthetic specialists or members of the elite. Culture is the speech and behavior in everyday life' (Shor 1993: 30–1).

These definitions suggest that all human beings have and make culture and that culture is reflected in people's everyday activities, relationships and social processes. They point toward culture as involving the making and sharing of meanings, the capacity to frame and use concepts and to think conceptually and, through this, the capacity to create: to 'add to the world we find'. They are 'larger' notions of culture than the everyday ones I began with, accommodating those examples and making clear how our everyday notions – varied and contradictory as they are – are nonetheless intelligible uses of the term 'culture'. These latter definitions point to a richer and deeper conception of culture, in which language is integral and central, and which I will explore here.

Culture and cultural process: nature, culture and consciousness

Bearing in mind Gee's earlier comments (this volume: xv) we can begin with an anthropological view of culture which distinguishes broadly between the world of culture and the world of nature. The world of culture consists of 'all human activity that is not the pure expression of *biological* characteristics of the species *Homo*' (Mann 1983: 74, first emphasis added). Everything else belongs to the world of nature. The natural world consists of everything animal, vegetable and mineral, and the myriad events, forces and processes, comings and goings and 'doings' applying to animals, vegetables and minerals, *except* for events, processes and products that reflect human activity other than purely biological functioning and being. The activity of bees making honeycombs, beavers building lodges, squirrels storing nuts, and chimpanzees chattering belongs as much to the world of nature as does the activity of water on rocks or lava flows on vegetation. By contrast, such human activities as setting nets for fishing, teaching a child a game, clearing land for cropping, forming a committee, or conversing about all and sundry belong to the cultural world.

The world of culture begins where humans act outside the limits of their biology or genetic constitution alone. Culture is seen as a consequence and a function of the *social* dimension of human life; cultural process is a consequence and an expression of 'human consciousness of the world and intentionality toward the world' (Freire 1974; Freire in Davis 1980). This view points directly to the central place of meaning and language within culture and cultural process. It reflects the way 'culture' is used generally within social theory to refer to 'the symbolic and learned, non biological aspects of human society, including language, custom and convention, by which human behaviour can be distinguished from that of other primates' (Abercrombie *et al.* 1988: 59).

According to the Brazilian educator Paulo Freire, the distinctiveness of humans as social and cultural beings is that they 'engage in *relationships* with others and with the world' (1974: 3, emphasis added). This, for Freire, is at the heart of cultural process, and of our conception of humans as social, historical, and cultural beings. Freire expresses these links very clearly:

> Because they are not limited to the natural (biological) sphere but participate in the creative dimension as well, [humans] can intervene in reality in order to change it. Inheriting acquired experience, creating and re-creating, integrating themselves into their context, responding to its challenges, objectifying themselves . . . [humans] enter the domain . . . of History and of Culture. . .
>
> As [humans] relate to their world by responding to the challenges of

the environment, they begin to dynamize . . . and to humanize reality. They add to it something of their own making, by giving temporal meaning to geographic space, by creating culture.

(pp. 4–5)

Culture, history and society: the circumstances of social existence

What sorts of things do humans add to reality through their cultural activity? How do we add to reality, and why? Under what kinds of conditions or circumstances do we act culturally?

Cultural 'products' include much more than concrete and visible artefacts alone. The additions humans have made to 'the world they find' include ideas, purposes and goals, concepts, beliefs, values, rules, theories, interpretations and, indeed, entire social institutions and patterned (or organized and ordered) social relations. Hence systems of laws and regulations are cultural phenomena, along with the endless variety of conventions observed in human societies. So also are symbols, signs, and whole systems of communication and making meaning, together with bodies of knowledge, information, ideology, dogma, ritual and customs.

Take something as basic as transportation. Humans have added to the world of 'natural mobility/movement' – such as animals using their legs for walking and birds their wings for flying – by developing vehicular forms of transport in accordance with their evolving purposes, values and means. Material artefacts here include everything from chariots and galleys, rickshaws, push-bikes and motorcycles, to the latest motorcars, hydrofoils and jet aircraft, depending on the social groups and historical epochs in question. Along with these artefacts go ideas (e.g. notions of more efficient engines), concepts (acceleration, braking), beliefs (non-polluting forms are best), values (we want maximum ease and speed of mobility), rules (e.g. of the road), theories (good design will improve safety), interpretations (it looks like the road could be slippery, so I'll slow down), social institutions (road transport divisions, Ministry of Transport, traffic policing), and entire signification systems (traffic-related symbols, road signs, maps).

Cultural phenomena also include systematic social relations and their associated power relations that operate within and between groups of human beings. Indeed, the very organizing of our lives within structured social groups, based on shared understandings and beliefs about how interactions should occur, and what will be done where protocols are breached, is also cultural. And so along with cultural productions of modes of mobility and transportation come recognized and patterned relationships between social actors – for example, between traffic officer and driver, between drivers themselves, between drivers and cyclists. There are designated ways for each to interact with the other in particular situations. These social relations also embody power relations that are enshrined in laws and other codes, and that we learn and observe. For instance, the traffic police have certain legal power advantages over motorists, drivers on one side of the give way rule have a legal power advantage over those on the other, and so on.

As we have come gradually to understand more about space and time, and about how they are related – e.g. in terms of distance and speed – humans have changed reality by making continuing changes in transportation. From wearing and cutting early tracks and trails to constructing superhighways and freeways, we have changed our reality materially in tangible ways. We have also changed other aspects of reality in the process, such as our capacity to cover large distances rapidly. This in turn makes all sorts of new social activities and relationships possible – such as long-distance trade and commerce, intellectual exchange, multiethnic communities. These continue to evolve as we create new ways to move ourselves, our products, our information, etc.

All this involves adding *meanings* of many different kinds to the world: meanings linked to the purposes of social groups and their available means for giving shape and expression to reality in accordance with their purposes. Geographic space is cluttered with ever-changing meanings (partly ideas, partly practices) of what it is to be a traveller, to take a journey, to go to work, to speed up or slow down, to be coming home at 6 p.m., to be going out again at 8 p.m. Indeed these amount to very different meanings in different contexts – for example, between rural Patagonia and urban New York. Humans give and receive, share and live around diverse meanings bound up with ideas and practices of transportation. Within modern societies these meanings span the range from the prosaic meanings of road signs to more elaborate meanings of entire social roles, like what it means to be a jet pilot, a traffic officer, a commuter. And what holds true for transportation as a realm of cultural process and cultural creation holds equally true for the myriad dimensions that make up daily life.

At a quite different level we might consider Fiske's example of how we have given temporal meaning to geographic space around popular cultural activities and processes such as those associated with 'the beach'. As *nature* the beach is simply a meeting point of sea and land. In fact, in nature the physical phenomenon we call the beach has no meaning whatsoever. It is unidentified; it is simply 'there'. Nothing exists in nature to say 'this is a beach'. There *is* no beach – just (what humans call) water and land. The very act of identifying a given piece of geographic space as 'beach', and distinguishing beach from sea and higher land, or rock, is precisely a cultural act. As *culture* 'beach' – or 'the beach' – is given diverse meanings through cultural practice. As Fiske notes,

[p]eople use beaches to seek out certain kinds of meanings for themselves, meanings that help them come to terms with their off-beach,

normal life-style . . . [D]ifferent people use the beach differently, that is, they find different meanings in it, but there is a core of meanings that all users, from respectable suburban family to long-haired dropout surfer, share to a greater or lesser extent.

(1989b: 43)

The cultural productions of meanings, artefacts, values, etc. – and, indeed, the wide array of Discourses and discourses (Gee 1990) – that coalesce around the beach belong predominantly to 'popular' culture. Other cultural productions, however, centre around pursuit of meanings that are associated more obviously with what is deemed 'high' or 'elite' culture. It is important to recognize that this distinction between popular culture and high culture reflects the differential power among social groups to have *their* meanings and pursuits assigned high status and value. It does not indicate that inherently different kinds of processes take place between productions of high culture and popular culture respectively. As will become apparent when we examine *how* humans add culturally to the reality they find, people are doing pretty much 'the same kind of thing' when they compose a symphony, review a Van Gogh exhibition, or listen appreciatively to a Chopin sonata, as when they organize a barbecue, write a column for a bikers' magazine, or follow a netball match.

This is to recognize the dialectical relationship between culture, as addition to the world, and *Discourse*. Composing symphonies, reviewing art, organizing barbecues, and following sport are all examples of human Discourses (or discursive practices). To this extent we can view Discourses in terms of what humans add to the world culturally. The world of nature is, so to speak, 'Discourse-free'. In creating the world of culture, humans have added Discourse(s) to the world they 'found'. On the other hand, Discourses must also be understood in terms of how humans add to the world through cultural engagement. Discourses are about making *meaning* – i.e. about creating, giving, receiving, and sharing meanings. At the same time, Discourses are about making meaning (or meaningful activity and inter-action) *possible*.

Meaning is absolutely central to human life and human being, as a social-cultural phenomenon. This, of course, is not simply linguistic meaning, but the idea also that human life is meaningful in the sense of being purposeful and ordered. As we have seen, social groups organize their lives around concepts, purposes, values, beliefs, ideals, theories, notions of reality, and the like. Through Discourse human life is organized into shape and form which can be recognized and understood – it can be 'read' as having 'meaning' – by ourselves and by others.

Gee describes Discourses as 'saying (writing)-doing-being-valuing-believing combinations': 'forms of life' or 'ways of being in the world', which integrate such things as words, acts, attitudes, beliefs and identities, along with gestures, clothes, bodily expressions and positions, and so on. Through participation in Discourses individuals are identified or identifiable as members of socially meaningful groups or networks, and as players of meaningful social roles (Gee 1990: 142–3). More than this, it is in and through Discourses that human individual and group *identities* are constructed and evolve. Human identities are systems of meaning and, as such, are among the cultural creations that humans add to reality.

As with language, so with Discourse more generally. Only once norms and rules (for use) are established and observed can linguistic meaning be 'stamped' and communicated, and people participate in speaking the language as part of the process of giving shape to human life. Likewise, as the terrain of the larger project of creating, shaping, and bounding social life, discursive practice is characterized by norms and conventions which permit cultural meanings beyond language alone to be made and communicated. Both the norms governing linguistic meaning and those governing cultural meaning-making in and through discursive practice have to be transmitted and learned. Education, socialization, training, apprenticeship and enculturation are among the terms we use to refer to processes by which individuals are initiated into the Discourses of their identity formations. Outside of Discourse there is no human life as social and cultural life. Knowledge of Discourses is not innate. Initiation into Discourses is cultural activity, and the Discourses themselves are, simultaneously, *means and outcomes* of cultural process.

Why and how do humans engage in cultural activity?

The question *why* humans participate in cultural processes may seem odd since humans do not have any choice in the matter. 'Cultural activity' is the inevitable result of humans (as conscious, intentional, social beings) pursuing satisfaction of their needs. In *A Scientific Theory of Culture*, the anthropologist Malinowski (1944) portrayed culture as a response to human needs. The basic needs of material human survival have spawned a diverse range of discursive practices concerned with producing means of survival, for example cultural processes of productive work, where members of social groups interact consciously and reflectively with their natural and cultural worlds to create means for subsistence – whether directly (growing, preparing and cooking one's own food), or indirectly (working for wages to exchange for direct means of subsistence). Cultural activity undertaken to meet basic natural (biological, physiological) needs often generates further needs and desires which are not at all, strictly speaking, basic or essential. For example, when translated from group to group into cultural processes, the biological need for food generates all manner of desires and perceived needs for particular kinds of food and/or eating experiences. These desires are met through discursive practices which generate the appropriate artefacts (exotic crops and delicacies, particular cuts of meat, elegant restaurants and sophisticated decors), values (how to conduct a meal, how to eat elegantly), customs (procedures of polite conversation, formal orders in which food is served and to whom), standards (overcooked, well cooked, nice presentation), and so on. All such evolving 'needs' and meanings become further cultural additions to the world. Similar examples could easily be provided for other basic biological and physiological needs, such as the need for shelter, the need to procreate, and so on.

Moving beyond basic physiological and biological needs we can consider other kinds of basic human needs and see how they too are associated with cultural processes, as consciousness and intentionality is brought to bear on reality. Recreational needs have been constructed culturally into wide-ranging quests for meaning and diverse productions of meanings including, among others, those coalescing around the beach, as noted above and elaborated by Fiske (1989b). Needs for emotional expression and release have spawned cultural processes as different as Discourses centred on music and the plastic arts (whether in 'highbrow', popular, or folk, etc. forms), counselling and therapy, headbanging, and graffiti – to name but a few. Among different social groups 'generic' Discourse varieties take on more or less distinctive specific forms. For example, the folk music and folk dance forms to be found among Guatemalan Indian groups differ from those folk forms occurring in Appalachian communities. All of them, however, are identifiable as 'folk' music and dance forms, as distinct from more 'highbrow' or 'popular' forms of music and dance apparent in Guatemala and the US.

It is obvious also that as social beings humans are literally 'born to culture'. To be born into a human setting is, precisely, to be born into 'a particular set of institutions and [social] relations'. These, of course, vary in detail from person to person and group to group. The important point, however, is that whatever particular set of institutions and social relations a given human being is born into, s/he is thereby born into a *cultural* milieu, a discursive universe. Clarke *et al.* (1981: 54) put this as follows:

> A social individual, born into a particular set of institutions and relations, is at the same moment born into a peculiar configuration of meanings, which give her access to and locate her within 'a culture' . . . These structures – of social relationship and of meaning – shape the ongoing collective existence of groups . . . [E]xisting cultural patterns form a sort of . . . reservoir . . . which groups take up, transform, develop. Each group makes something of its starting conditions – and through this 'making' culture is reproduced and transmitted.

The process of being socialized into the way of life of one's group begins immediately an individual is born. It is not as if, once born, a human being can *live* and then somehow 'do' culture as an optional extra. Human beings are literally born into cultural participation, framed initially by the conditions and circumstances encountered in their 'primary Discourse' (Gee 1990, 1991).

How do humans engage in cultural activity? What, so to speak, are the 'mechanics' and the 'inherent characteristics' of cultural activity and cultural processes. Humans draw on resources made available to them by the Discourses of their cultural field to engage in meaning-making activity by participating in what Clarke *et al.* call 'sensuous human praxis' (1981: 53). 'Sensuous' means here that the praxis involves/engages our senses. 'Praxis' refers to a unity of reflection and practice. Praxis is action which is reflective, and reflection which is incorporated in action. Such praxis can be remarkably 'everyday'. Take an ordinary conversation, for example. To engage in (a) conversation – knowing what is appropriate, and participating appropriately – is 'sensuous' in that it involves sound and, in the case of face-to-face conversation, sight and often touch. It is 'praxis' in that it involves both action (in the form of talking, listening, gesturing, etc.), and reflection (in the form of interpreting what is said, framing a response, judging whether one has communicated, etc.).

Karl Marx (1970) underscored the significance of consciousness and intentionality by distinguishing between natural processes of production and cultural processes of production in his celebrated comparison of the work, respectively, of 'natural' and 'social' beings:

> A spider conducts operations that resemble those of a weaver, and a bee puts to shame many an architect in the construction of her cells. But what distinguishes the worst of architects from the best of bees is . . . that the architect raises his structure in imagination before [construct-ing] it in reality. At the end of every [such] process we get a result that existed in the imagination of the labourer at its commencement. [Labourers] not only effect a change of form on the material on which [they] work, but . . . also realise a purpose of [their] own that gives the law to [their] modus operandi, and to which [they] must submit [their] will.
>
> (p. 174)

Architects draw on resources for making and communicating meaning in the process of pursuing their purposes that are not available to bees, but are available to humans through Discourse. In producing a planned construc-tion, an architect gives expression to intent in ways that can be recognized, understood, interpreted and evaluated by others, and according to concepts, norms, and conventions against which to monitor how far s/he is succeeding in giving material form to the original idea (Braverman 1974: ch. 1). In this we see, on multiple levels, the making, giving, and receiving of meaning: that is, the cultural process.

At this point it is worth noting three general features of the circumstances under which human beings engage in cultural processes.

First, humans participate individually and collectively in cultural processes as social beings who have been initiated into the particular range of Discourses associated with the life of the group – or groups – to which they belong. While these Discourses enable us to function as cultural beings in the first place and, thus, to participate in cultural processes, they also inevitably impose limits and constraints on what we are able to do and how we are able to live culturally. Discourses are important 'raw materials' of cultural participation and production, but like any raw materials they are both finite and limited in what they 'permit' to be done with and through them. Increasingly, educational theorists working from bases in social linguistics and family resource theory are providing evidence of how the Discourses and associated language practices of particular social groups contribute to limiting educational access and achievement (Kress 1985a, 1988; Gee 1990, 1991, 1993a, 1993b; Nash 1993). This leads to the next point.

Second, within complex plural societies different social groups participate in 'the cultural mainstream' from positions of relative advantage or disadvantage. Such societies consist of numerous social groups, each with its own particular 'discursive heritage'. These different social groups include different class groups and sub-groups, as well as different race, ethnic, religious, etc. groups. These categories intersect and overlap to make a very complex cultural matrix, which is further complicated when we add gender to the mix. There are two key points to be noted here so far as this chapter is concerned:

- Societies like our own are hierarchical, in that groups and classes are ranked above or below each other in respect of their wealth, power, relationships within economic production, and their cultures. The various cultures within such societies stand in domination or subordination to one another, along 'a scale of cultural power' (Clarke *et al.* 1981: 54).
- While the lives and 'beings' of different social groups go on alongside and independently of each other to some extent – e.g. in worship, in clubs, in close-knit communities – they are also 'gathered together' in a range of highly important social processes and settings. Education and employment are two of these. We find here that more dominant and powerful social groups are able to define educational culture and the culture of (especially corporate) employment in ways that advantage those with 'Discourse histories' most like their own and disadvantage those whose Discourse histories are different. In practice it is simply not true that all social groups are equal when they stand before The School or The Corporation.

Third, as Clarke *et al.* (1981: 54) observe, the cultural 'starting conditions' of social groups at any given point in time are 'not of their own making'.

Neither, however, are they fixed and unchangeable – either in and of themselves, or in relation to the starting conditions of other groups. Social groups 'take up, transform [and] develop' their particular 'pre-constituted "field-of-the-possibles"' in all sorts of ways (p. 54). These include ways that seek to resist, challenge, and transform the overall shape of the cultural field, in order to expand the range of meanings a group can make and to enhance the status and rewards accruing to those meanings.

These features of the circumstances under which humans engage in cultural processes will become crucial to the discussion of language as a 'medium' and a 'broker' of culture and cultural process.

Language, culture and cultural process

Language is integral to culture and cultural process. There is, says Gunther Kress,

> a very close fit of ideas and language; indeed, some ideas/forms of language seem to exist in one culture and not in another. Language and culture are very closely interwoven; social structures and linguistic form are intimately intermeshed. This is so across larger cultures, as much as it is the case in the social and cultural diversity within one society.
>
> (1988a: ii)

Much more could be said about language and cultural process than is possible here. Nonetheless, we can make reasonable inroads into the territory by taking the three themes identified at the outset:

1 language as a precondition of culture and an outcome of cultural process;
2 language as a medium of culture; and
3 language as a broker of cultural process.

Language as precondition and outcome of cultural process

The distinctions between 'sensing' and 'making sense of', and between '(merely) sentient beings' and 'conscious beings', provide a good starting point for understanding language as both a precondition and a consequence or outcome of culture.

To call a being 'sentient' is to say it experiences sensations; it senses phenomena (of a wider or narrower range). Not all sentient beings, however, *make sense of* the phenomena they sense. A sheep which has broken its leg senses what we would call pain. But it does not make sense of that sensation as *pain*, or of the experience as a *painful* one. Its pain behaviour will doubtless include writhing, fast breathing, and bleating. But so far as we know, there is no sheepish equivalent of the realization/thought/statement 'I am in agony; this hurts so bad; I've never felt pain like this before.'

By contrast, conscious beings sense pain as *pain*. They are conscious of an experience they undergo as being of *this* type – painful – rather than *that* type – pleasant. Having made sense of such experience and ascribed a value to it – e.g. pain is an evil, it is to be alleviated if possible – humans can and have set about creating further meanings and meaningful practices with the purpose of dulling pain, distracting people's attention away from their pain, and so on. This is cultural.

A parallel argument applies beyond the experience of sensations. For instance, when it gnaws branches and assembles them in a particular way, a beaver does not consciously recognize its activity as building, far less as building a lodge rather than building a dam. This is precisely what we mean when we speak of the beaver's behaviour, and certainly the bee's, as instinctive or reflexive; as belonging to the natural rather than the cultural domain.

How is cultural activity possible? How do (conscious) beings get to make sense of X as X and, consequently, become capable of making meaning in the diverse, complex, and subtle ways that humans in fact do? How do humans become capable, for example, of making sense of a given stretch of terrain as a 'beach', a site for recreational activity, a place to hang out, and so on? How do people come to recognize and understand a given kind of activity as building, or playing? And how do they come to envisage and create new ways of playing? And what does language have to do with this?

We can ask questions at two levels here. Both are important for understanding language in relation to cultural process.

First, how do human beings in fact become capable of classifying, categorizing, conceptualizing, and generally making sense and meaning out of their experiencing? The short answer here is that they *learn* to do so through a sociocultural process which initiates them into, or apprentices them to (what have been called) 'forms of life', 'domains of social practice', or 'Discourses'. This apprenticing is done in socialization, training, education, and so on.

The second-level question is more subtle. It asks what the necessary conditions are for conceptualizing, classifying, and meaning-making to go on *at all* – as opposed to teaching people how to do it given that it is already established in human practice.

I will take this second question in some detail now, and address the first in the following section on language as a medium of culture.

For humans to have concepts and categories at all, with which to make sense of reality and to interact consciously with it, there has to be a way of establishing them and fixing them objectively. For example, to be able to pick out a particular object as a tree, or a particular sensation as a pain, we have to have some way of knowing that *this* (object, sensation) is another one of *those* (tree, pain) that occurred on previous occasions. We are only able to do this as individuals because other people are picking out the same things in essentially the same ways. In other words, we and they are drawing on the same rules and criteria and norms for making the same identifications, distinctions, 'pickings out' and so on. For you and I to share the same meaning for concepts, categories and signs – such as signifying a greeting by a nod of the head – we have to be drawing on shared criteria and rules (which govern nodding and 'receiving nods' in certain contexts and under certain conditions). To be shared they must be public. And the possibility of public rules and criteria emerges from the existence of common/shared *material* practices.

Meanings and language are possible because humans engage in material practices which are regular and patterned. In other words, they go on frequently and have similar shapes and routines from one occasion to the next. This regularity is largely linked to the fact that these practices have purposes and goals. They comprise exactly the kind of context in which concepts and signs *can* emerge and become fixed, in relation to things that are going on and that participants can be *aware* are going on, because they have a material dimension that is open to perception and other modes of experience by all involved. Language does not (and originally did not) emerge autonomously or in isolation, but rather as embedded in larger shared and public practices. Thus two beings encountering each other every morning in the course of their routines might evolve a particular behaviour – e.g. a nod – as a meaning; they might 'fix' that meaning over time by mutually reinforcing the use of what becomes their sign (the nod) *only* in association with *first* seeing each other in the day, and not in association with other things and events, such as passing again at the end of the day – where they might evolve a different sign-meaning combination (wave-farewell) instead. Here we have the production and fixing of a *concept* (greeting), a *category* or categories (morning/bidding greeting versus evening/farewelling greeting), and a *sign* (nod, wave).

When public rules, criteria and conventions emerge to make shared concepts and wider meanings possible – becoming attached in the process to signs (verbal or non-verbal) which objectify and *realize* the rules and criteria and permit meanings to be checked out, consolidated, transmitted, reflected upon, and used in the course of enhancing, refining, developing, and transforming social practices – we have language.

However, it is not as though we have meaning and *then* have language – in order to express our meaning. Rather, language is integral to realizing meaning. Language *is* social practice in which meanings are made, fixed, and shared publicly. Language *is* the practice of linking signs, rules and patterns in agreed ways within larger shared and purposeful material practices. This is 'the kind of agreement that occurs when groups of people come to share values, beliefs and ways of doing things over time' (Emmitt and Pollock 1991: 8).

The patterns and regularities providing the necessary material conditions for the public character of language were, no doubt, originally grounded in common behaviours and purposes operating at the level of instinct and reflex – i.e. belonging to nature. With the 'arrival' of language these behaviours and purposes, and thus the relationship of humans to their world, became conscious and intentional. They became objectified and opened to reflection, making possible the kinds of enlarged social practices and processes we identify as *cultural*. In this sense, then, language can be said to 'beget' culture and be a necessary precondition of cultural process.

There is, however, a reciprocal side to the language-culture relationship. Cultural practices and processes in turn 'beget' language. This can be illustrated by reference to some highly visible changes that have occurred during the past decade within cultural sites of education. These changes were influenced powerfully by developments within Discourses of economics and organizational management.

In the education case there was growing pressure through the 1980s to reorganize and administer schools and other educational organizations much more closely along the lines of private institutions, like businesses. This was, in effect, to force public service institutions to become more like private institutions (see Drucker 1985).

The crowning goal of private institutions is to make a profit. This is a very clearly defined and tangible goal, amenable to exact measurement. Profits are enabled by such processes as minimizing costs, maximizing efficiency, and achieving an optimal balance between productivity and quality. Management science and business economics and administration have generated theories, strategies, and languages for guiding the cultural practices of profit-maximizing private institutions.

With the evolution of welfare states, an array of public service institutions were funded out of tax revenues and charged with providing benefits – such as health and education – for their publics. As goals, benefits are much less clearly defined and amenable to (exact) measurement than the profit goal of private institutions. With economic recession came moves to 'reconstitute' public service institutions and make them operate more like private institutions. This brought a dramatic change in education language, accompanying equally dramatic changes in the cultural practice of administering and operating schools, universities, polytechnics, etc. Suddenly, educational activity was steeped in and increasingly shaped by talk of 'mission statements' and 'school charters'; 'cost centres' and 'cost–benefit analyses'; 'performance criteria', 'performance contracting', and 'performance indicators'; 'efficiency'; 'accountability'; 'devolution'; 'flat management structures'; 'low cost production' of 'deliverables', and so on. Changes in discursive practice saw changes in language.

Of course, new language did not *really* 'flow' in behind a wave of cultural change, no more than language flowed into nature, trailing culture in its wake. Rather, the process is dynamic and the tendencies are in play simultaneously. Cultural practices of education administration changed along with a changing language of education administration: the cultural language of educational administration changed along with a changing administrative practice. But cultural change there *was*. With it came language change. And the two shaped and promoted each other, as co-constitutive elements. And *we*, of course, changed to a greater or lesser extent in the process.

Language as medium of cultural process

To understand how far and in what ways language serves as a medium of cultural process we need to understand the relationship between the 'language bits' in Discourses and Discourses *per se* (Gee 1993c: 14); or, to use different terms, between language and 'forms of life' (Wittgenstein 1953). I will approach this in two stages.

First, what can we say about the mediating role of language in the cultural processes of groups initiating their members into (or apprenticing them to) Discourses, by means of which they become capable of 'doing culture'? How, in other words, is language related to the larger process of being socialized and educated into forms of life?

This can be treated quite briefly since the main ideas have already been addressed. Discourses, or forms of life, involve agreed-upon combinations of linguistic and non-linguistic behaviours, values, goals, beliefs, assumptions, and the like, which social groups have evolved and which their members share. The important point here is that the language component is inseparable from the other elements in these 'combinations'. Language is interwoven with them to make up each particular Discourse or form of life. In this way, the 'rest' of the Discourse is presupposed within its language component. The term 'performance indicator' means what it does to 1990s academics only because of what is involved in the larger social practice of performance-driven research and teaching within many contemporary universities.

Applying these ideas to a group socializing its young, we can say that Discourses are the 'fields of reference we learn to work within' when we are trained in the language of our group. Hence, to learn a language is to learn 'the outlook, assumptions, and practices with which that language is inseparably bound and from which its expressions get their meaning'

(Grayling 1988: 84–5). Teaching language explicitly and deliberately to youngsters becomes a major focus for pulling together 'language, behavior, values, and beliefs to give . . . shape to [their] experience' (Gee 1990: 151). In addition, of course, teaching the language of a Discourse to any human being at any stage of their life assumes similar significance – as, once again, the example of the new language of educational restructuring makes clear. Within these terms language operates as a *medium* of cultural process, both of the process of cultural transmission (as initiation into Discourses or forms of life), and of the process of learning 'how to do culture' through initiation into Discourses which provide crucial 'raw materials' for cultural engagement.

Second, there is a further aspect of language as medium of cultural process to be considered here. This has to do with the actual process of cultural creation under the empirical conditions of multiple sets of Discourses associated with different social groups operating within complex societies.

Gee (1991) distinguishes between primary and secondary Discourses. We acquire our primary Discourse in 'face-to-face communication with intimates' in the course of being socialized within a family or kinship unit. Our primary Discourse provides our first ways of 'thinking, feeling, valuing, and using our . . . language': our first sociocultural 'tools' for giving shape to and making sense of our life experience. Primary Discourses may (and often do) vary considerably from one social group to the next. Secondary Discourses are encountered through participation in social institutions beyond the primary group. In societies like our own these include schools, clubs, churches, government departments, etc. Secondary Discourses involve uses of language and ways of behaving, valuing, believing, etc. that present new and extended, *and possibly very different*, ways of giving shape to experience and making sense of the world from those made available in our primary Discourse. For some groups, the differences between secondary Discourses and their primary Discourse may be so great that these groups make very different meanings from and sense of their secondary discursive experiences from members of other groups, who experience a closer 'fit' between their primary and secondary Discourses. Indeed, for some groups making any viable sense at all of life within secondary institutions becomes a major challenge.

School ethnographies provide some very interesting accounts of the cultural process, as seen from the standpoint of different social groups giving expression and shape to their life experience within the secondary institutional sphere. One I continue to find particularly interesting, in respect of the operation of language within the cultural process, comes from New Zealand (see Jones 1986, 1991). I will describe just one facet of this study: namely, the cultural production and operation of two very different classroom literacies and pedagogies by members of two very different social groups studying in the same all-girls high school.

Alison Jones studied two 'ability streams' of students at the same school grade level. One was a low-to-middle stream class comprised almost entirely of students from Pacific Island migrant working-class families: 5M. The other was a top stream composed overwhelmingly of students from white middle-class (especially professional and business) families: 5S. Jones observed closely these students in their classrooms during two years, the second being the year of their first national certification exam, School Certificate.

Both groups believed strongly that school success was the route to good life chances, and that success in academic exams involves a combination of ability and hard work. Both groups wanted to succeed in School Certificate and both expressed commitment to working hard. Indeed, Jones found that both groups *did* work hard. What she also found, however, was that the two groups had very different views of the work to be done, and that these corresponded to very different views of how to operate language within learning.

The 5M students drew on discursive experiences which emphasized, among other things, strong deference to authority. They saw the teacher as *the* authority on school knowledge. As a result, they worked from a view of academic and exam-oriented literacy that amounted to getting the teacher's knowledge down as notes to be learned up later. These students made sure their notes were always up to date, neat, and typically ornately illustrated. They spent much time putting together their 'notes'.

This conception of academic literacy had some interesting – and unfortunate – features. First, it contributed to the production of a distinctive pedagogy in 5M classrooms. Jones shows how the respective beliefs and values of 5M students and teachers interacted to produce culturally this particular pedagogy and its consequences. Basically, the pedagogy consisted of the teacher dictating notes. 5M students saw this as the teacher's proper role: imparting knowledge. If she departed from this role – e.g. by involving the class in discussion, comment, questioning, etc. – the class would 'play up'. The teacher would have to come back to dictating in order to restore control and get students 'on (some acceptable) task'. On the other hand, whenever the class *did* get briefly into question-based pedagogy, teachers would typically simply ignore wrong or inappropriate answers offered (seriously) by the students, and revert to dictating the right answers, or putting their own words into students' mouths – seemingly as the only way they could see of making up for the massive gaps evident in these students' curricular knowledge.

The dictation literacy-pedagogy was, of course, compatible with students involving themselves in inappropriate activities during class time. So long as *someone* was taking notes, that could be borrowed and written up later, other students could read or daydream as they wished, or catch up on other notes!

Moreover, students often took notes down inaccurately. In the first place, it seems that much curricular knowledge was far from their previous experience (as evident in a student suggesting with full seriousness and sincerity that they shut the windows to keep germs out). They often had little notion of what was being spoken about (e.g. in economics and science). In addition, however, they had no apparent idea that claims advanced as knowledge/information should be checked for accuracy and sense against recognized authoritative sources. Yet this is an essential aspect of enacting the appropriate 'saying (writing)-believing-valuing-doing combinations' involved in academic-exam literacy specifically, and academic Discourse generally.

In almost exact contrast, 5S students would punish the teacher if she dictated notes at any length. Also, they would challenge her if they thought her information or point of view might be mistaken. 5S saw the teacher as just one of the resources available to them for the purpose of getting the knowledge they needed. Moreover, they knew the knowledge required for scholastic success (particularly in 'prestige' subjects) goes far beyond merely absorbing and repeating information, but includes also developing and defending viewpoints via structured argument, taking detached positions, analysing and synthesizing information from diverse sources and perspectives, displaying flair, and so on. Consequently, for them hard work involved very different language and literacy practices from those of 5M. They insisted on classroom language being a medium of discussion, debate, and the development and rehearsal of views and positions. They would question, probe and challenge, and remain on task in this mode.

5M and 5S come from very different social groups, having very different prior and ongoing discursive experiences and histories. They met on the same site, but from very different 'starting conditions' and with very different 'raw materials' available to them. They made very different 'senses' of their exam-focused school-based life experience. They played active roles in the process of producing and operating very different pedagogical processes and school literacies. They made very different meanings, in the form of artefacts (notes versus developed positions), social relationships (teacher as authority versus teacher as one resource among others), structured routines and practices (dictation versus discussion), and so on. These two groups took their respective sets of 'raw materials of their existence' and turned them into quite different 'distinct patterns of life', thereby giving different 'expressive form to their life experience'.

Here the notion of 'cultural process' spans very different detailed cultural processes. Language was absolutely integral to the difference. Indeed, the respective language uses and practices of 5M and 5S were themselves very different. These differences both reflected and contributed to the ongoing process of creating and maintaining social and cultural differences between different groups within the one complex society. A growing corpus of studies point in their own ways, and with greater depth and sophistication than I can convey here, to the nature and role of education as medium of cultural process. Readers may refer to the following as representative exemplars of quality work in this area: Shor (1980); Hirshon (1982); Heath (1983); Chris Searle (1984, 1993a); Luke (1988); Baker and Freebody (1989); Delgado-Gaitan (1990); Gee (1990, 1993b); Green (1990); Delgado-Gaitan and Trueba (1991); Edelsky (1991); Gowen (1992); Kantor *et al.* (1992); Anderson and Irvine (1993); Hull (1993); Apple (1993, 1995, 1996).

Language as broker of cultural process

This concluding theme focuses on language in relation to cultural politics within complex hierarchical societies characterized by contending cultural forces. Dominant social groups use raw materials of the larger societal culture – including established institutions and institutionalized procedures – in ways that help preserve their dominance. On the opposite side, subordinate social groups in pursuit of enhanced cultural status, greater material wealth, social mobility, and improved social conditions, will try in various ways to use cultural raw materials to gain greater recognition of and reward for their own cultural meanings and heritages. Once again, language will be integral to this process of cultural struggle in various ways (Kress 1985: 52). The metaphor I use here of language as a 'broker' is intended to focus on ways in which dominant and subordinate groups alike (try to) enlist the 'services' of language to act as an 'agent' on behalf of their respective interests. (A broker is an agent acting on behalf of a principal to buy and sell goods, securities, etc., in the interests of the principal.)

I will look first at some of the ways dominant groups can draw on language to (help) maintain their dominance, i.e. how language functions in the service of elite interests in the production and distribution of (cultural, social, economic) power. Second, I will note some examples of subordinate groups fastening on to language in attempts to improve their social and cultural standing and to win greater access to power.

Language in the service of dominance within education

The kinds of differences in language and literacy evident in Jones's study are closely associated with systematic patterns of academic-exam success and failure. Moreover, the circumstances of 5M and 5S are part of a much larger picture. The 5M students almost universally failed School Certificate, while 5S passed. This is part of a well-known pattern. Insofar as students like those in 5M secure passes in competitive exams at all, they are very often in low status subject areas. Within prestige subjects particularly, like English and the sciences, exam success is tied closely to abilities, attitudes, and dispositions that go far beyond the mere recall and reproduction of information. Scholastic achievement draws heavily on discursive practices and associated language uses which emphasize developing positions and viewpoints by argument and debate; amassing evidence in support of one's position; demonstrating flair in arguing a point of view; manipulating and relating abstract ideas; and assuming detached standpoints when matters of objectivity or hypothesis arise.

The required modes of speaking, writing, and thinking generally come easily – or, at least, much more easily – to students from social groupings represented in 5S than to those in 5M. Growing evidence from studies across a range of disciplines indicates that the primary Discourses, cultural capitals and family resources of students like those in 5S position them advantageously to master the dominant literacy of writing exams, and to enjoy maximum opportunities to *learn* in classroom settings those 'meta-level competencies' tested in scholastic exams (compare Wells 1987; Gee 1990, 1991: 8–10; Nash 1993).

Dominant social and cultural groups have been able to establish *their* language, and *their* knowledge priorities, learning styles, pedagogical preferences, etc., as the 'official examinable culture' of school. Their notions of important and useful knowledge, their ways of representing truth, their ways of arguing and establishing correctness, and their logics, grammars and language are established as the institutional norms by which academic and scholastic success is defined and assessed (Luke 1993a: 21). This is not necessarily a conscious process, far less a conspiracy. It is simply what tends to happen, with the result that the Discourses and discourses of dominant groups become those which dominate education, and become established as major legitimate routes to securing social goods (like wealth and status). As a result, educational success is patterned along distinct lines of prior discursive experience associated with membership of particular social groups.

While this becomes most apparent at the point of scholastic examination, it is actually a trend that is evident from the very outset of formal education.

Consider, for example, the practice of privileging within formal education the standard form of an official language over other languages and non-standard dialects. The standard variant of a language is that which is usually used in print and is normally taught in schools and to non-native speakers learning that language. 'It is . . . the variety which is normally spoken by educated people, and used in news broadcasts and other similar situations' (Trudgill 1983: 17). In Australia, for instance, Standard Australian English exists alongside Aboriginal English and non-standard Australian English as a dialect of English spoken in the community. However, it is Standard Australian English that is officially identified in Australia's language and literacy policy as 'the form of English associated with public affairs . . . the primary and dominant language of education', and hence the form of English which must 'be accessible to and accessed by all Australians' (DEET 1991b: 32). At the same time, as Allan Luke notes, Australia has become increasingly diverse ethnically and linguistically, to the point where in many urban and outback areas across Australia,

> schools now feature a majority of students with non [standard] English speaking backgrounds . . . [ranging] from children who speak Aboriginal languages, Creoles and non-standard dialects to those children who speak the languages of community ethnic groups which have migrated to Australia.
>
> (Luke 1993a: 19)

While Australia's language and literacy policy explicitly acknowledges the inherent equality of the various languages and dialects spoken inside the country, and legislates for preserving languages and dialects other than Standard Australian English, as well as for providing opportunities for all Australians to experience and understand non-standard varieties, to all intents and purposes Standard Australian English is, precisely, the standard within formal education.

Of course, the situation of Standard Australian English within Australia is the same as that of other English standards (e.g. British, American) within their respective societies: namely, it

> has no linguistic status or characteristic which separates it off from all of the other dialects of English. It is simply the dialect of English which is spoken by the more powerful, dominant groups in society, and which has therefore become the language of education, the media, government and the law.
>
> (Eades 1993: 1–2)

However sensible and necessary it may be to recognize one language variety as the official language of public life in a society, and to endeavour to ensure that it is accessible to and accessed by all citizens in that society, the fact remains that extending legal recognition to Standard Australian English as the dominant and primary language of education constitutes it as a 'broker' on behalf of the interests of dominant cultural groups. This establishes a crucial form of educational advantage for those who acquire high levels of proficiency in Standard Australian English as a 'natural' consequence of their discursive birthright.

Language brokes dominance and advantage for 'already dominant social groups' within the daily routines of formal education in more subtle ways as well.

Following Hymes (1972), numerous linguists and educationists have examined the relationship between home/social group/community language uses and those of schools via the notions of 'speech events' (Hymes 1972) and 'literacy events' (Heath 1983: 386). These are the ideas, simply, that *all* language uses – whether grounded (primarily) in speech or in written/visual texts – are situated within larger rule-governed social practices which shape the events within which language is used and meanings taken. How children learn to speak, what they learn to say and how they come to say it; how they learn to interact with printed text, what texts they learn to interact with, and how they come to interact with them; these will vary from social group to social group in accordance with differences in the form of the speech and literacy events integral to their respective Discourses or forms of life (compare Cazden 1979; Heath 1983: 386; Gee 1990, 1993b). A child's language socialization within her primary group will relate either more closely or less closely to the *mainstream* language events and language uses of the school (Heath 1982, 1983; Luke 1993a). The cultural productions *of* language, and *with* language, that occur in homes and communities are by no means necessarily the same – or even close to – the 'taken as normal' mainstream cultural productions of the school.

The best-known and most thorough work in this area remains Heath's ten-year ethnographic study of language practices in two working-class communities – one black (Trackton), the other white (Roadville) – in the south-east of the United States, and her comparison of these with language socialization practices in the families of 15 primary school teachers in a middle-class school-oriented community (Maintown). Heath describes in detail the differences between these communities in terms of their 'patterns of language use' and 'the paths of language socialisation of their children'. She found that the 'ways with words' in Trackton and Roadville differed from one another as much as each did from the Maintown 'way'. Moreover, the different ways each community interacts with printed text to make meaning and derive knowledge, and the different ways they *use* this knowledge, are linked closely to the different ways children in each community learn to talk through social interactions with caregivers (Heath 1982: 50).

Heath is at pains to insist that her study deals with specific sites and should not be generalized into any kind of macro explanation of patterned difference in education mediated by language. Moreover, her study has much wider purposes than suggesting the relative *efficacy* of the three group-based 'ways with words' in relation to school literacy and learning. Nonetheless, her work provides a powerful detailed illustration of how language may 'broke' dominance and subordination within formal education in specific sites. It shows, for example, how Roadville literacy events – notably, bedtime story reading – involve specific habits and forms of questioning that serve the children quite well in the initial stages of schooling. However, by fourth grade new kinds of questions – e.g. calling for imagination or supposition – and new kinds of language-related habits become increasingly important and frequent in the classroom. Roadville children have not been familiarized with these through their language socialization. Consequently, Roadville children's initial successes

> in reading, being good students, following orders, and adhering to school norms of participating in lessons [e.g. question-answer routines] begin to fall away rapidly . . . [and increasingly] they have no way of keeping up or of seeking help in learning what it is they do not even know they don't know.
>
> (Heath 1982: 64)

This is because the 'ways with words' of dominant social-cultural groups – as typified in the literacy events of Maintown teachers' own homes – constitute the mainstream language uses and practices of school. To use Luke's metaphor, children from different sociocultural backgrounds bring their different language competencies 'to the linguistic "market place" of the school'. The school 'acts to select children on the basis of who brings the most mainstream, school-like approaches to speech and literacy events' (Luke 1993a: 31). Classroom speech and literacy events are characterized by certain forms of questioning, particular conventions for speaking and acting around texts, and a selected tradition of genre and text types (Luke 1993a). Hence, caregivers and other intimates who speak and read to children in the course of their socialization in ways that reflect similar turn-taking patterns as occur in classrooms, and who 'scaffold' dialogue (Cazden 1979) and operate the 'initiation-reply-evaluation sequences' repeatedly described as 'the central structural feature of classroom lessons' (Heath 1982: 51; Knobel 1993), are in effect preparing children from infancy for their subsequent schooling (see Luke 1993a: 31). These are 'mainstream' caregivers, families and social groups: the dominant social and cultural groups whose children populate the 5S-type classrooms of societies like our own.

What holds for written forms of language holds equally for oral language. Discursively shaped forms of spoken address prevalent in communities like Trackton have traditionally been utterly at odds with 'mainstream' school language uses. Gee (1993b) provides a telling illustration here by reference to the 'sharing time' contribution of a 7-year-old black girl, Leona. Leona's 'Cakes' story is a classic of its particular oral narrative genre. Gee analyses its many and complex literary features, establishing a clear-cut case for its structural, thematic, syntactic and poetic sophistication, not to mention its sheer style! He notes that Leona's classmates enjoyed her sharing time stories immensely – when the teacher gave her the chance to complete them. The 'problem' for Leona was, in part, that she told her stories during sharing time, when a quite different genre is called for. The teacher would regularly cut Leona off because, contrary to the demands of the mainstream school Discourse of 'sharing time', she was never 'talking about one important thing' (p. 289).

Leona did not know the rules of sharing time, which call for 'fact-by-fact reports that use explicit and literal language typical of essayist writing'. Moreover, even if the teacher were to have made the rules explicit it is questionable how far Leona could have met them. She has been apprenticed to an entirely different discursive tradition, 'connected to thousands of years of cultural history' (p. 289). Mastering the rules of sharing time calls for an extended apprenticeship that entire groups of students have not had. Teachers, however, often omit to make the rules of classroom Discourses explicit, largely because they are not conscious that rules are actually operating. Such is the 'invisibleness' of our own Discourses to us. Because we have always been 'in them', they become so much a 'part of us' that we do not 'see' them: it does not occur to 'look' for them. We just play them out. In 'playing out' dominant Discourses, teachers unwittingly become agents in the cultural politics of language 'brokering' dominance. Indeed, where they don't ignore them altogether, teachers may well construe the linguistic competencies of students like Leona as 'behavioural problems' (Luke 1993a: 31).

Not only does Leona's home-based Discourse fail to translate to sharing time. *It fails to translate to any mainstream school practice* (see Gee 1993b: 290). It thus fails to provide a basis for status and recognition at *any* point within the reward structure of school learning. It is truly a subordinate Discourse. As language, it 'brokes' subordination.

Up from under: language in the service of cultural recognition and reward in school

While the norm in hierarchically ordered societies is for cultural process to 'naturalize' the dialect and Discourses (including discourses) of dominant groups (Fairclough 1989), making them into norms for school language and learning, it is also true that efforts on behalf of subordinate groups to 'denaturalize' standard dialects and dominant Discourses are increasingly evident. To conclude, I will look briefly at three sorts of contemporary initiative within the cultural politics of language.

Bilingualism as an educational demand/ideal

Within English-speaking countries, challenges to English holding a monopoly on 'linguistic legitimacy' stem from two main underlying factors: the existence of indigenous precolonial populations and cultures, and migration by peoples from non-English-speaking backgrounds. Students from both types of population figure disproportionately in educational underachievement.

Given this, indigenous and migrant peoples face a 'double loss' by going along with practices of formal education grounded in the language, dialect, and Discourses of dominant groups. They stand to lose their language(s) and cultures through cultural assimilation, while at the same time failing to achieve educationally. To put it bluntly, the 'reward' for going along with the mainstream may be the right to end up on the wrong side of school achievement statistics. This has prompted a range of initiatives based on the view that education should promote bilingual (or even multilingual) competence, and that languages other than English should feature as both a medium of instruction and as curriculum subjects. Two examples from the many available will indicate something of the range of positions that have been taken.

During the 1980s the Kura Kaupapa Maori (Maori Philosophy and Language) primary schooling movement emerged in New Zealand (Aotearoa), *outside* the existing state and private systems (Smith 1990). This was a response to long-standing recognition by many Maori of the 'double loss' syndrome, and that successive education policy reforms had failed to promote more equal educational outcomes for Maori as well as to accommodate Maori aspirations for cultural and linguistic integrity and health (see Sharples 1988).

The 1970s had seen the flourishing of Te Kohanga Reo (Maori language nurseries). Here, preschool children were immersed in Maori language and Maori 'ways' – including distinctively Maori ways with words – among kin and other intimates who had retained these ways, and within maximally authentic settings and protocols. (Numbers of European/Pakeha parents who sought bilingual education for their children enrolled them in Kohanga Reo.) Upon graduation from the kohanga, hundreds of children annually faced the prospect of having no primary school available that would meet their language and pedagogical needs.

Kura Kaupapa Maori take the validity and legitimacy of Maori knowledge, pedagogy, and cultural practice as givens, and place high priority on ensuring the revival and survival of the Maori language. These kura (schools) 'use *total immersion* methodology, teaching and learning wholly through Maori language' (Smith 1990: 78). They have developed, outside the state system, 'through the initiative and collected resources of the parents and communities involved' (p. 78). By 1990 there were four kura, with more planned. Participants maintain that normal participation outside of school hours in the routines of the mainstream society will ensure familiarity with English language and Pakeha cultural ways. In summary,

Kaupapa Maori schooling is Maori derived and implemented . . . Maori needs are given priority and care . . . Maori language and culture are central and important components. Maori people are able to select those curriculum items which *they* consider important for their children, and which provide increased choices enabling children to participate more fully in the *total* New Zealand society. The outcome of total immersion Maori language schooling *is* bilingual and bicultural competencies; expertise in both Maori and English languages and cultures.

(p. 79)

'Bidialectism' in education

Outside of settings where the issue is mainly about non-English language variants, other initiatives aim at resisting the 'naturalized' monopoly of linguistic legitimacy within education by Standard English. And in some places where they don't exist, pressure is mounting to force a change. Eades (1993), for example, laments that education systems in Australia have much still to do by way of recognizing and accommodating the special needs of Aboriginal speakers of English. She pays special attention to the needs of those Aboriginal children who come to school as 'fluent and competent communicators' in some variety of Aboriginal English:

Few would deny that these children have the right to learn SE [Standard English], which is after all a prerequisite for equal participation in areas such as employment and further education. Yet AE-speaking [Aboriginal English] children should also have the right to education in their own dialect, and to learn SE as a second dialect.

(p. 5)

The current situation in Australia, however, is 'far from adequate' (Malcolm 1992). Training teachers to recognize AE and its speakers' needs is barely under way. As is common in other multidialect societies, teachers still commonly misclassify Aboriginal students as 'slow learners' – largely on account of discursive differences from the mainstream in ways of communicating and, especially, of responding to teachers' questions. Eades (1993) cites a 1979 legal case from Michigan, where parents successfully established that the School Board had failed to ensure an adequate education for their children. With assistance from linguists, they established that Black English Vernacular (BEV), spoken by their children, was so significantly different from Standard English that the Board's failure to provide for instruction via BEV constituted neglect of duty. The court ordered the School District to recognize BEV, to 'develop a program to help teachers to recognise it, and [to] offer teachers methods of using that knowledge in teaching Black children SE' (p. 5. See also Chambers 1983).

Anderson and Irvine (1993) report an interesting case of tensions between West Indian Creole dialects and Standard English involving students at the University of the Virgin Islands. These students channelled their anger at being assigned to a non-credit remedial English class into a critical investigation of language and dialects, discovering in the process much about the politics of dominance and subordination mediated by standard and non-standard dialects. Focusing on their own shared belief that they spoke 'broken English', they studied linguistics, stimulated by a West Indian linguist who advanced concepts and evidence which established Creole as a (genuine) language. The students

> experimented with writing essays in Creole, discovering that composing an essay is difficult in any language. In the process they had to agree on which of their varieties of Creole would be the standard for creating an orthography, and discovered the reasons for conventions in standard English at the same time. Their sociolinguistic research documented which settings and topics [under existing norms and conventions] called for Creole and which for standard English.
>
> (Anderson and Irvine 1993: 94–5)

The fruits of this critical investigation of dialects impacted on student language practices in class and out of class. Students learned that choice of dialect is more than a matter of simply choosing a formal code, but also includes choices about 'the social uses and values associated with different forms (essays, letters, or songs) . . . the audiences and purposes for the intended . . . products [and] on students' educational goals' (p. 96). Thereafter, these students in honours and remedial classes wrote consciously in a variety of genres: using standard English for research papers, letters to editors, etc.; Creole for fictional stories addressed to other West Indians on themes of shared interest; and Creole for letters of thanks to guest speakers from the community, etc.

'Multidiscoursal' education

There is more to Anderson and Irvine's example than is evident from considering it in terms of bidialectism (or multidialectism) alone. The achievement of the students involved much more than winning some recognized curricular space for Creole dialects. These students had been placed in a remedial class on the assumption that it was in their educational and larger interests to increase their mastery of Standard English. If, however, this strategy is confined to the logic that (so far as language is concerned) the way to improve the conditions of disadvantaged groups and to help them become upwardly mobile 'is to teach [them] standard English, the language of power', it fails to address 'the primary issue': namely, 'challenging the inequality between groups' which produces and maintains cultural and linguistic hierarchies in the first place (Anderson and Irvine 1993: 95).

It is never simply a given *dialect* that is stigmatized but, rather, the entire way of life and the integral identities associated with it as discursive practice. To accept the standard language-dialect as the necessary condition for advancement is to take a chance on an assimilatory logic that rejects the language *and the way of being* of those who speak the non-standard variety.

To succeed within this logic entails a rejection of one's own language, family, and community (Anderson and Irvine 1993). It is to reinforce further the cultural politics of domination and subordination. The important point evident from the case of the Virgin Islands students is: through critical investigation of language in relation to a problematic experience they successfully challenged the monopoly of educational legitimacy assumed by standard English; at the same time they increased their mastery of standard English and learned when to draw on it to achieve success and status; in doing so they discovered they could 'choose to learn the standard for various functions without having to reject their own language, family, and community' (p. 95); and in the process they engaged in a cultural politics of opposition to and transformation of existing patterns and structures of domination and subordination.

Recognizing the principles underlying such cases, and the larger democratic and egalitarian ethics and politics they exemplify, many educators call for school classrooms and classroom pedagogies to provide sites in which all students are exposed 'to a variety of alternative primary and secondary Discourses' (Gee 1991: 10). In such classrooms and pedagogies, Leona's primary Discourse would find its place alongside those more dominant Discourses inherent in currently mainstream school routines like sharing time, scholarly report writing, and academically oriented exams. This would recognize the educational goal of enabling all students 'to critique their primary and secondary Discourses, including dominant secondary Discourses' – acknowledging that 'this is what good teaching and learning are good at' (p. 10). More generally, such a pedagogy of difference enables students

> to cross over into diverse cultural zones that offer a critical resource for rethinking how the relations between dominant and subordinate groups are organized, how they are implicated and often structured in dominance, and how such relations might be transformed . . . Difference in this case does not become a marker for deficit, inferiority, chauvinism, or inequality; on the contrary, it opens the possibilities for constructing pedagogical practices that deepen forms of cultural democracy that serve to enlarge our moral vision.
>
> (Giroux 1993: 375)

Conclusion

The relationship between language and cultural process is complex. Indeed, we do better to think in terms of diverse languages, manifold cultural processes, and the innumerable relationships that operate among and between them. In this introductory investigation of language and cultural process, we have seen that language is both a necessary condition for cultural process and an outcome of that process. Language also functions in complex ways as a medium of cultural process generically, as well as of myriad specific cultural processes. Finally, from the perspective of cultural politics, language can be seen as very much a 'broker' of cultural process. These are just three of many themes worthy of further exploration in what continues to be underexplored terrain.

A number of the key ideas and examples introduced in the course of this discussion will be picked up in greater depth or from different angles in subsequent chapters: notably the Discourse-discourse distinction, the idea that literacy is many rather than monolithic, and the fact that literacies and Discourses are ordered hierarchically within the politics of daily life. These notions are especially pertinent to discussing critical literacy and issues of empowerment in relation to literacy: themes which are taken up in the next two chapters.

two

CRITICAL SOCIAL LITERACY FOR THE CLASSROOM: AN APPROACH USING CONVENTIONAL TEXTS ACROSS THE CURRICULUM

This chapter aims to develop a workable approach to critical social literacy across the secondary school curriculum: an approach that deals with both practical and conceptual-theoretical aspects.

This is quite a challenge, for various reasons. Part of the difficulty stems from the fact that, like the notion of empowerment discussed in Chapter 3, being 'critical' is very much in educational vogue right now. Educators are increasingly being called on to develop 'critical approaches' with their students. Unfortunately, many such calls come from quite disparate theoretical positions – or from no discernible theoretical position at all. Consequently, as a descriptor term 'critical' often suffers from having too little meaning, or from having too much. What does this mean?

Some empirical observations

'Critical' seems often to be invoked as a 'magic bullet' term (see Chapter 3). In such cases it has too little meaning. 'Critical thinking', 'critical awareness', 'critical pedagogy', 'critical literacy' and so on are commonly appealed to as solutions to some problem or need, without any real indication being provided of what actually counts as critical practice in the particular cases. For instance, developing critical thinking skills throughout the workforce is often touted as an answer to sluggish economic performance. Similarly, a critical literacy approach to language learning is widely advocated as a means to making learners more powerful/empowered language users. Often in such cases little or no attempt is made to describe, interpret, or theorize *the critical*. It is seemingly believed or assumed that merely inserting the word 'critical' into curriculum and policy documents (or rhetoric) will point the way – perhaps, even, lend material assistance – to meeting educational goals and overcoming existing problems. In such cases, 'critical' goes into battle without any clear meaning, but with a lot of work to do.

On the other hand, while 'magic bullet' appeals to critical approaches leave the concept with too little meaning, many educationists *do* in fact elaborate conceptual and theoretical views of what is involved in thinking, judging, analysing, reading and writing *critically*. The snag here is that the views advanced vary greatly and there are many of them. The development of critical acumen is a perennial educational value. To the extent that being critical contrasts with being naive, superficial or acritical, it is hardly surprising that educators should espouse a 'critical' approach. In this respect, 'critical' is like other positive value terms such as 'freedom', 'democracy' and 'empowerment'. As with these other terms, concepts, theories and practices of the critical are constructed in disparate ways, and for much the same reason: namely, to derive the benefits of the positive connotations of 'critical' while at the same time giving expression to larger values, purposes, and traditions that vary greatly from interest group to interest group. Viewed from this perspective, 'critical' has altogether too much meaning.

A survey of contemporary educational theories and pedagogies reveals quite different approaches to critical literacy. Allan Luke and Christine Walton (1994), for example, distinguish 'conventional' variants of critical literacy from what they call 'critical social literacy' approaches. Within recent and current educational theory and practice we can discern 'reader affective response to literary texts', 'higher order skills with text', and 'liberal rationalist' constructions of critical reading and writing, among many others, as examples of *conventional* variants (see Luke and Walton 1994; also Lankshear 1982). Luke and Walton discuss 'critical pedagogy/Freirean-based approaches' and 'discourse analytic approaches' as examples of *critical social literacy* variants.

To these might be added others as diverse as approaches derived from systemic functional linguistics, on the one hand, or from the gamut of poststructuralist, postmodern, postcolonial, etc. constructions of textuality and 'reading/deconstructing texts' on the other (see Kress 1985; Martin 1985; Morgan 1992; McLaren 1993; Peters and Lankshear 1994).

How might educators espousing commitment to some critical ideal or other of literacy specifically, and education more generally, negotiate their way across the gulf that exists between critical literacy having too little meaning and having altogether too much meaning? How might we choose appropriately among the variants we become aware of? – bearing in mind that proponents of each variant jostle enthusiastically for our allegiance.

Alternatively, how might we construct a theory and practice of critical literacy that we can subscribe to and engage with conviction?

Getting started on thinking about critical literacy

A good place to start is by accepting that 'critical literacy' is not a name for some finite established entity. Rather, it implies more the idea that there are standards or criteria on the basis of which we may distinguish *critical* conceptions and practices of reading and writing and viewing, etc. from *non-critical* or *acritical* literacies.

Unfortunately, this does not take us far. The criteria or standards in question are by no means established. 'Critical' is an essentially contested concept. Representatives of quite different and often incompatible views claim for their respective values, purposes and practices the status attaching to 'being critical', and there is no settled way of saying that some views are bona fide and others are not.

Moreover, this is far from a matter simply of conceptual competition. The stakes are higher than mere dispute about conceptual meanings. What is at stake here is competition among Discourses.

As argued in Chapter 1, it is within and through Discourse(s) that human beings conceive, enact, and thereby give shape or form to values and meanings. We construct motherhood, loyalty, courage, citizenship, scholarship, learning and so on, within and through discursive *forms* of doing and being these ways.

This is not to imply that the norms governing and defining a particular Discourse and membership within it are necessarily precise; still less is it to imply that they are settled or immutable. Neither is it to suggest that values and purposes come first and are then made into live forms. Nor is there just one discursive construction corresponding to each Discourse descriptor. There *are* multiple variants of motherhood, or of being a linguist, although the possibilities are bounded. There *are* limits.

The key point here is that each and every Discourse and (Discourse variant) is historically contingent (McLaren 1993). As we have seen already, Discourses are social constructions, and therefore are not *necessary*. That said, however, the formal constructing of a given Discourse nonetheless imposes requirements for recognized participation in that Discourse, for as long as it remains operative. One cannot, for example, practise 'being critical' without adhering to *some* set or other of recognized values and procedures. To the extent, however, that all identifiable Discourses of critical practice are contingent there is no superior basis for identifying any one of them as being 'the real thing'.

How, then, do we identify, give allegiance to, or become involved in shaping up a Discourse of critical literacy? How might one begin to develop and defend a position on critical literacy?

At least two approaches are available. One involves 'unpacking' existing discursive constructions of engaging critically with and through texts, identifying the standards and criteria in relation to which they are deemed *critical* and, if necessary, providing grounds for preference against other constructions. An example of this approach is provided by John Searle (1990), who elaborates one established practice of critical literacy based on 'the canon' and argues its superiority over both what has been called a liberal rationalist approach and what he sees as 'overtly political' constructions of critical literacy (see Lankshear 1994a).

The second approach involves beginning from minimal assumptions about critical social practice and actually constructing a critical literacy in the light of the strengths and weaknesses of actual and conceivable alternatives.

It is this second approach that I will take here.

From the ground up: constructing critical literacies

A helpful start to 'tidying' up our thinking about critical literacy can be made by drawing some distinctions. Two are especially helpful. The first involves recognizing two essential elements of any and *all* critical practice. The second deals with an ambiguity within the idea of critical literacy itself.

The adjective 'critical' and its related terms, 'criticism', 'criticize' and 'critique', imply judging, comparing, or evaluating on the basis of careful analysis. There are, then, two necessary aspects to any critical orientation. There is the element of evaluation or *judgement*. There is, in addition, the requirement of knowing closely and 'for what it is', that which is being evaluated: the *object* of evaluation or judgement To *criticize* X (i.e. to judge X positively or negatively) is to comment on X's qualities or merits. This requires identifying them through some kind of analysis.

These two 'moments' of critique are readily apparent, for example, in Peter McLaren's (1989, 1995) conception of critical pedagogy. Insofar as schooling itself comprises the object of critique, critical pedagogy is grounded in an analysis of schooling as a form of cultural politics. That is, schooling 'always represents an introduction to, preparation for, and legitimation of particular forms of social life' (McLaren 1989: 160). Furthermore, schooling always involves power relations, social practices and privileged forms of knowledge 'that support a specific vision of past, present and future', and 'rationalise the knowledge industry' in ways that 'reproduce inequality, racism and sexism [and] fragment democratic social relations' by emphasizing 'competitiveness and cultural ethnocentrism' (p. 161). In response to the cultural politics of schooling, critical pedagogy engages students and teachers together in making explicit the socially constituted character of knowledge, and asking in whose interests particular 'knowledges' are thus constituted, legitimated, and perpetuated. In accordance with an *analysis* that is grounded in a theory of schooling as a form of cultural politics, and in accordance with detailed findings derived in the analysis, we might advance a substantive *evaluation* or judgement of schooling in general, or of particular cases and aspects of schooling that exemplify the larger cultural politics in question.

So far as critical *literacy* is concerned, we need to establish its object of critique: what is it that is to be known 'through and through'? Here we find ambiguity at the very base of the idea of critical literacy. This ambiguity corresponds loosely to Gunther Kress's distinction between 'knowing *about* language' and 'knowing *through* language' (Kress 1985: ch. 2, 1989), and Catherine Wallace's distinction between critical reading as a matter of 'responding to particular texts' versus critical reading as involving 'awareness . . . of what reading itself is' (1992: 61).

These distinctions suggest at least three potential *objects* of critique in respect of critical literacy. A critical literacy might involve any or all of:

- knowing literacy in general, or particular literacies, critically; that is, having a critical perspective on *literacy* or *literacies per se*;
- having a critical perspective on particular *texts*;
- having a critical perspective on – i.e. being able to make 'critical readings' of – wider *social practices, arrangements, relations, allocations, procedures*, etc., which are mediated by, made possible, and partially sustained through reading, writing, viewing, transmitting, etc., texts.

The first of these 'foci' (for want of a better label) may be thought of in terms of having some meta-level understanding of literacy/literacies as social practice(s): that is, to know literacy for what 'it' is. Of course, accounts of 'what it is' are necessarily informed by some theory or other and will be contentious. For example, many literacy scholars and educationists professing a critical perspective conceive literacy – and, indeed, language generally – as an inherent component of Discourse, where Discourse(s) are inescapably value-laden, power-ridden, and interest- or purpose-serving. Hence, for them literacy is irredeemably ideological and implicated in creating and maintaining social hierarchies, differences, advantages and disadvantages, etc. Furthermore, all literacy (like all Discourse), is historically contingent, socially constructed and, to that extent, *transformable*. To act transformatively on literacy will to a greater or lesser extent be to act on Discourse. The example provided in Chapter 1 by Anderson and Irvine, of the Creole-speaking Virgin Islands students is a case in point here.

The second and third 'foci' of critical literacy in theory and practice relate more specifically to *texts*. Clearly, what a text *is* can be viewed in different ways. In a narrow and formalistic conception, a text is simply a passage of print or a slice of speech, or an image: it is more or less frozen in time and space, and largely cut off from its sociality, its *context*. Beyond this, however, lies a richer conception of text, with particular significance for critical literacy. It too can be conceived in narrower or wider terms, marking the difference between our second and third 'foci' respectively. Gunther Kress (1985) takes us directly to the non-formalistic sociocultural conception of text that underpins my emerging account of critical literacy.

Kress argues that so far as our interest in language and literacy is grounded in the social and cultural rather than the merely formalistic, texts comprise the 'relevant units of language'. Moreover,

> The forms and meanings of texts are determined by discourses – systems of meanings arising out of the organisation of social institutions – and by genres – formal conventional categories whose meanings and forms arise out of the meanings, forms and functions of the conventionalised occasions of social interactions. Clearly, both of these sources of the forms and meanings of texts are entirely social and cultural. Nor are discourses and genres unrelated – social institutions tend to have their own particular occasions of interaction, and so it seems at times that when we are talking about genre we are talking about discourse, and talking about characteristics of discourse when we are discussing genre. Clearly too, certain discourses tend to have preferred relations with certain genres, and some genres are incompatible with certain discourses.
>
> (Kress 1985: 31)

Texts are 'given' form and meaning by discourse and genre. We give and receive textual meanings in discursive settings and in generic ways. Furthermore, we are *formed* discursively as givers and receivers of textual meaning. We become givers and receivers of meaning in virtue of our discursive histories – our accumulated experience of discourses.

It is helpful here to revisit the distinction suggested by Gee between Discourse and discourse. Discourse (with a capital 'D') refers to social practices which amount to 'ways of being in the world' (e.g. being a teacher, being Catholic, being a linguist, being a feminist, etc.). This is the use employed above. discourse (with a lower case 'd') refers to the language (saying, listening, reading, writing, viewing) components of a Discourse. There is no (and cannot conceivably be) Discourse without discourse, and vice versa. They simultaneously form and inform each other. All literacies are embedded in Discourses.

Thus specific texts, understood as sociocultural phenomena, are simultaneously more or less specific 'chunks' of Discourse, or 'moves' within a Discourse, and 'exemplifications' of or participations in *the character of the*

Discourse as a whole. It is this distinction between 'a chunk of Discourse' and 'an exemplification of a larger discursive logic' that distinguishes the second and third 'foci' for critical literacy noted above.

More needs to be said, however, to clinch this point. The notions of 'speech events' (Hymes 1972) and 'literacy events' (Heath 1982, 1983) are helpful here. Language 'events' are more than just words. Allan Luke's (1993b) account of speech and 'speech events' makes the point I seek. Luke notes that speech is not developed in isolation, or in some pure form. Rather, learning to speak

> entails learning, negotiating and contesting ways of conducting social relations with elders, siblings and other community members. Language use occurs in boundaried *speech events* (Hymes 1972). These events are not random or arbitrary, but are rule governed and structured. Although they may seem spontaneous, events such as mealtime conversations, ordering in a restaurant, the rituals of preparing for bedtime and telephone conversations follow identifiable protocols and patterns: some topics and kinds of language are acceptable, particular social roles and relationships are called into play. Hence, for a child, learning how to participate in a mealtime conversation requires apprenticing at a set of rules that govern who can nominate which topics, how to get the floor, what kinds of gestures can and can't be made, when and who can interrupt whom, who has the final 'word', where slang and profanity might be appropriate, even volume levels. The rules and conventions mark out what the philosopher Wittgenstein called 'language games'.
>
> (Luke 1993b: 23)

Now, for language, communication and meaning to be *social-cultural* is for them to be *political*, for them to be inseparable from the production and operation of institutionally structured *power*. Language is deeply and inescapably bound up with producing, reproducing and maintaining arrangements of power which are unequal. To this extent the meanings which are given and received in language, through texts, are not 'innocent'. They are not merely descriptive, performative, factual, or propositional. They are also *ideological*. Developing critical readers and writers of texts has, then, necessarily to do in part with enabling them to detect and handle the inherently ideological dimension of literacy, and the role of literacy in enactments and productions of power.

Such is the nature of all language and literacy. Specific texts can be approached both as discrete moves within some language game or other within a Discourse, *and* as participating in the 'logic' of the Discourse as a whole. To read a text critically in the narrower sense identified above would be to read it as a discrete move in a language game and, having thus analysed it, to respond to it evaluatively. To read critically in the wider sense would be to respond to a particular text as an embodiment of a larger discursive logic.

This leaves the question of what, in either case, constitutes a critical *response*. This is to ask about the relationship between critical literacy and what Freireans (among others) would call *praxis*. There is an obvious sense in which the practice of critical literacy as outlined so far might remain at a linguistic level: at a level of articulation or comment. For example, students might analyse a text in terms of its sexist ideology – whether as a move in a sexist language game or as an exemplification of some sexist Discourse – without *challenging* the Discourse in any substantive material way. To make a critical move in a language game as a *praxis* of critical literacy, however, would involve addressing the Discourse in the process of addressing its discourse.

Much of what I have tried to say so far is encapsulated in Pam Gilbert's view (1993: 324) that a critical literacy for the 1990s must 'address the practices by which words enact social meaning, and the practices by which we, as social subjects, make meaning'. In particular, classroom practices of critical literacy must explore how and why social subjects can 'make the range of meanings' (or readings of texts) they can in fact make – i.e. the 'repertoires' of readings they can access and, hence, the social meanings that are authorized and silenced by their available practices of reading, writing, viewing, and compositing (Green 1995).

> A grasp of 'critical' literacy – of what I would call the social contextualisation of language practices – necessitates a grasp of how language operates in a social sense [the first of the 'foci' identified above – author] . . . Such understandings are learnt in functional settings and cannot be divorced from social practice. To work with a commitment to *critical* literacy, therefore, will inevitably necessitate an engagement with the politics of language practices . . . To explore the social context of language practices is . . . to explore . . . networks of power that are sustained and brought into existence by such practices. It is to explore how language practices are used in powerful institutions like the state, the school, the law, the family, the church, and how these practices contribute to the maintenance of inequalities and injustices. For teachers, it means engaging with issues that are often controversial, certainly contemporary, and perhaps quite volatile.
>
> (Gilbert 1993: 324–5)

These later comments resonate with the second and third 'foci' above.

Having sketched a broad concept of critical literacy I will now consider some pedagogical practices that can bring it to life in classrooms, beginning with some examples of Catherine Wallace's work in London with migrant EFL (English as a Foreign Language) students. Despite the context of adult second language learning, Wallace's practices can easily be seen to apply to more mainstream classroom settings.

'Critical language awareness': critical reading as pedagogical practice

Wallace begins from the view that critical reading has two senses. In its narrower sense critical reading is about responding to particular texts. More widely, however, critical reading involves 'awareness . . . of what reading itself is' (Wallace 1992: 61). The problem with much – if not most – literacy teaching is that critical reading has not generally been encouraged in either sense, regardless of whether the learners have very limited English language proficiency or are quite advanced learners of English.

Readers in general tend to adopt overly deferent stances toward texts, says Wallace, and there is insufficient use of texts 'which are provocative' and inadequate attention paid to developing methodologies for interpreting texts which address 'ideological assumptions as well as propositional meaning' (p. 62).

Wallace describes aspects of her own pedagogy which she developed to 'help readers to resist certain kinds of assaults presented by written texts: to challenge, that is, particular ways of talking about persons, places, events and phenomena and ways of talking to the reader – of positioning her/him in particular ways' (p. 61).

Her aim as a literacy teacher is to enable learners to see texts and the reading of texts as problematic, to understand the political-ideological character of literacy as a social phenomenon, and to become more assertive in interacting with written texts. It is worth noting here that while Wallace is concerned explicitly with critical *reading*, her ideas, of course, apply equally to the other dimensions of linguistic activity.

Her pedagogy emerged as practical activities prompted by three questions which, together, cover the wider and narrower aspects of critical reading.

(1) What reading practices are characteristic of particular social groups, for example, what kind of reading behaviour typifies a particular family or community setting?
(2) How is reading material produced in a particular society, that is how do texts such as newspapers, advertisements, leaflets and public information material come to us in the form they do, who produces them, and how do they come to have the salience they do?
(3) What influences the process of interpreting texts in particular contexts?

(p. 63)

Let us consider some of the ways she addressed these in her pedagogy.

Reading profiles

The class drew on a model of profiling people's reading experiences to develop a framework for thinking about the role of reading in their own personal lives, and of how far this role had been shaped by early family and school experiences. The framework (Wallace 1992: 64) comprised:

- first memories of reading (what, where, with whom?);
- favourite reading as a child;
- favourite reading as an adult;
- most important book/s or author/s in your life;
- main roles and purposes of reading (e.g. as parent, professional, for pleasure, religious purposes).

Using this framework learners interviewed other people and brought the profiles back to class for discussion and analysis. They also did 'family literacy' surveys, asking people about their reader roles as family members. (See also Heath 1983 for further possibilities.) These exercises and subsequent discussions revealed 'how much can be learned from [reading behaviour and reading material] about social class membership, education [and] political views', as well as about 'taken for granted assumptions about gender, class and race' (Wallace 1992: 65). The group discovered, for instance, the 'near invisibility' of entire social groups (Asians, disabled, etc.) in a sample of children's books. (They had examined children's books in view of the fact that many of the learners were parents.)

Reading and written texts as problematic: the production and consumption of reading material

Wallace aimed to problematize power in relation to published reading material and the consumption of texts. For example, what factors tend to influence 'what gets published and where and in what form' (p. 66)? Is our press *free*? What counts as news and where is it sourced? Is it significant who owns specific media? 'Does it matter that *The Times* and *The Sun* are both owned by the same man?' (p. 66).

To address such issues in a classroom setting, Wallace had members assemble a diverse range of authentic (or in daily use) texts – such as advertisements, letters, newspapers, bills. Groups of learners classified and discussed the texts around the following task(s):

(i) Try to classify the texts on each table. Suggested categories might be: requests from charities or causes; public information leaflets; professional reading material.

   (ii) When you have worked out five or six broad types of text, try to
        identify the following:
        (a) who produces them? e.g., public bodies, commercial enter-
            prises, local authorities
        (b) for whom are they produced, i.e., who are the consumers or
            expected readers of the material?
        (c) why has the text been produced?
        (d) is this type of text of interest or relevance to you? why/why
            not?
        (e) choose one text from each category which particularly appeals
            to you, either because of its style or content and discuss with
            other members of your group.

                                                                    (p. 66)

Reading specific texts critically

These previous components of Wallace's pedagogy were designed to
stimulate a critical awareness of what reading *is* in general terms: to situate it
socially and in terms of broad political effects. To augment this general level
of approach, Wallace also developed pedagogies for teaching critical reading
of specific texts. These included procedures for collecting materials, as well as
approaches to reading texts critically.

Students were invited to collect texts they come across in everyday use and
from a range of genres (ads, magazine articles, public notices, newspaper
reports, etc.) to work with in class. Wallace would add texts (on student-
chosen topics) written from different positions or perspectives from the
original text. Students had to provide reasons for choosing their particular
text as being appropriate for the group as a whole to work with.

This would encourage learners in pre-reading activity to focus on such
meta-level considerations relevant to critical literacy as the *history* of texts
(where a text comes from, why it is what it is, the circumstances under which
it was produced, etc.); *intertextuality* (presumptions about the reading
experiences of others in the group, an attempt to relate this particular text to
others in a series, to identify texts within a common genre, or across genres,
etc.); and *discourse* (identifying the links between ways of talking and writing
and conventions associated with social institutions – hence the fact that ways
of talking about people, phenomena, places, events, etc. are ideologically
shaped and constrained, and that language is part of the discursive process of
establishing and maintaining power differentials between different 'types of'
people). For example, good reasons for working with a given text might
include the belief that it drew on common experiences of daily routines and
pressures, connected with prior reading histories, positioned readers in given
ways, and contributed to maintaining X or Y states of affairs.

Wallace chose to work with a pre-reading/while-reading/post-reading procedure which was constructed around an explicitly critical ethos. In the pre-reading phase, for example, rather than asking students for 'their personal opinions' on the topic of a text, Wallace would focus attention on why the topic was selected for text production in the first place. Specifically, she built classroom procedure on Kress's (1985: 7) three questions,

1 Why is this topic being written about?
2 How is this topic being written about?
3 What other ways of writing about the topic are there?

adding two further orienting questions of her own,

4 Who is writing to whom? and
5 What is the topic?

Thus, pre-reading tasks may include asking what range of ways might be available for writing on the topic (of a selected text) of X; and why might the text have been written; and (drawing on a scan of the headline, pictures, photo, sub-headings, etc.) what the text is (seemingly) about.

Tasks for 'while reading' centre on how material in the text is presented. Those employed by Wallace drew on a range of linguistic devices identified as important by 'critical linguists' in the vein of Gunther Kress and Norman Fairclough: such as, who takes what subject positions in sentences? how are active and passive constructions allocated? what modal constructions are employed? and so on. These questions focus attention on questions of power in discourse, on reader positioning, the construction of 'a possible world', and so on.

Post-reading tasks employed by Wallace invited opinions on to whom the text was (primarily) addressed, and a *post hoc* consideration of other ways in which the text could have been written – hence which options were not taken up textually, why not, and with what consequences or effects. Such tasks involve classroom readers and writers in active processes or rereading and rewriting: processes which have obvious potential for spilling over into students' larger discursive practices both inside and outside school settings.

By such means classroom teachers can go a long way toward meeting the demands for critical literacy practice identified by Gilbert. The special contribution made by Wallace is that the pedagogy she describes serves as an initiation for teachers into a practice of critical literacy within the very process of teachers working to develop a critical literacy pedagogy for their students.

To complete this present attempt to translate elements of a concept and theory of critical literacy into pedagogical practice, I will draw on some recent work I have done with Michele Knobel to construct a critical literacy practice around a specific set of texts and across several areas of the secondary school curriculum.

Critical literacy across the curriculum: media texts and interdisciplinary critique

Drawing on a range of concepts and techniques elaborated by theorists and teachers working in various areas of critical language study, Michele Knobel and I have been developing activities around a simple media text we believe has interesting possibilities for an interdisciplinary practice of critical literacy. We suggest working with the newspaper in conjunction with a set of rather different but relevant texts to address questions adapted from linguists and literacy educators like Norman Fairclough, Allan Luke and Gunther Kress.

Our approach calls for a context where teachers across several subjects – e.g. English, geography, modern history, social education, environmental studies – agree to work cooperatively and in an integrated way to explore texts critically through their disciplines. Our approach has two cornerstones: the English teacher and the teacher librarian.

The English teacher helps students 'break texts open' by using available procedures for critical study of texts as described and modelled by people like Fairclough (1989, 1992), Kress (1985), Luke (1988) and Gilbert (1993). In English, then, texts will be broken open in ways that require three kinds of resources to inform alternative 'readings': information associated with other disciplines or subject areas; texts grounded in a range of theoretical-ideological perspectives; texts that cross historico-cultural time and space. The English teacher, then, creates a need for exploration of issues traversing a range of subjects and from different standpoints.

The teacher librarian, in collaboration with subject teachers, coordinates resources across the subject areas. S/he locates and assembles – for each subject area involved – texts conveying information which reflects different theoretical, ideological and cultural perspectives pertaining to issues and themes that have been identified by 'breaking texts open' linguistically and subsequently allocated to particular subject areas.

The starting point is a front page story from a major Australian daily newspaper, 'The Face of Starving Africa'. The story is dominated by a 22 cm by 16 cm black and white photograph (which, because of copyright conditions, is not reproduced here) of a young unclad Somali boy sitting in the dust. The child is starving, almost to the point of death – he is literally skin and bone and his face is etched with the pain of starvation. The photograph, a study in pathos, carries the byline of Phoebe Fraser, daughter of a former Australian prime minister. In addition to this front page story, the same issue of the newspaper carried further coverage on page 7, dealing with specific aspects of the drought in Somalia. 'The Face of Starving Africa' pointed readers to these additional stories.

The Face of Starving Africa

A Somali boy, one of 30 million Africans suffering from the effects of drought – Picture: Phoebe Fraser.

AFRICA today. A starving child waits to die in the dust of Somalia.

Hundreds of Somalis collapse every day, unwilling and unable to live any longer in the worst drought to grip their continent for 100 years.

More than 30 million Africans, from Ethiopia to Mozambique, have left their villages in search of food and water.

This photograph was taken by Care Australia's program officer, Ms Phoebe Fraser, the daughter of former prime minister, Mr Malcolm Fraser, who is president of Care.

'Somalia is desperate,' she says. 'In a country where hundreds of bodies line the streets, most of them children, you can only hope the world is watching.'

Yesterday, the United Nations said it would send 500 armed soldiers to protect aid supplies to Somalia, which has been ravaged by drought and civil war, following agreement by warring factions to allow the safe delivery of aid.

The Australian's readers have helped raise thousands of dollars to buy food and medicine by sending donations to the addresses of aid agencies alongside articles on Africa's heartbreaking story.

Aid should be sent to: Care Australia, GPO Box 9977, in your capital city; World Vision, GPO Box 9944, in your capital city; Red Cross, GPO Box 9949, in your capital city; Save the Children's Fund, GPO Box 9912, in your capital city; Austcare Africa Appeal, PO Locked Bag 15, Camperdown NSW 2050; Community Aid Abroad, GPO Box 9920, in your capital city.

(*The Australian*, Friday 14 August 1992: 1)

In the beginning: critical language analysis in the English class

Drawing on work by linguists and literacy scholars, Allan Luke advances some very effective means for undertaking critical language analysis across a range of text types, including media stories (Luke 1992). These can be used productively with a text like 'The Face of Starving Africa' to explore how it constructs reality textually and positions readers. A preliminary 'opening up' of the text provides a basis for exploring its practical discursive and ideological implications through wider subject study, which is integrated with more specialized language study in English.

Activity: preliminary critical language analysis of the text

Luke notes that texts employ devices of various kinds to construct reality textually, and to position readers. For example, there are multiple and diverse ways in which the reality in Somalia might be represented or constructed textually. A given text, such as 'The Face of Starving Africa', will represent it one way (a 'possible world') rather than others. At the same time, the text will, by various means, position readers to make meaning from it in a particular way. It 'positions readers in relation to a particular worldview or ideology' (Luke 1992: 6), which in this case has implications for how we act in the world and see ourselves as local and global citizens, as political beings, moral agents, and so on.

Text analysis exercise

Read 'The Face of Starving Africa', and explore the following questions:

1 What version of events/reality is foregrounded here?
2 Whose version is this? From whose perspective is it constructed?
3 What other (possible) versions are excluded?
4 Whose/what interests are served by this representation?
5 By what means – lexical, syntactic, etc. – does this text construct (its) reality?
6 How does this text position the reader? What assumptions about readers are reflected in the text? What beliefs, assumptions, expectations (ideological baggage) do readers have to entertain in order to make meaning from the text?

(adapted from Luke 1992; Fairclough 1989)

Objective and rationale

As we see things, an important part of the English teacher's job is to enable students to understand what these questions (and similar ones) are asking, and to acquire a relevant meta-language of linguistic and semantic concepts and 'tools' by which to break the text open through such questions. Such understandings are best acquired in contexts which incorporate precisely the kinds of text and activities in question here.

We should note, however, that much of what is needed in order to identify versions that have been excluded, the interests served by a particular representation, etc., is best pursued in wider subject settings. Thus, the English class breaks the text open in ways that call for elaboration from other subject areas, from whence further inquiry and critique can proceed in the English class. At this point in the inquiry, the English class might only get as far as addressing the construction of reality and aspects of reader positioning.

A possible (sample) response to text analysis exercise

Construction of reality

1 Those people starving in Somalia – and, indeed, the 30 million Africans from Ethiopia to Mozambique – are suffering from the effects of drought.
2 This drought is the worst in 100 years.
3 Somalia is also ravaged by civil war, which contributes to starvation.
4 The situation is so desperate the only hope is international sympathy and goodwill (aid).
5 Readers have contributed money to aid agencies.
6 Aid agencies address the situation in Somalia.
7 Six agencies are named, to whom donations should be sent.

Putting these together we find a construction of the Somalia reality in terms of an extreme drought happening in a setting where there is also a war. In such circumstances, aid agencies coordinate relief. The role for ordinary people is to donate aid. The action is undertaken by the aid agencies, with assistance from some (special) history-making individuals like the Frasers. Aid agencies exist to respond to calamitous happenings like droughts.

Reader position

1 The reader is positioned to make meaning from an emotive rather than a rational or informed standpoint. The photo dominates, and the text conveys virtually no *factual* detail of consequence. (In terms of the matters we will address below, it should be added that the page 7 stories, like most reporting in the mass media of the famine in Somalia, construct essentially the same reality.) Wordings like 'Africa's heartbreaking story', 'desperate', 'hope', 'starving child', 'collapse', etc. set the tone.
2 Outside of an emotive basis for making meaning, the reader is presumed to respond to a propaganda device commonly known as 'testimonial'. A former prime minister and his daughter are invoked here as authoritative support for the particular construction of reality, as well as for constructing the reader-citizen as *donor*.
3 To make meaning the reader is required to operate from the following sorts of assumptions and beliefs which, it will become apparent, are profoundly ideological: '(natural) disasters happen'; 'disasters are addressed by money, converted to aid or relief'; 'aid and relief agencies are the officially valid mediums of action'; 'some causes are genuine (hence worthy of our

generosity)'; 'children are always innocent victims'; 'we can extend generosity by donating – their circumstances are unrelated to us'; 'extending charity freely is a virtue – a *human* act', and so on.

Some implications of this analysis for other subject studies

Let us assume that something like the above response might emerge from a careful probing of the text given a reasonably typical range of (English) teacher and secondary student understandings. To go further, however, and envisage other possible versions of reality, ideological and interest serving aspects, and implications for citizenship, calls for a wider curriculum base.

References in the original text to drought, civil war, the creation of a continent-wide refugee population, and the operation of aid agencies, create openings for further exploration across several subject areas.

Activity: subject teachers with teacher librarian

1 Locate for each subject area a range of texts relevant to situations like that in Somalia (viz. disasters).
2 Ensure that among them the texts reflect different perspectives.
3 Identify and describe key differences in the perspectives, in terms of their underlying theories, the questions or issues with which they are most concerned, their key assumptions, whose standpoint they most reflect, where you would locate them on a continuum.

Four possible sample texts

'[A] whole variety of things [makes] people susceptible to drought'. [A] factor that contributes to vulnerability is history. Many developing countries have inherited inappropriate economic structures and relatively weak positions in the global economy. In particular, colonisation fostered the orientation of whole national economies towards exportation of one or a few products . . . Such exclusive focus on one or two sources of export revenue increases vulnerability in many respects. Notably, it deprives the country of food crops for domestic consumption and leaves it at the mercy of international markets. Also, due to scarce resources, only enough staple crop is grown to satisfy immediate needs, leaving the population without a buffer of stored grain to carry it through periods of drought.

(Castellino 1992: 8–9)

'The extensive plunder-culture [of plantations under colonization] meant not only the death of the forest but also, in the long run, of . . . fertility. With forests surrendered to the flames, erosion soon did its work on the defenceless soil and thousands of streams dried up.'

This process is continuing in many parts of the world. The desert in West Africa is spreading. With the growth of refrigeration the number of food crops that can be exported for luxury consumption in the developed countries has increased. In Upper Volta peasants . . . organised themselves into unions to demand the right to grow crops for themselves rather than vegetables to export to France.

(Hayter 1982: 54. The quotation is from Galeano 1973)

The fundamental causes [of Africa's food crisis] are varied and complex . . . The cumulative effects over many years have resulted in decrease in per capita food production, deforestation, desertification, increasing reliance on imported foodstuffs, and a mounting foreign debt. Such consequences are rooted, however, not in impersonal 'market forces' or climatic conditions, but in political decisions involving the allocation of resources . . . [For example] when resources were allocated to infrastructure and extension services in the agrarian sector, the bias was toward revenue-generating export crops, rather than food production.

. . . African states were colonial creations with a fragile history of internal cohesion. That which existed has been rent by harsh economic realities . . . These divisions have been played upon by outside interests for their own ends. In Angola the CIA-backed UNITA rebels fought a protracted civil war against the Marxist government. The South African government gave military support to RENAMO bandits in an effort to destabilise Mozambique . . . The militarisation of Africa, frequently funded by loans under the guise of development aid is yet another drain on scarce resources. The ending of the Cold War threatens to release even greater quantities of surplus arms onto Third World markets.

(Dorward 1991: 5–10)

[In Ethiopia] massive deforestation contributed to a decline in precipitation, which . . . with other factors has been responsible for the country 'losing 1 bn tons of topsoil a year'.

Apart from adverse environmental factors, existing social institutions combined with inappropriate government policies were also instrumental in engendering famine. During Haile Selassie's reign, large segments of the agricultural sector were under the tutelage of the royal household, the military, feudal lords, or the church. Heavily taxed peasants lacked motives to innovate and increase production . . . Ethiopian food production was among the world's lowest.

. . . Following . . . the 1975 land reform program [of the new Marxist government] 'production began to fall markedly' [and] the government arrogated to itself exclusive rights 'to market peasant produce, for which it paid little, on occasion less than cost'. Coffee was so heavily taxed that . . . production halved. With steady rises in prices and limited availabilities of consumer goods, farmers scaled down food deliveries . . . the government . . . countered by requisitioning crops. Immediately prior to the 1984 famine, 'soldiers . . . confiscated surplus grain at gunpoint', and in so doing deprived peasants of the very reserves needed to ride out the drought.

(Stein 1988: 10)

An authorial intrusion: what these texts suggest

We see such texts suggesting a number of things that relate back to the construction of reality in 'The Face of Starving Africa' and help focus possible activities in other subject areas. They suggest, for example:

- Droughts are often not purely *natural* disasters.
- Droughts do not 'act on their own' to cause famines and death by starvation.
- Famines are to an important extent created *socially*: they are consequences of human actions and inactivity.
- Certain policies and institutions have contributed to causing starvation.
- Some people/countries benefit from activities that contribute to causing droughts, floods, famines, etc.
- People and countries across the entire world are implicated directly and indirectly in processes, relationships and structures that contribute to famine.
- These same processes, structures and relationships are integral to the social creation of *refugees*.

Activity: subject teachers working as a team

Around the texts located, develop complementary exercises in each subject area to reveal aspects that may have been left out or distorted in the original media story and initial (orienting) exercises.
(N.b. space limits us to considering just a few of the potential subject areas here, and a limited range of orienting exercises.)

Geography exercise 1

1 In which countries do famines mainly occur?
2 Which social groups do they affect most?
3 Are famines *natural* disasters?

4 Find texts that provide significantly different accounts of particular famines.

Environmental studies exercise 1

1 Identify ecological variables (e.g. precipitation, soil) that are important to food production.
2 In what ways have human activities impacted on ecological variables?
3 What consequences can this impact have on food production?
4 Are there different views about the nature and the extent of human impact on ecology? If so, how do they differ?

Modern history exercise 1

1 Identify some countries that have been badly affected by famine.
2 In which cases was 'political instability' a factor?
3 In those instances where it was a factor, what different accounts are provided of the causes of the 'instability'?
4 In the different accounts, who is seen to 'be behind', or benefit from, the factors causing instability? How do these interests differ according to the accounts provided?

Activity: to be undertaken in each subject area

Using the photograph that accompanied the story 'The Face of Starving Africa' – or any photographs from popular media which depict starving children – see if you can interpret the meaning of the image in a range of different ways, drawing on the diverse information available in texts used in exercise 1.

Back to English

In the light of work done around the exercises in other subject areas, students can return to questions posed at the outset, and elaborations of them:

- From whose perspective is 'The Face of Starving Africa' presented?
- What other possible (and actual) versions have been excluded or elided here?
- Whose interests are served (and whose undermined) by the original representation?
- Comment on the effect of the reader position evident in 'The Face of

Starving Africa'. What other reader positions do you now see as possible for different texts on the same subject?

The question of critical response: literacy, discourse and praxis

Let us for the sake of argument accept that the pedagogical approach and activities described here amount to a viable classroom practice of critical literacy. In what might the *critical response(s)* to the original text be seen to consist? To what extent in the examples given are we talking of a (merely) linguistic (or otherwise academic) critical response to a piece of frozen text? Alternatively, to what extent might we have here the potential for some larger and more embodied critique of discursive practice in the real world of human actors?

With what Discourse(s) might the original text be associated? That is, to what Discourse(s) might 'The Face of Starving Africa' be 'helping' to apprentice and/or confirm readers? Clearly, such texts serve at least partially to constitute us as newspaper readers, as consumers of information, and so on. Less obviously, perhaps, they are also implicated in constituting us as some kind of informed (i.e. in some sense of 'informed') *citizens*, and as concerned moral beings who 'act' through and within an aid Discourse to contribute toward building a (more) viable world.

I would argue that texts like 'The Face of Starving Africa' can be seen as involved in the discursive production of unduly passive and underinformed citizens. To be sure, they play an important role in helping mobilize essential material resources (aid) in moments of human catastrophe, and that fact must not be overlooked, downplayed or trivialized. At the same time, to the extent that they channel us toward passive 'curative' and poorly informed approaches to addressing global and local challenges crucial to the survival and thriving of the human race, they are part of the 'problem logics' that contribute to creating social disasters in the first place.

Ideally, then, in conjunction with practices of critical literacy around such thematic texts as that on the Somalia famine, teachers and curriculum developers need also to open up possibilities for discourse critique which, as Gee (1990, 1991, 1993b, 1993c) argues, aims at *changing* Discourses. To be able to critique a Discourse presupposes apprenticeship to alternative Discourses. Through this we obtain the meta-level knowledges, capacities for analysis, practical experiences, and standpoints outside the Discourse necessary for evaluating and transforming it through conscious thought and action.

So, for example, if we posit 'development' and 'active and informed citizenship' as alternative discursive practices to 'aid' and the constitution of 'passive and underinformed citizens', we have a basis for integrating critical engagement with text into full-fledged D/discourse critique. Classroom apprenticeship to a Discourse of development will, of course, involve critical scrutiny of texts constructed from a development perspective. These texts will be discussed and worked with in ways that are organic to the practice of development as social activity. Just as students may read texts like 'The Face of Starving Africa' and become active in fund-raising for aid, so may students read relevant texts in the discursive tradition of development and be apprenticed to activities and projects steeped in the distinctive values, purposes, theories, social relations, world-views, vocabularies, knowledges, and conceptual universes of an alternative (viz. development) Discourse.

The same holds for initiation into a quite different Discourse of citizenship from those encountered – where they are encountered at all – by young people in postmodern times. I have discussed elsewhere (Lankshear 1992; Lankshear and Knobel in press) some aspects of what this might involve.

To close, I would suggest that the ideal I envisage for critical literacy is one that will accord with a social ideal of democratic life, justice, and human emancipation expressed in broad detail by educationists as otherwise different as Maxine Greene, Paulo Freire, Courtney Cazden, Myles Horton and bell hooks. In the final analysis, the educational goal that is simultaneously progenitor and outcome of such a social ideal is marked by the attainment of a critical consciousness which has four component qualities. Ira Shor describes these as follows:

1 *Power Awareness*. Knowing that society and history can be made and remade by human action and by organized groups; knowing who exercises dominant power in society for what ends and how power is currently organized and used in society.
2 *Critical Literacy*. Analytic habits of thinking, reading, writing, speaking, or discussing which go beneath surface impressions, traditional myths, mere opinions, and routine cliches; understanding the social contexts and consequences of any subject matter; discovering the deep meaning of any event, text, technique, process, object, statement, image, or situation; applying that meaning to your own context.
3 *Desocialization*. Recognizing and challenging the myths, values, behaviors, and language learned in mass culture; critically examining the regressive values operating in society, which are internalized into consciousness – such as racism, sexism, class bias, homophobia, a fascination with the rich and powerful, hero-worship, excess consumerism, runaway individualism, militarism, and national chauvinism.
4 *Self-Organization/Self-Education*. Taking the initiative to transform school and society away from authoritarian relations and the undemocratic, unequal distribution of power; taking part in and

initiating social change projects; overcoming the induced anti-intellectualism of mass education.

(1993: 32–3)

I believe that our best prospects for further developing and refining a theory and practice of critical literacy integral to this ideal lie in working at the intersection of different but complementary theoretical and pedagogical initiatives. To those readers who wish to take up the challenge I heartily recommend exploring the conceptual and methodological work of people like Norman Fairclough, Paulo Freire, James Gee, Gunther Kress, David Bloome, Courtney Cazden and Judith Green, among others, in conjunction with examples of classroom pedagogies provided by Catherine Wallace, Chris Searle and the students of Earl Marshal School (1993b, 1994, 1995), Hillary Janks (1993a, b) and Mary Hamilton, David Barton and Roz Ivanič (1994). While theirs are by no means the only perspectives and approaches consistent with the ideal of critical literacy outlined here, they are exemplary developments of that ideal. And if they are not the end point of our quest, they certainly provide admirable points from which to set out.

three

LITERACY AND EMPOWERMENT

Understanding 'empowerment'

Since the mid-1980s 'empowerment' has become an educational buzz word *par excellence*. Unfortunately, it runs the risk at present of becoming trivialized and losing its semantic integrity and persuasive force as a result of unreflective overuse. The idea of empowerment often surfaces as a kind of 'magic bullet' for fighting educational causes on behalf of disadvantaged groups. At times it seems to name a goal for educational programmes and policies sought on the grounds of social justice, equity, and like ideals. Elsewhere it appears to serve more as a means or a principle for enabling learning to take place. But whether it is invoked as a goal or as a means – which itself is often unclear – 'empowerment' is all too rarely given adequate conceptual or theoretical attention by those who set most store by it.

Empowerment talk often suffers from having too little meaning. This occurs whenever 'empowerment' is used to '*name* the space where theoretical work is needed, rather than to *fill* that space' (Dale 1991: 417, second emphasis added) – that is, where we simply assume the meaning and significance of empowerment to be self-evident. A common instance of this is where empowering pedagogy or empowering literacy are advanced as self-explanatory recipes for addressing educational and social needs of disadvantaged groups:

Q1: How should we assist disadvantaged learners?
A1: By empowering them.
Q2: How?
A2: By using an empowering pedagogy.

From a different angle, however, empowerment talk can be seen as having altogether *too much* meaning. It has connotations of positive value which appeal to people across different and often incompatible ideological and normative positions. These connotations often substitute for substantive meaning. While all-comers may agree that pedagogies and literacies should be empowering, and that learners should be empowered, *shared* meaning and values here are typically more apparent than real. This is not a good basis from which to pursue educational advances.

There is a further problem. If people do not recognize and address the vague semantics and ambiguity of 'empowerment', they may well fall for educational agendas they would otherwise have rejected on the grounds that they are in fact manipulative or oppressive. In the opening pages of *Literacy for Empowerment*, Concha Delgado-Gaitan (1990) describes how at first she resisted using empowerment as the central analytic and explanatory construct in her study of education with southern Californian migrant communities. This was because empowerment has 'been used to mean the act of showing people how to work within a system from the perspective of people in power' (p. 2). Delgado-Gaitan had to address this problem to her own satisfaction before she was prepared to use 'empowerment' as a frame for her work with the migrant communities.

This chapter suggests ways in which literacy work might benefit from addressing conceptual and theoretical matters surrounding 'empowerment'. I begin by suggesting a conceptual model of empowerment which adapts work done by Joel Feinberg in philosophy more than two decades ago on social concepts of freedom. There are some good grounds for believing that Feinberg's approach may be useful here.

First, it has long been recognized that within everyday usage 'freedom' is prone to the semantic pitfalls already mentioned: sometimes being unduly vague and ambiguous, and at other times connoting too much. Similarly, freedom has been used to name diverse and often incompatible educational and sociopolitical ideals and practices (MacCallum 1967; Berlin 1969: 118–72). Second, with freedom as with empowerment, it is important to make clear the educational and ethical values held by those seeking to influence social practices by appeal to persuasive concepts; such values should be opened to scrutiny and debate. We need ways of opening up substantive debate about desirable pedagogies, literacies and the like, rather than closing them down by definitional fiat or by recourse to persuasive, trendy or emotive terminology. Finally, like freedom, empowerment is a *relational* concept referring to social arrangements and outcomes produced within discursive practices. This needs to be reflected in the way we approach and treat such ideals conceptually and theoretically.

Building on still earlier work by Maurice Cranston (1953) and Gerald MacCallum (1967), Joel Feinberg (1973) argues that statements about freedom are 'elliptical', or abbreviated. When people appeal, for example, to economic freedom as a political or social ideal, we need to know whether they mean freedom of the economy to operate according to market forces, untrammelled by government intervention; or the freedom of individuals to meet their material needs by having access to adequate economic resources; or something else again. Feinberg endorses Cranston's claim that we should 'call for the full version of all such abbreviated slogans' (Cranston 1953: 12), otherwise we don't know what we are supporting, demanding or trying to bring about.

According to Feinberg's analysis, which is still as fruitful as any I know of for dealing with freedom as a social ideal, 'freedom' is a relational concept involving three variables: a subject, a constraint, and an outcome. To provide the full version of statements about freedom we need to specify who or what is free (or unfree); from what they are free (or unfree); and what it is they are free (or unfree) to do, be, have, become, and so on. As Feinberg (1973: 11) puts it, we have to be able to fill in the blanks in the schema:

— is free from — to do, be, have, etc. —

Like 'freedom', empowerment is a relational concept – although it involves at least four variables. For claims about empowerment to be clear they should spell out:

1 the *subject* of empowerment;
2 the power *structures* in relation to which, or in opposition to which, a person or group is being empowered;
3 the *processes* or '*qualities*' through or by which empowerment occurs; and
4 the sorts of *ends* or *outcomes* which can or do result from being thus empowered.

In other words, claims about empowerment should spell out the contents of *A–D* in the following schema:

A (the subject) is empowered in respect of B (some aspect of the discursive structuring of power) by/through C (a process or quality) such that D (some valued ends or outcomes) may – and ideally *will* – result.

I present this model as a way of teasing out what I think is involved in claims about empowerment that are informed by any kind of adequate social theory. It is intended to encourage and assist educators to declare and clarify their ideas and values when they talk about empowerment – particularly in relation to literacy.

It is one thing to present a conceptual model and make claims for its usefulness in guiding educational practice; it is quite another, however, to demonstrate its usefulness by means of examples and creative applications. I will elaborate and explore this approach to empowerment by relating it to Gee's work on literacy and Discourse mentioned in the previous chapter. In particular, I will describe and adapt Gee's concepts of *dominant* literacies and *powerful* literacy to suggest various ways in which literacy might be said to empower.

Literacies, dominant literacies and empowerment

In this section I return to some of Gee's ideas, although in greater depth than in the opening chapters. In *Social Linguistics and Literacies: Ideology in Discourses* (1990), Gee distinguishes Discourses (with a capital 'D') from discourses (p. 142), and defines literacy by reference to what he calls *secondary* Discourses (p. 153). Building on a further distinction between dominant and non-dominant Discourses, he distinguishes dominant from non-dominant literacies (p. 153). He then identifies an ideal of *powerful* literacy, whereby we use a literacy as a 'meta-language' to critique other Discourses and literacies and the way 'they constitute us as persons and situate us in society' (p. 153).

Let us recall that for Gee, Discourses are 'saying (writing)-doing-being-valuing-believing combinations': 'forms of life' or 'ways of being in the world', which integrate such things as words, acts, attitudes, beliefs and identities, along with gestures, clothes, bodily expressions and positions, and so on. Through participation in Discourses individuals are identified or identifiable as members of socially meaningful groups or networks, and as players of meaningful social roles (pp. 142–3). Language, of course, is integral to Discourse(s), but Discourse is always much more than language alone. Gee uses 'discourse' (with a lower case 'd') to refer to the 'language bits' (Gee 1993c: 14) in Discourses: 'connected stretches of language that make sense, like conversations, stories, reports, arguments, essays' (Gee 1990: 143).

Outside of self-contained face-to-face communities, humans participate in both primary and secondary Discourses. We encounter and develop our primary Discourse through 'face-to-face communication with intimates' (Gee 1990: 7), or what sociologists call primary socialization. Primary Discourse is grounded in oral language, our *primary* – first – use of language. Through the process of enculturation among intimates we learn to 'use language, behaviour, values, and beliefs to give a . . . shape to [our] experience' (p. 7). Although each person encounters just one primary Discourse, primary Discourses and language uses vary across sociocultural groups distinguished by race, ethnicity, social class, and so on. Thus the particular shape given to experience within primary Discourse varies socioculturally.

We develop our secondary Discourses 'in association with and by having access to and practice with . . . secondary institutions' beyond the family or primary socializing unit, e.g. schools, churches, workplaces, clubs, bureaucracies and professional associations (p. 8). Secondary institutions require us to communicate with non-intimates in ways and for purposes beyond those of our face-to-face world. Secondary uses of language are those developed and employed within our multiple secondary Discourses. Secondary uses of language include classroom talk, filling forms, interviewing, writing letters, inputting data, running stock inventories, writing policy, translating, and so on.

Gee defines being literate as having control of *secondary* language uses, that is, fluent mastery of language uses within secondary Discourses. This is a matter of using the 'right' language in the 'right' ways within particular discursive settings. Being literate is not a *singular* competency or attribute, however. Literacies are myriad. According to Gee, there are 'as many applications of the term "literacy" as there are secondary Discourses, which is many' (p. 8. See also Street 1984).

Discourses, Gee argues, are intimately linked to 'the distribution of social power and hierarchical structure in society' (Gee 1990: 4–5). Having control over certain Discourses – and, hence, of their literacies – can result in greater acquisition of social goods (money, power, status) by those who enjoy this control; lacking control, or access to control, of these Discourses is a source of deprivation. Gee calls Discourses which are avenues to social goods 'dominant Discourses', and identifies dominant *literacies* as secondary uses of language which can (help) provide privileged access to social goods (inside existing discursive arrangements) for those who have control of them. Subordinate literacies, by contrast, offer little or nothing in the way of privileged access to social goods.

Here again the cases of 5S and 5M in Alison Jones's study, discussed in Chapter 1, are relevant. Both classes were sitting their first national school examination (School Certificate). Within 'prestige' subjects like English and science, exam success is largely a function of the ability and disposition to reason and argue in particular ways and to extrapolate from and interpret what is given in texts, as well as (to some extent) to absorb, recall and reproduce information, including that provided by teachers in class (see p. 29–30; this volume).

Whereas the kinds of understandings, styles and dispositions required for exam success were more or less universal among the 5S students, the girls in 5M did not command the required style of thinking, the detached and analytic relationship to subject-matter, or the appropriate writing genre. Jones's data suggests that this is because the individual and collective discursive and experiential histories of the 5M students were far removed from the way academic examination writing was constituted as a dominant (school) literacy.

As noted in Chapter 1, it seems that the enculturation of most 5M students steeped them in values of uncritical reverence for the teacher as authority and 'font of knowledge'. This underpinned their view of school literacy as being a matter largely of transcribing the teacher's words as notes and 'learning them up' later. They did not seem to realize that claims advanced in texts or in classroom lectures should be checked and cross-checked for accuracy and meaning against (a range of) 'authoritative' sources. Yet operating such checks is an essential aspect of the Discourse of taking academic exams, of being an academic or scholarly student. It is one essential move in the discursive process of effecting the 'right' saying-writing-doing-believing-valuing, etc. combinations presupposed in being exam literate. As it happened, 5M students frequently copied information inaccurately. With regard to the function of haemoglobin, for instance, Ruth wrote that it 'helps blood clots', when the teacher had said 'it helps the blood to clot'. 5M students seemed to lack a conception of such ideas as intrinsically complex and calling for accurate understanding – which they might lack. Inevitably, they 'mislearned' such material, despite considerable 'hard work' – including meticulous illustration and ornate print – as they understood it to be. They failed the exam, overwhelmingly.

While this might be described and explained in numerous ways, recent developments across a range of theoretical perspectives – including postmodern social theory, and adaptations from poststructuralist theories in particular – lend support to attempts which focus on aspects of the mismatches between individuals' primary Discourses and dominant secondary Discourses and literacies, and/or between dominant secondary Discourses and literacies and their other secondary Discourses and literacies. Individually and collectively, 5S and 5M students respectively practised different literacies within the context of exam-oriented school learning; despite sharing common syllabi and curricula and even, in some cases, the same teachers.

The generic practice of academic-scholastic examination is an obvious case of what Gee calls a dominant Discourse, offering as it does avenues to a range of social goods and powers, material as well as symbolic. Having control of the associated secondary language use here is to have mastery of a dominant literacy – to *command and practise* a dominant literacy. The view advanced here – although it calls for considerable further development and scrutiny – is that 5S have control of the dominant literacy (i.e. they are exam literate) and 5M do not. As a dominant literacy, academic examination literacy might be distinguished from such other secondary language uses as reading teen romances, writing shopping lists, browsing Sunday papers, or reading bedtime stories to children, *all of which were doubtless controlled by 5M students*. The discursive processes of producing and 'allocating' power can be seen here to bestow advantage in the acquisition of social goods – mediated by literacy – on one group at the expense of another.

Gee himself offers a further example of a dominant literacy by reference to literary criticism as a dominant Discourse. His example refers explicitly to talk of empowerment:

> [D]iscourses are intimately related to the distribution of social power and hierarchical structure in society. Control over certain discourses can lead to the acquisition of social goods (money, power, status) in a society. These discourses empower those groups who have the fewest conflicts with their other discourses when they use them . . . [T]o take [an] example, the discourse of literary criticism was a standard route to success as a professor of literature. Since it conflicted less with the other discourses of white, middle-class men than it did with those of women, men were empowered by it. Women were not, as they were often at cross-purposes when engaging in it. Let us call discourses that lead to social goods in a society 'dominant discourses' and let us refer to those groups that have the fewest conflicts when using them as 'dominant groups'.
>
> (Gee 1991: 5)

Let us accept that literacy criticism is a dominant Discourse *par excellence*, and that to practise its associated language uses successfully is to have control of a dominant literacy. The matter to be clarified is *how* dominant literacies are related to power and, to that extent, empower those with command of them.

There are two important things to note here about Discourses and their literacies. The first is that a given Discourse – any Discourse, dominant or otherwise – is constituted around specific objects and purposes. It privileges certain concepts, viewpoints, perspectives and values, at the expense of others. It consequently 'marginalize[s] viewpoints and values central to other Discourses' (p. 5). Successful participation by individuals in a given Discourse and its characteristic conception and practice of reading and writing can, then, be impeded in at least two ways: by a 'lack of fit' between the given Discourse and language use and their other Discourses – and especially their primary Discourse; and/or by value conflict between their other Discourses and the Discourse in question (e.g. peer group and class-cultural discourses that make it 'uncool' to succeed academically).

The second facet of a Discourse is its place within the discursive ordering of access to social goods: that is, its status within the hierarchy of dominant and subordinate Discourses. In this respect the literacies associated with literary criticism and scholastic exams are inherently different from those associated with Discourses central to the being of many women, ethnic minority and migrant groups, and working-class populations. They stand in opposite relations to the power to access social goods. The literacies of formal criticism and exams provide avenues to acquiring social goods. The others do not. Nor, moreover, do they cohere (or 'fit') well with dominant Discourses.

What sense can we make of literacy and empowerment against this background of concepts and examples, and in terms of the conceptual model of 'empowerment' outlined earlier? What would it mean to say that 5S students are empowered by 'exam literacy', whereas 5M students are not? In what sense do dominant Discourses and their associated language uses 'de-power' groups and individuals, by marginalizing their discursive histories and allegiances? What conception and theory of power is implied?

The view of social power assumed here is that power is produced in the process of certain 'qualities' being related to social 'goods' (or means to 'goods') through Discourse. To *have* access to power is to possess qualities that have been related positively to goods or means to accessing them. To actually *exercise* power is to draw on these qualities, to 'cash them in', as it were. To *be* empowered is to have the qualities one possesses (or has available) made discursively – that is, through Discourse – into 'currency' for acquiring goods and benefits, or for having them bestowed.

Students from the kinds of social groups represented in streams or classes like 5S have social power by virtue of certain of their discursively acquired qualities (e.g. a disposition and ability to interpret, argue, debate, abstract, adopt a position) having been positively related – discursively – to exam success. 5M students – and others more or less like them – lack power as a result of being positioned discursively in the opposite relationship to exam success. Students like those in 5S are empowered by secondary Discourses centred around school having made these qualities – which are available to them on terms denied to the social groups most represented in 5M – into 'legal tender' for exam success. As a dominant Discourse, scholastic examination 'de-powers' those social groups whose discursive histories and allegiances impede their attaining control of the requisite language uses and related dispositions, attitudes and performances.

To employ the conceptual schema outlined earlier, we can say that:

> as individuals or as a group, *students like those in 5S* are empowered in respect of *school exams* (as a dominant discourse which affords access to social goods), by *their facility with appropriate language use* (which itself reflects a coherence between their larger discursive universe and the language demands of exams and scholastic work) such that under prevailing conditions they are able to *enjoy exam success* and access to associated social goods and powers.

Within existing discursive orders, dominant literacies empower certain groups (and depotentiate others), by making what they *already* have (or have privileged access to) into currency for acquiring social goods and benefits. These groups are empowered as a 'natural' discursive consequence of who and what they already are, or will, in the normal course of events, become.

Powerful literacies: empowerment and critique

While dominant literacies can be seen to empower groups who are, so to speak, 'on the right side of Discourse', they are not the same as *powerful literacy*, and they empower in a different way. To develop this argument I will begin from Gee's account of powerful literacy and adapt and modify his central idea for my own purposes.

Gee defines powerful literacy as control of a secondary use of language used in a secondary Discourse, that affords us a meta-language with which to understand, analyse and critique primary Discourses and/or other secondary Discourses – notably, *dominant* Discourses – and the ways they constitute us as persons and situate us in society (see also Gee 1990: 153, 1991: 8–9). By a meta-language he means 'a set of meta-words, meta-values [and] meta-beliefs' (1990: 153). Practising a powerful literacy, so defined, can provide the basis for reconstituting our selves/identities and resituating ourselves within society. We should note here that a powerful literacy is *a particular use* of a literacy (or discourse/secondary language use) and not a particular *literacy*.

The key to Gee's conception of powerful literacies is the notion of operating secondary language uses as *meta-languages* of analysis, critique and transformation. He argues that understanding and critiquing a Discourse by means of a powerful literacy grounded in some other Discourse presupposes meta-level knowledge in both Discourses. The point here is that we can operate entire Discourses with fluent mastery and control of their literacies – including dominant varieties – *without* having (good) meta-level understanding of these Discourses, of how they constitute us and position us in relation to other individuals and groups, with what implications and consequences for them and us, and so on. How could this be?

The explanation rests on a distinction framed by Stephen Krashen (1982, 1985) between 'acquisition' and 'learning'. Very briefly, 'acquisition' is defined as a process of more or less unconscious attainment, resulting from exposure to models and to trial and error within meaningful and functional natural settings. Most people come to control their first language through acquisition. 'Learning' is defined as a process of gaining conscious knowledge via explanation, analysis, and similar *teaching* processes. Learning, then, 'inherently involves attaining, along with the matter being taught, some degree of meta-knowledge about the matter' (Gee 1991: 5). Where our proficiency has simply been *acquired* – as distinct from being underpinned with 'meta-level' knowledges that only become available through processes of *learning* – we may indeed enjoy benefits of dominance, and of distinctive forms of power and modes of empowerment accessed by dominance. We will, however, remain cut off from access to other forms of power and modes of being empowered that depend on having learned as well as having acquired.

These are what mark the difference between a powerful literacy and a dominant literacy.

The link between literacy (as secondary language use), meta-level knowledge of Discourses, and operating a powerful literacy is quite straightforward. Viewed from one perspective, secondary language uses are integral aspects of their respective Discourses and must be controlled in order to participate coherently and successfully in these Discourses. From a different perspective, however, secondary language uses can be seen as providing the means for understanding Discourses themselves for what they *are* – generically and in distinction from one another. This is a matter of grasping the relationship between 'the language bits of Discourse' (as signifiers, bearers, and 'enactment vehicles' of the various values, beliefs, norms, theories, etc. that constitute given Discourses), and the Discourses themselves.

Meta-level knowledge, then, is knowledge *about* what is involved in participating within some Discourse(s). It is more than merely knowing *how* (i.e. being able) to engage successfully in a particular discursive practice. Rather, meta-level knowledge is knowing about the nature of that practice, its constitutive values and beliefs, its meaning and significance, how it relates to other practices, what it is about successful performance that makes it successful, and so on. Meta-level knowledge of Discourses impacts in at least three ways so far as accessing power through literacy is concerned. I will refer to these as three modes of empowerment.

First, to have meta-level knowledge of a dominant Discourse and its literacy enhances our prospects of mastery and high level performance within that Discourse as it is currently constituted, thereby increasing our (potential) access to social goods and their associated forms of power and privilege. Let us call this Mode A.

Second, meta-level knowledge enhances possibilities for analysis and for applications of analysis. Being able to control secondary language uses as a means for analysing a Discourse enables us to see how skills and knowledges can be used in new ways and new directions within that Discourse. This is Mode B.

Third – and this is Mode C – meta-level knowledge of Discourse(s) is required in order to critique a Discourse and seek to change it, or at least to change its identity constitutive and social positioning effects on oneself and others.

Meta-level knowledge of Discourses is necessary for their critique because all Discourses, necessarily, are largely immune to internal critique. To critique a Discourse and envisage possibilities for resisting or transforming it, we need a critical place to stand outside that Discourse. Critique presupposes both meta-knowledge of the Discourse itself – knowing that we are in it, and what it is we are in – and meta-knowledge of some other Discourse against which we understand the first and from which we compare and evaluate it. As Gee puts it: 'One cannot critique one discourse with another (which is the only way to seriously criticize and thus change a discourse) unless one has meta-level knowledge in both discourses' (1991: 9). Hence (for instance), for women to critique patriarchal Discourses and pursue their transformation, they need(ed) meta-knowledge of what patriarchal Discourses are and do. This presupposes a perspective from the standpoint of (some) non-patriarchal Discourse – such as a feminist Discourse, and meta-level knowledge of that Discourse, as well as meta-level knowledge of and a meta-language for understanding, describing and analysing *experience* of being constituted and situated by patriarchal Discourses.

By identifying typical examples we can note some of the ways in which 'powerful' literacies, construed as meta-languages of analysis and critique, differ from dominant literacies in terms of how they *empower*. The following examples are by no means exhaustive. They are intended only to suggest some ways in which we might clarify and extend our conception and practice of empowering learners through constructing and teaching powerful literacies.

Empowerment: Mode A

Let us begin with the notion of meta-level knowledge enhancing prospects of mastery and high level performance within an established dominant Discourse by enabling the operation of a *powerful* literacy.

I can recall an instance of this from my own experience, where I completed a successful MA thesis in Analytical Philosophy of Education without having a clear understanding of why what I had done was 'right'. I had seemingly controlled the appropriate literacy without experiencing *being in control* of it. This produced considerable perplexity and insecurity. It was not until I became a tutor in an introductory course (and followed the excellent instructions and exercises covering the skills of analysing claims into different categories, making conceptual distinctions and analysing concepts, and evaluating arguments in terms of their validity and soundness) that I began to bring to consciousness what I'd been doing (by imitation, intuitive 'feel', and with a good deal of supervisory help) in the thesis, and to understand why it had been given a good grade. It seems that in the act of moving from being a student apprentice of the Discourse to being a teacher my hitherto absent and tacit understandings of the Discourse became (more) *explicit*: largely, I believe, because the teaching guides spelled out important elements of procedure, purpose, integral theory and so on, which had previously escaped my conscious knowledge.

The process of attaining a meta-level knowledge of educational philosophy as a discursive field and a literate practice continued slowly during my doctorate, and more rapidly after it. I felt increasingly in control of the

Discourse and literacy of analytical philosophy of education and able to make them work for me, rather than experiencing *them* controlling *my* work (and my *being*) as I struggled to understand their demands. It became progressively easier to conceive and produce publishable work: to operate (knowingly) the literacy with greater fluency and confidence. With that came the usual sorts of social goods and benefits attending relative success in a Western academic arena. In this way I experienced greater power in the form of being able to operate the Discourse and to access the goods it made available discursively. Elements of social and personal power were closely intertwined here.

Three implications seem noteworthy here.

First, so far as this example goes, there was no transformation of the Discourse involved. Nothing changed outside of one individual becoming increasingly able to operate a literacy – and, to that extent, a Discourse – more successfully and to access benefits ordained by the discursive structuring of power within an existing state of affairs.

Second, my 'coming to power' may actually have reduced the career prospects of others whose ability to operate the Discourse in a way that 'unlocked' social goods was surpassed by my growing confidence and 'productivity'. This marks an important difference between 'having control of a dominant literacy' and 'operating a powerful literacy'. Those who are empowered in terms of access to social goods merely as a result of 'their' acquired Discourses being constituted as dominant, are vulnerable. They are in danger of being displaced by those whose literacy within a dominant field of social practice becomes more *powerful*. In short, one can be dominant without being *powerful* in important respects, and that lack of personal power may result in eventual loss of social dominance. Not all who are born to rule live and die as rulers, so to speak.

Third, to the extent that empowerment through control of dominant literacies is empowerment patterned by class, ethnicity and gender, pedagogies aimed at promoting powerful literacy have potential for democratizing access to social goods within existing power structures.

To invoke the empowerment schema by (hypothetical) reference to the example drawn from Jones's study of the girls grammar school:

> S (an individual who is otherwise 'bound for 5 M') would be empowered in respect of *school exams* (a discourse offering access to social goods), through attaining *meta-level understanding of exam demands* (reflecting the triumph of pedagogy over socially ordained deficit), such that S could *succeed in exams*, and be better positioned to access associated social goods.

This is an approach to empowerment by which (1) members of non-dominant groups (2) can access social goods (3) through personal power developed around pedagogies of powerful literacy (4) within substantially unchanged discourses and power structures. Dominant literacies largely operate a 'closed shop' of empowerment. Powerful literacies can help 'open the shop'.

There is an important pedagogical requirement here, namely, that educators

> realize that *teaching and learning* [in the technical sense derived from Krashen] are connected with the development of meta-level cognitive and linguistic skills. They will work better if we explicitly realize this and build the realization into our curricula. Further, they must be carefully ordered and integrated with *acquisition* if they are to have any effect other than obstruction.
>
> (Gee 1991: 9–10)

At the same time, we must avoid unrealistic expectations of explicit teaching as a means for redressing 'shortfalls' in the prior acquisitions of non-mainstream students so far as dominant D/discourses are concerned. While rendering the rules, values, procedures, etc. of dominant D/discourses overt and explicit – i.e. concrete and accessible – to all students is binding on teachers at all levels, this is 'not an educational panacea [for non-mainstream students] and . . . involves complex problems' (Gee *et al.* 1996: 12). Making 'the rules of the game' overt can never be done exhaustively, since we cannot put all that is involved into *words*. And even if we could, what we could say in classroom settings would be merely the tip of the iceberg. In addition, such overt knowledge 'would not ground fluent behaviour [in, say, exam preparation, choice of examples, exam writing] any more than overt knowledge of dance steps can ground fluent dancing' (p. 12). This observation, however, does not detract from the ethical and vocational obligation to *teach well*, which includes rendering the implicit explicit, and the abstract concrete, where it is possible and appropriate to do so.

Alternatively, if we shift the empowerment emphasis away from a strict focus on accessing *social* goods and attend more to the dimension of *personal* power, we might complete the schema in ways that stress, say, autonomous and independent competence. Within the social relations of knowledge production, degree candidates and future authors can win their own voice of competence and become independent of mentors by becoming powerfully literate in the discourse.

Empowerment: Mode B

The notion of empowerment through enhanced possibilities for analysis and applications of analysis can be dealt with quite simply. Let us take the practice of quality control in the modern workplace as an increasingly relevant example from a key site of daily life.

According to a commentator on changing work conditions, 'ten years ago we saw quality control as a screening process, catching defects before they got out the door . . . Today we see quality as a process that prevents defects from occurring' (Wiggenhorn 1990: 71–2). Quality control as Discourse changed, and enterprises are forever on the lookout for improvements to the practice that may help them win a market edge over competitors. Quality control is but one aspect of the way in which, in Wiggenhorn's words, 'all the rules of manufacturing and competition [have] changed'. Motorola's management learned 'that line workers had to actually understand their work and their equipment', and the relationship between them (p. 72).

This, in effect, is a call for greater meta-level understanding of manufacturing Discourses on the part of workers. There are implications here for workers' employability, career prospects and control over their own work, as well as for corporate profits. Workers who have and operate a meta-language of quality control can analyse the purposes and processes of quality control and, by application of this analysis, contribute to enhancing and transforming quality control practices – including, specifically, the literacy components of quality control. This may well presume that they have meta-level understanding of Discourses and secondary language uses of *quantity*-oriented Discourses of manufacture or other forms of production. The terms of the empowerment schema can be embodied in various ways in relation to this example. The subject variable can range over individual workers or groups (cells or teams) of workers, who in turn may vary by gender, ethnicity, prior experience, first language, and so on. The second variable could range variously over decision-making procedures, the system of wages and rewards, career ladders, and hierarchies of responsibility. The achievement or quality variable refers, of course, to command of a meta-language of quality control. The outcome variable could range over better wages, promotion prospects, control over work conditions, relative autonomy from management, and enhanced possibilities of finding (better) work in other enterprises. Hence, shopfloor workers might develop innovations on the basis of their understandings of a discourse (e.g. quality assurance, quality control), have these recognized, and be promoted as a consequence. Alternatively, by harnessing inventiveness to meta-level understandings of markets and niches, such workers might 'go entrepreneurial' and sell their innovations to high bidders, take out patents, and so on. Many contemporary work D/discourses, markets, niches, routines, etc. are sufficiently new and different to mitigate some of the differences among employees in prior experiences and acquisition, enhancing prospects of empowerment through relevant meta-level knowledge.

Empowerment: Mode C

Gee's particular emphasis in his discussion of literacy and empowerment falls squarely on the possibilities afforded by powerful literacy for *critique* and *transformation* of Discourses.

With regard to classroom pedagogies of powerful literacy, Gee calls for teaching to be constructed around a critical intent aimed at enabling children from all social groups to critique their primary and secondary Discourses. This entails using texts and other resources to expose children 'to a variety of primary and secondary Discourses' in ways that promote meta-level knowledge of these Discourses (Gee 1991: 10). Meta-level knowledge makes possible meta-languages of critical preference among Discourses and knowledge of how to act on critical preference. And with critical awareness of alternative Discourses, and the possibilities of meaningful choice among them, comes power – including the power to resist the way particular Discourses constitute us as identitied persons and situate us within society and the social hierarchy of Discourses; and so, too, comes the power to *choose* apprenticeship to participation in other Discourses that will constitute and situate us in certain ways we have come to see as desirable or preferable – for various reasons, including ethical and political reasons.

This approach is reminiscent of successful forms of feminist pedagogy which offer women the option – albeit often a tough option secured at high cost – of refusing ways in which patriarchal discourses (would) constitute and position them as women (Bee 1993; Rockhill 1993). Beyond this, feminist pedagogies make it possible to envisage and embark upon a long historical march through sexist discourses and institutions, with a view to their eventual transformation in accordance with values and conceptions drawn from examples and visions of alternative discursive practices.

Variations on D/discourse analysis and critique approaches to promoting powerful literacy are apparent in pedagogical initiatives currently under development in Australia. These are associated with the work of people like Carolyn Baker, Peter Freebody, Pam Gilbert and Allan Luke – to name just a small sample of those working in Queensland. (For examples of their work, see Baker and Freebody 1989; Freebody *et al.* 1991; Luke 1993b.) Insights informing this approach and its broad lines of development are neatly described by Luke and Walton:

> Written texts are . . . refractive; that is, they actively construct and represent the world. To read critically . . . requires awareness of and facility with techniques by which texts and discourses construct and position human subjects and social reality . . . Instruction based on text and discourse analysis aims to give students insights into how texts work and, more specifically, how texts situate and manipulate readers. In so doing, its purpose is to engage readers directly and actively in the

politics of discourse in contemporary cultures, to open institutional
sites and possibilities for alternative 'readings' and 'writings'.

(Luke and Walton 1994: 1196)

Near the heart of this approach we find Kress's (1985) view that texts
construct 'subject positions' and 'reader positions'. Texts represent and
construct *subjects* in the world and also position and construct model
readers. Via a range of lexical, syntactic and semantic devices, texts portray a
view of the world and position readers to read and interpret that portrayed
world in particular ways.

The uncritical (unpowerful) reader is not aware of these processes and
devices, submitting unknowingly to their ideological and 'subject-
constitutive' effects. Critical (powerful) readers, by contrast, understand how
a diverse range of linguistic techniques employed in texts position readers,
defining and manipulating them, and employ an understanding of how
syntax, grammar and words themselves act to shape human agency, cause
and effect, and how the world is portrayed (Kress 1985; see also Fairclough
1989). In so reading the text they can resist, as appropriate, the meanings and
subject positions it coaxes them to adopt.

Such meta-level knowledge of texts and how they operate is, precisely,
knowledge of the ways power is produced and enacted through language.
The powerfully literate reader can contest texts, resisting meanings and
positions these would otherwise 'impose'. This is to be empowered as a
recipient or 'object' of text. As a writer of texts the powerfully literate person
develops 'powerful competencies' with a range of genres and techniques
which may be employed in pursuit of personal, ethical and political purposes.

Such approaches to powerful literacy as described here likewise sustain
meaningful conceptions and pedagogies of empowerment. They address the
power of Discourses and their literacies to shape what we become as
persons and what we are impeded from becoming, and thereby what is (and
is not) available to us in the way of social goods, benefits and opportunities.
They suggest pedagogical techniques that allow readers to understand these
discursive and textual processes in relation to the politics of daily life in
general as well as of particular spheres, like home, school and work. In so
doing, they address elements of ideological-symbolic domination and
control as well as more material forms of regulation – since Discourses
involve both. Discourse critique promotes meta-level understanding of
Discourse(s) as well as familiarity with the substance of multiple Discourses,
in respect of what they make available and withhold. Learners, then, are
enabled to see how they are, or have been, constituted by Discourses. They
are enabled also to envisage embarking upon new and different possibilities
for 'self-construction' or identity formation by engaging in alternative
Discourses.

Final remarks

There are advantages in taking the conceptual demands of empowerment seriously along the lines sketched here. The more closely and clearly we specify particular learner-subjects, the more likely we are to identify forms and processes of power which limit their options within everyday settings and to envisage or negotiate learning processes and outcomes in line with the ends we seek. Similarly, the better our theory is of how power is produced and distributed, the more we will understand the varying circumstances and aspirations of different learners, and the better informed will be the means and processes employed toward (negotiated) learning outcomes.

Moreover, the approach adopted eschews chauvinism and pre-empts certain dangers associated with restrictive forms of political correctness. Rather than usurp the ideal of empowerment for a sole (typically unargued) pedagogical or ideological position, it leaves the way open for proponents of differing values to state their case clearly and to develop their pedagogical models in an informed and directed way. We can then engage in focused substantive debate, knowing with clarity and a good deal of precision what it is we are agreeing with or disputing. At present we can all agree on empowerment as an educational goal and proclaim the virtue of an empowering literacy, since 'empowerment' means all things to all people: which is to say that it means nothing clear. And 'nothing clear' is a poor pedagogical guide.

In the final analysis, if we believe literacy for empowerment marks an educational ideal worth striving for, having concern for clarity, coherence, and critique makes a good starting point.

part 2

LITERACY AND
SOCIAL JUSTICE

four

LANGUAGE, LITERACY AND THE NEW WORK ORDER

James Paul Gee and Colin Lankshear

Introduction

In this chapter we consider some of the 'key words' of an emerging genre of business texts, namely, what we call 'fast capitalist texts'. These texts, written by business managers and consultants, seek to attend as textual midwives at the birth of a new 'work order' within a new capitalism, books such as *Workplace 2000* (Boyett and Conn 1992), *Liberation Management* (Peters 1992), *Post-Capitalist Society* (Drucker 1993), *Reengineering the Corporation* (Hammer and Champy 1993). They announce a new 'enchanted workplace' where hierarchy is dead and 'partners' engage in meaningful work amidst a collaborative environment of mutual commitment and trust.

Fast capitalist texts are important, however, not just within the sphere of business and work. Their vision and values have deeply informed contemporary calls for reform both in adult education and training, as well as in schools across the 'developed' world. Such reform efforts (e.g. Australia's call for 'smart workers' in a 'clever country') stress the need to prepare children and adults to participate effectively as 'knowledge workers' in 'enchanted workplaces'. In turn, those areas that supply theories and practices to educational debates, such as educationally relevant cognitive science, are beginning to align themselves with fast capitalist values (Gee 1994b). For instance, both educationally relevant cognitive science (for classrooms) and the fast capitalist literature (for workplaces) heavily stress collaboration, active problem solving, learning in context, alternative assessment, communities of practice, and the integration of technology. Finally, the fast capitalist literature, with its stress on the destruction of hierarchy, borders, divisions and stasis, at times takes on some of the language of postmodern critical theories, theories that are otherwise often quite critical of any form of capitalism (Gee 1994b). Thus, we suggest that fast capitalist words are of wide relevance as part of important emerging realignments in the relationships among different spheres in society.

It is, of course, easy to be cynical about the new capitalism and its textual ancillaries. It is also possible that such cynicism, unaccompanied by authentic engagement with the global changes portended in these texts, will leave enterprises like 'critical literacy' and 'critical theory' on the sidelines of history. In this chapter, as a form of both critique and engagement, we want to argue for the importance of critical language awareness for all (willing and unwilling) participants, whether educators, leaders, workers or students, in the practices and texts of the fast capitalist world. We will suggest an approach to critical language awareness by reference to two 'key words' in fast capitalist textual visions of the 'enchanted workplace': 'self-directed learning' and 'empowerment'. There are, however, many more such words that our approach would apply to with equal effect.

Whose reality? Competing views of the new work order

Before we get to critical language awareness, however, we need to survey briefly the 'story line' – part 'reality', part prediction, and part hope – that underlies fast capitalist texts. Of course, the story line we will give is a composite from many texts, and is, as such, not entirely fair to some of the differences and nuances in specific texts. Nonetheless, we believe that our story line is a fair representation of the 'big picture' that emerges from these texts. (See the Appendix at the end of this chapter for a sample of the texts we have used in constructing this story line. This sample is representative of what is now a very large literature.) It is only against such a story line that any analysis of the words of these texts will make full sense.

The 'story' is, then, that the very structure and needs of a new and transformed capitalism (sometimes called 'post-capitalism', e.g. Drucker 1993) is leading to a more meaningful, humane, and socially just, though more stressful, workplace. The 'old capitalism' was based on the mass production of (relatively uniform) goods by large, hierarchically structured corporations serving a commodities-starved, but progressively richer post-World War II population in the 'developed' world. Workers, hired 'from the neck down', needed only to follow directions and mechanically carry out a rather meaningless piece of a process they did not need to understand as a whole, and certainly did not control (this is the heart of so-called 'Fordism').

The new capitalism is based on the design, production and marketing of 'high quality' goods and services for now-saturated markets. In the 'developed' world today economic survival is contingent on selling ever more perfect(ed) and newer 'customized' goods and services to 'niche' markets, that is, to groups of people who come to define and change their identities by the sorts of goods and services they consume. The emphasis now is on the (active) knowledge (and flexible learning) it takes to design, market, perfect and vary goods and services as 'symbols' of identity, not on the actual product itself as a material good. And, thanks to technological and social changes, this sort of 'quality' competition is now fully globalized. The 'winners' design 'customized' products and services 'on time', 'on demand' faster and more perfectly than their global competition, or they go out of business:

> I like the word 'ephemeral' almost as much as 'fashion' or 'fickle.' In fact, I'm fond of speaking of 'the four ephemerals': ephemeral 'organizations' . . . joined in ephemeral combinations . . . producing ephemeral products . . . for ephemeral markets . . . FAST.
>
> (Peters 1992: 15–18)

As this quote attests, the 'logic' of fast capitalist competition implies a good many changes in organizational structures and, ultimately, in society as a whole. Only those businesses that are 'lean and mean' (no extra, i.e. non-value-adding people) and 'close to the customer' (that is, local and personal in effect even if huge and global in reality) will succeed. One result is that the large, hierarchically structured, depersonalized corporations of the old capitalism must be broken into smaller, more personal and locally-flavoured workplaces where hierarchy is greatly lowered (we get so-called 'flat hierarchies'). The 'middle' (i.e. middle managers) of old-style corporations disappears.

The middle had previously existed to supervise the workers and to pass information up and down the hierarchy between the (insulated) bosses and the workers; additionally, middle managers were the ones who were supposed to understand the processes and systems of the workplace. The logic of the new work order is that the roles and responsibilities of the middle will pass to the 'front-line workers' themselves (formerly the bottom of the hierarchy). Workers will be transformed into committed 'partners' who engage in meaningful work, fully understand and control their jobs, supervise themselves and actively seek to improve their performance through communicating clearly their knowledge and needs.

Such 'motivated' workers (partners) can no longer be 'ordered' around by 'bosses', they can only be 'developed', 'coached', and 'supported'. Hierarchy is gone, egalitarianism is 'in'. Workers increasingly assume managerial roles within settings where work centres around collaborative (team-based) 'projects'. Concomitantly, they must take responsibility for their own 'careers', and not leave such responsibility to businesses or governments. When their 'project' is over (perfected), they must be willing to move on to develop their own 'portfolio' of skills and achievements. They must not expect the business to sustain them in the long run; it may need, as it develops new products and services, to hire new teams for new projects. It is not uncommon in fast capitalist literature to find the metaphor of work projects as analogous to making a movie for a studio. The team works together until the movie is finished, and then leaves the studio. Let's hear Peters again on some of these themes:

> The message is clear [to chiefs]: (1) trust, (2) 'they' can handle 'it' (whatever 'it' is), (3) you're only in control when you're out of control ('head' of a flat, radically decentralized 'organization').
>
> (Peters 1992: 758–9)

> Another big step, it turns out: the entrepreneurizing of every job. One hundred percent of employees turned into 'business people' is, I contend, no pipe dream . . . With a bit of imagination (okay, more than a bit), the average job − actually, every job − can become an entrepreneurial challenge . . . Letting go means letting the person alone to experience those Maalox moments − that is, true, genuine, no-baloney ownership in the gut. If there's no deep-seated, psychological ownership, there's no ownership. Period.
>
> (Peters 1994: 67, 72, 80–1)

As we observed at the outset, the world of these fast capitalist texts has served, like a magnet, to attract and change the shape of educational debates in the 'developed' world, whether these be concerned with vocational and adult education, workplace training and literacy, or schools. Just as it is not enough for workers in the new capitalism to simply follow directions, as it was in the old, it is not sufficient (it is argued) for students or workers-as-learners just to 'pass tests'. They must develop 'higher order thinking', 'real understanding', 'situated expertise', the ability to 'learn to learn' and to solve problems at the 'edge of their expertise'. These have become leading motifs in the literature in educationally relevant cognitive science, for instance (the leading edge of school reform in the US). Indeed, this literature has recently become quite overt in its equation between 'excellence' in education (what constitutes 'higher order thinking', for instance) and 'quality' and 'pro-ductivity' in the new work order of fast capitalism:

> Although 'quality' is no easier to define than 'excellence', and in everyday language means approximately the same thing, the quality movement has given the idea substance. As conceived by W. Edwards Deming and other gurus of the movement, quality bears a very close resemblance to the concept of expertise that we have been trying to develop here. It is a continuing process, not a state or outcome. It involves all the members of an organization cooperating in pursuit of an ideal goal that can never be attained, but that can be approached

endlessly. Although not identified as such, progressive problem solving seems to be implicit in the idea.

. . . So close is the resemblance of quality improvement to the process of expertise, that we might even characterize it as the process of expertise translated into a practical program for organizations.

(Bereiter and Scardamalia 1993: 242–3)

This quote is from a book on the psychology of education concerned with children and schools. Only at the end does it draw an explicit connection between its project and the fast capitalist project. Given the low status (in the US, at least) accorded to adult education and workplace concerns, and the high status of childhood education, this connection is all the more striking. In this perspective, fast capitalist texts should be of interest and concern to all those interested in the construction of knowledge and learning, as well as educational sites.

Fast capitalist texts are not mere attempts to describe a reality already in place; they are what we might call 'projective' or 'enactive' texts (Gee 1994b). Written by business leaders and consultants to business, they are almost always parts of larger projects to enact (to call into being) a vision of a new world. Further, their vision of new values, new social purposes and practices, and new social identities is strikingly totalizing. Just as new identities are being formed (worker as partner; boss as coach, designer of others' learning processes, and visionary leader), so, too, old divisions, such as that between 'public' and 'private', are being effaced: 'What these "work hard, play hard" companies want is nothing less than total responsibility and over-the-edge loyalty . . . Employees are constantly on view and the line between work and play, the line between public and private becomes fuzzy' (Kirp and Rice 1988: 79, cited by Boyett and Conn 1992: 40).

We have, thus far, sketched the story line of our fast capitalist texts, and argued their wider significance. It is clear, however, even from such a cursory sketch, that this textual world is deeply paradoxical, something that we will see yet more clearly when we turn to our discussion of fast capitalist key words. At present, though, we turn to two paradoxes of fast capitalism that betoken aspects of its 'darker' side.

The first paradox we deal with is really the underside of 'enchantment' in the newly meaningful, equalitarian and 'empowering' workplace. 'Enchantment' can mean 'delightful'; as such, it can stand for the claims that the new workplace will be more deeply meaningful and fulfilling than the old. But it can also mean 'to be under a spell'. And, indeed, our fast capitalist texts are aware of the tensions between workers who are in control and thinking for themselves and the possibilities that they might question the very ends and goals of fast capitalist businesses themselves, which would make them very poor fast capitalists indeed. But, then, what sort of 'freedom' and 'empowerment' do workers have if they cannot question the 'vision', values, ends and goals of the new work order itself? Boyett and Conn, in *Workplace 2000*, see this as a core tension in the new capitalism:

> (Robert Howard says:) 'The contradictions inherent to this emerging ideology of management make it easily vulnerable to abuses of power and the elaborate manipulation of people and values . . . The promise of the enchanted workplace is promise of meaning, with the corporation as the mediator between work and the self. In order to cash in on the meanings of the enchanted workplace, however, the workers must cleave to a set of ends – "superordinate goals," "corporate culture," whatever – that "like the basic postulates of a mathematical system," is posited in advance. Workers rarely have the opportunity to influence the content of those ends, let alone play an active role in their formation . . . As a result, the necessity of allegiance to a set of ends over which one has little control can become a recipe for a dangerous corporate intrusiveness that produces not autonomy and freedom, but enforced conformity, not genuine participation, but a kind of high touch coercion.'
>
> (Boyett and Conn 1992: 114–15)

It is interesting that this quote comes from a fast capitalist book, not a critique of capitalism. These texts are quite overt about this paradox and constantly seek a solution to it, one of which is to trust ('irrationally') in visionary leadership:

> Workplace 2000 leaders will have a vision of the future . . . Well, it isn't 'build market share' and certainly not 'make money.' A vision is much broader and more compelling. It's a dream and an ideal. It's nothing less than 'changing the world.' The leader visualizes an ultimate purpose or mission for the organization that is so inspirational followers will voluntarily suspend rational judgment about the probability of success . . . Leaders visualize a larger reality and transmit that vision to others.
>
> (Boyett and Conn 1992: 147)

The second paradox to which we turn constitutes an even darker side to our fast capitalist texts, because they are, for the most part, deeply silent about it, though it often lurks just below their surfaces. The paradox is this: just as 'enchanted' (fulfilled or cast under a spell) workers follow from the logic of fast capitalism, so, too, do even greater numbers of what we might call 'disenchanted workers'.

Enchanted workers are part of the 'core' participants in the new work order. While they may have to move on after their 'project' is accomplished, they are (we are told) 'partners' who sell their 'knowledge work' for a share in the benefits and risks of the enterprise. But 'lean and mean' enterprises require a large, cheap and flexible workforce to work 'on demand' only as and when required to carry out the remaining low level tasks that are a waste of the (better paid) core participants' time and efforts. These are the 'peripheral' workers in the new capitalism. In theory, 'knowledge' is the true 'value added' of the new capitalism, and that capitalism will only pay for value added. Thus, workers who have little knowledge to sell or whose knowledge is not needed or wanted are 'logical' candidates for deep exploitation. And, indeed, temporary, part-time, and subcontracted workers are, in fact, the fastest-growing segment of the workforce over the last few decades (Reich 1992; Parker 1994). Such workers often collect few or no fringe benefits and often cannot collect unemployment benefits. They absorb seasonal or cyclical fluctuations in business activity.

These peripheral workers constitute a massive supply of underemployed and periodically unemployed workers together with the growing hordes of 'service workers', who sell not knowledge but the brute delivery of the services connected to ever newly designed 'lifestyles'. Peter Drucker, one of the senior gurus of fast capitalism, has argued that the growing numbers of low-paid service workers (and we can add the under and unemployed in general) will represent the main social 'class' problem of the new capitalism:

> The social challenge of the post-capitalist society will, however, be the dignity of the second class in post-capitalist society: the service workers. Service workers, as a rule, lack the necessary education to be knowledge workers. And in every country, even the most highly advanced one, they will constitute the majority.
>
> (Drucker 1993: 8)

Drawing on research by people like Atkinson (1988), Christopherson and Storper (1989), Kumazawa and Yamada (1989) and Pollert (1987), Peter OConnor (1994) summarizes this paradox of the new capitalism, the large reservoir of disenchanted workers that seems to be a 'necessary' accompaniment of the new enchanted workplace. He touches on our first paradox, as well:

> In order to achieve maximum flexibility, companies will increasingly [subcontract] a range of functions, and further reduce and segment their workforce by maintaining a core workforce which is multi-skilled, flexible, and can be used across operational functions, and a peripheral workforce which is more disposable, based on part-time and temporary work, short term individual contracts and fewer employment rights and entitlements . . . [Indeed] the core remains the domain predominantly of men, providing more skills flexibility and development and diverse work, while the periphery is predominantly the domain of women workers, with fewer opportunities and further deskilling and control.

... [It is possible that this] 'core-periphery' dualism merely extends and intensifies labour market segregation by gender, race and age, [and that] we may simply be experiencing a switch in management strategies which rather than delivering democracy and greater opportunity in the workplace, further enhances and extends managerial control.

(O'Connor 1994: 13–14)

The fast capitalist world, then, holds out deep opportunities and risks for those of us interested in education. If we as educators accept the fast capitalist vision uncritically we risk becoming party to 'enchantment' as a spell cast on workers to achieve a new 'high tech' hegemony. We risk, too, collusion with processes which create enchanted conditions for some, but at the expense of possibly deeper disenchantment for many, and, ultimately, perhaps, society as a whole. If we fail to engage with fast capitalism altogether, we risk being left on the sidelines as education at all levels simply aligns itself with the values, visions and practices of fast capitalism.

We believe that critical awareness of language in practice and context is a crucial place where we can accomplish both critique and true engagement with the texts and practices of fast capitalism. Fast capitalist texts stress the need for leaders and workers to understand the systems they are part of, and not just their local places ('jobs') within those systems (Senge 1991; Senge *et al.* 1994). In today's complex systems, given changes in technology and global relations, actions that locally appear quite rational can ramify through the system with disastrous, though 'unintended' consequences – thus, the need to think and act in terms of the complex and extended relations of systems as wholes. If this skill is crucial for 'higher order thinking' in the new capitalism, we argue, too, that understanding systems in a critical way and at a 'meta-level' is crucial for all of us to protect ourselves from the intended and unintended dangers of our changing economic and social systems. And one crucial way to attain this sort of understanding is to engage in critical language awareness with regard to fast capitalist texts and their implementations within businesses and organizations.

Enchanting language: same words, different practices

Thus, we argue that a careful examination of the language in which portraits of an enchanted future are being painted is important for developing the critical perspective necessary to face complex changes and alignments with a clear and clearly articulated vision of one's own. This requires close investigation of key terms in the vocabulary of fast capitalist texts: terms like 'empowerment', 'self-direction' and 'self-directed learning', 'partnership', 'collaboration', and the like (Gee 1994b). These are words that cross discursive boundaries, spanning multiple world-views, interests, and value systems. They all carry positive connotations and name ideals to which people who embrace different – and often incompatible – aspirations, purposes, interests, and investments claim allegiance. The problem is that when matters come down to the level of lived social practice, these seemingly shared terms refer to very different ideals across different communities.

Some of the most 'motivating' words in our language can have quite different and incompatible meanings. Take, 'freedom', for example. 'Freedom' can mean the absence or removal of constraints to one's actions, a concept often referred to as 'negative freedom'. However, there is another concept of freedom – often referred to as 'positive freedom' – where being free is being able. According to this conception it is not enough simply to have restrictions removed – lack of means, e.g. support, money, access, may well serve as quite effective constraints to one's freedom. In this second sense of 'freedom', a poor person is not 'free' to go to a prestigious private school, however much he or she may be 'free' to do so in the first sense.

It is obvious that in such cases there is more at stake than mere differences in linguistic (referential) meaning. Words like 'freedom', and many others that Gee (1990) has called 'socially contested terms' (terms describing social relationships which one can choose to use in any of several different ways and where such choices carry significant social and moral consequences), get caught up in the operations of very different Discourses. 'Discourses', with a capital 'D' (Gee 1990, 1992), are ways of thinking-believing-acting-interacting-speaking-listening-valuing (sometimes, too, reading and writing) at appropriate times and places with appropriate objects so as to signal membership in (to be 'in sync with') a particular social group. There are many Discourses, ranging from (certain sorts of) African-Americans, boardroom executives, feminists, Soviets, doctors, street gang members, physicists, and so forth.

Carol Gilligan (1982) has pointed out how differences like those between our two senses of 'freedom' get connected to larger discursive systems and concomitant social identities. Some groups in their words, deeds and values focus on a sense of moral responsibility based on not restricting others' 'freedom', while other groups focus on supporting and enabling people within social networks. Many women, and people like police, soldiers, and minority groups that live under a sense of threat, belong to Discourses that integrate this second sense of 'freedom' and related words like 'responsibility' and 'rights'.

Socially contested words get caught up with different Discourses – different ways of being in the world, different forms of life, different integrations of words-deeds-values-objects signalling different social identities. That is why so much is at stake when textual practices like fast capitalist texts take up socially contested words and embed them in new and powerful

Discourses that attract and align other Discourses in new ways. A moral we can draw here, then, is this: arguing about what words (ought to) mean is not a trivial business ('just words', 'hair splitting', 'just semantics') when these arguments are over socially contested words. Such arguments are what lead to the adoption of social beliefs and the theories behind them, and these theories and beliefs lead to social action and the maintenance and creation of social worlds. Such arguments are, in this sense, also a species of moral argumentation.

One obvious implication here is that when we come into sites of social practice that bring together people from different discursive traditions and backgrounds, we cannot assume that the meanings we associate with given words/concepts are the same as other people's. Indeed, in many cases we can safely assume they are not. This is especially important where words which have positive connotations and generate strong allegiances across discursive borders are being employed in discursive contexts where projects of willing visions into reality are being enacted. In such contexts there are real dangers of being co-opted into agendas we might subsequently wish we had resisted, but where we could/did not resist because we failed to appreciate the extent to which the meanings of others were not our own meanings; possibly we did not even realize exactly how others with the power to ensure that their meanings prevailed were, in fact, framing what appeared to be shared concepts.

Critical language awareness for the new work order

Many key words used to articulate the vision of a 'new work order' in the fast capitalist literature, and related enterprises such as adult education and workplace training, operate across Discourse borders in the manner just described. While we will deal with the notions of 'self-directed learning' and 'empowerment' below, another good example is the word 'liberation', which appears in the title of one of Tom Peters's books (*Liberation Management*, 1992). The ways in which Peters, a leading fast capitalist writer/consultant, frames liberation and his vision of liberation management as Discourse, however, bespeaks very different allegiances, concerns, theories and beliefs – indeed, a different world-view – from, say, liberation theologists working on the left wing of the Catholic church (Gutiérrez 1973) or proponents of pedagogies of liberation along the lines developed by Paulo Freire (Freire 1972, 1973; Freire and Macedo 1987; Shor and Freire 1987). Given these often effaced differences, we argue that it is a key task, in the contemporary world, for proponents of different Discourses (say Freirean critical pedagogy and fast capitalism) to become clear, at a meta-level, about just where their differences lie in regard to socially contested terms like 'freedom', 'liberation', 'empowerment', 'equality', and so forth, and what grounds there may or may not be for making common cause in the creation of a more socially just world.

Likewise, both the fast capitalist literature and contemporary workplace education and training reforms put a high premium on collaboration and effective communication, as well as on empowering workers and on their being self-directed (learners). However, these terms take on quite different colouring depending upon whether people are mutually collaborating on generating purposes, goals, visions and ends, or simply cooperating to carry out a pre-given agenda within a system and vision they have had little say in forming, beyond yielding their allegiance as a 'committed' member of the team. Fast capitalist texts sometimes mention the necessity for 'bottom up' initiatives while more often talking about charismatic leaders conveying their vision almost mystically to their employees, who 'freely' (albeit irrationally) carry out the leaders' goals, ends and vision (recall here the earlier quotation from Boyett and Conn 1992: 147).

There are many aspects to critical language awareness (see Fairclough 1992; Wallace 1992), such as critical scrutiny of particular texts or specific units of language, or, at a more general level, awareness of the functioning of language and Discourses in society. We focus here, however, on the ways in which teasing out the possible meanings of socially contested terms can give rise to sets of questions and issues for debate and dialogue among Discourses, as well as deeper understanding of the values and ideological loadings that are at stake in any Discourse. We offer two 'case studies', one in regard to 'self-directed learning' and the other in regard to 'empowerment'. Readers will find a swarm of other such words in any fast capitalist text for further analysis.

Self-directed learning: whose self? Whose direction?

Fast capitalist texts uniformly stress the need for 'life-long learning' and the need continually to adapt, change and learn new skills in our changing times. They also stress that schools and universities, especially as they are currently structured, have no monopoly on these processes, and, indeed, are not always well suited to the task:

> 'In a knowledge age economy,' Lewis Perelman writes in *School's Out*, 'the learning enterprise is strategically crucial.' Far too crucial to leave to the schools, he adds. Perelman . . . imagines all the world turned into a giant learning network . . . The guiding principle is 'personal learning "on demand", "just in time", whenever and however the opportunity is wanted.'
>
> (Peters 1994: 183–4, 185; see also Perelman 1992)

One of the ways in which fast capitalist texts and school reform have aligned themselves recently is in the claim that it is not 'good enough' merely to be able to pass tests or learn in a classroom outside the context where one's knowledge needs to be applied and adapted. Both current educationally relevant cognitive science and fast capitalist texts stress that learners (students or workers) need to 'learn to learn', 'problem solve', and come to 'real' understanding applicable in new contexts (Gardner 1991; Perkins 1992; Bereiter and Scardamalia 1993). They need to be 'autonomous' learners, motivated and capable of 'self-directed' learning, not simply waiting to be told what to do, 'follow orders', or 'do school'.

The notion of 'self-directed learning', then, has become integral to visions of autonomous, motivated, self-activating students and knowledge workers operating in enchanted workplaces. At the same time, talk of self-directed learning is well established in the general theory and practice of adult education, even apart from the literature on fast capitalism and its needs, or that of educationally relevant cognitive science. Looking at issues germane to 'self-directed learning' is a good way to study the general implications of the pervasive talk about learning, knowledge and self-development in the fast capitalist texts.

A fruitful approach to reading accounts of 'self-directed learning' critically can begin from asking *what* constructions of 'self' and 'direction' are operating in this particular text, and *why* are they operating here. From this basis we may investigate what *alternative* constructions are available – what kinds of framings would best capture *our* ideals for learning, knowledge and personal development? Such questions lead very quickly to deep philosophical, moral and Discourse-related issues – which, of course, are precisely the sorts of issues that should emerge from any critical awareness about language.

In an influential and increasingly typical account advanced from a fast capitalist perspective, Piskurich frames self-directed learning as a training programme 'in which trainees master packages of pre-determined material, at their own pace, without the aid of an instructor' (1993: 4). Trainees work with packages – the 'basic units' of self-directed learning – until they master the skill, knowledge or competence with which a package is concerned. Learning materials and goals are 'given', and trainees work at their own pace within the rhythms and time constraints of their organization or workplace.

In this account 'direction' implies much more the notion of *command* (as in 'directing/commanding someone to do this') than the notion of 'where one is going'. Here, the self-directed learner is directing (= commanding, supervising) her/himself to acquire and master skills and content that have been established as important or necessary by 'external sources': by (for example) other persons directly, or, more impersonally, by quality standards or the need to adjust quickly to shifts in production. For self-directed learning as much as any other training design, 'certain essentials govern what is and isn't possible' (p. 4). These essentials are, primarily, the organization's 'bottom line', production schedules and corporate goals. Piskurich acknowledges that actual programmes of self-directed learning in competitive work settings will reflect decisions about content, materials, the type of media to be used and so on, that are compatible with self-directed learning being the 'optimal solution' to the contingencies of that setting.

Far from reflecting autonomous choice of direction, such constructions of self-directed learning seem to presuppose heteronomy: willingness to accept externally imposed directions (read 'directives') for learning. The only obvious 'play' of self may well consist in the individual's desire to remain viable as an employee in that organization. In other words, self-direction seems to be compatible here with a good deal of coercion and constrained choice.

This, in fact, is symptomatic of the kind of 'self-direction', 'self-development' and 'choice' increasingly available to workers within the new work order. To appreciate this, it is necessary to read fast capitalist texts on 'self-direction' in conjunction with the big picture of fast capitalism as a constellation of Discourses. Fast capitalist businesses cannot succeed without workers fully buying into the ends/goals/vision of the organization. They must proactively take responsibility for the total ramifications of their own work on the organization as a whole, including its results (productivity). This will only happen if workers actively choose to believe in the ends and vision of the organization, and to direct themselves in accordance with them. At the same time, the ends, goals and vision are established by visionary leaders and by the parameters of the Discourses (e.g. total quality management, just-in-time production, continual improvement, benchmarking, etc.) that together constitute social practice within the organization (see Gee 1994b).

Self-directed learning poses deep issues for fast capitalists. They face a paradox in that they want workers to experience in meaningful ways a sense of autonomous decision making, choice and self-directedness. At the same time, for organizational goals to be met it is necessary that workers make 'the right decisions/choices' and take 'the right directions' so far as their workplace learning is concerned.

The underlying issues here face the architects of practically *any* exercise in planned learning and knowledge transmission, namely: who has the right to direct what others will learn? If people learn best what they are personally interested in, how can we ensure they learn the things (we believe) they *need* to learn? What power are we entitled to draw on in order to ensure others learn what they 'need' to know? It is worth recalling here that in competitive and polarized job markets, 'self-directed' workplace learners may find themselves in a very tight spot: they either master what they need to know for the job, and do so quickly and efficiently, or they are out. Compulsory schooling itself seems scarcely less coercive in this respect. Close examination of 'self-directed learning' brings out an ambiguity that always infects the popular phrase 'on demand' (as in 'learning on demand'). This ambiguity is evident, for example, in Perelman's earlier-mentioned view of the guiding principle for learning in a knowledge age economy.

Furthermore, fast capitalists may find themselves pulled in opposite directions by their commitment to humanist pedagogical principles in the interests of building trust, culture and empowerment, on the one hand, and the pragmatics of meeting immediate training demands on the other. As a result, fast capitalists can be caught between a wish for the 'high tech' effectiveness of a learning method (which is what people like Piskurich do in fact choose), and the need for some more 'personalizing' approach that 'wins the hearts and minds' of employees.

In any event, fast capitalist constructions of self-directed learning will represent a broad set of responses to questions that impinge on *all* discursive constructions of learning and knowledge, questions like: what are the ideals and goals of learning/knowledge? How are these to be decided, and by whom? How is the power to determine learning goals, materials and methods produced and controlled? How is this (learning) Discourse regulated and policed? All Discourses, by definition, are bounded. All have their limits and all must be regulated. All discursive constructions of learning – self-directed or otherwise – present *opportunities*, but in doing so necessarily impose limits. Key variables in this equation are: what sorts of opportunities are made available by a particular learning Discourse? Who gets these opportunities, and who misses out? Who 'gatekeeps' learning and knowledge within this (or that) Discourse? How is this gatekeeping done, and with what consequences?

Accounts of self-directed learning advanced from other 'spaces' generate very different answers and values to the above questions and variables from those provided by fast capitalist texts and their associated practices. We might, for example, expect Brookfield's (1986) construction of self-directed learning from the standpoint of a left-liberal Discourse of adult education to vary markedly from fast capitalist accounts like that of Piskurich. Brookfield endorses an approach to self-directed learning in which 'critical reflection on the contingent aspects of reality, the exploration of alternative perspectives and meaning systems, and the alteration of personal and social circumstances are all present' (p. 59).

Different constructions of (self-directed) learning and knowledge produce different outcomes in terms of who benefits from or is disadvantaged by them, and in what ways. It is always of the greatest moral, educational and political importance to keep open the question: what are the consequences, and for whom, of organizing learning and knowledge in *this* way as opposed to *other* ways? Addressing this question seriously presupposes having access to experience of other Discourses of learning and knowledge, as well as the disposition and ability to frame up our own learning ideals, to make explicit our own theories and goals, to identify and contest competing constructions, and to insist always that spaces for such contestation be maintained within educational settings.

Empowerment: more than a feeling?

'Empowerment' presents another case of a key word which has positive connotations across multiple Discourse communities and has been adopted by fast capitalists and framed in accordance with values and purposes integral to their project.

Fast capitalists advocate the importance of visionary workplace leaders employing empowerment as a means for getting followers to carry out the goals of the organization. In *Workplace 2000: the Revolution Shaping American Business*, Boyett and Conn (1992) claim that leaders of 'Workplace 2000' organizations will insist upon their organization 'finding and following "the one best way"', but that the leaders will at the same time insist that employees 'be "empowered" to find a better way' (p. 156). Indeed, the process of empowering their employees

> will be the chief motivational tool of Workplace 2000 leaders and the primary way they get things done. People feel empowered when they feel confident and in control. Leaders empower people. And empowerment is an emotional and motivational high. No task seems too difficult. No outcome seems too impossible or, at least, unworthy of valiant effort. The leaders' efforts at empowerment are varied, but all aimed at the same outcome – followers who have ever increasing faith in their own abilities.
>
> (pp. 156–7)

In such accounts, successful leaders use empowerment strategies like 'building confidence through winning'. They create situations where employees are highly likely to win/succeed, and 'make success really matter', by being 'effusive with reinforcement'. Leaders committed to empowerment 'make work fun', and they 'coach', rather than 'control, order, demand, or criticize' (p. 156): they encourage employees to explain what they think they should do – what they 'want' to do – to solve their 'own' problems (i.e. the problems they face in meeting organizational purposes most efficiently).

Fast capitalist approaches to empowerment are very different from approaches developed inside other Discourses, such as the 'New Age' personal development movement (see Dyer 1991; Hay 1991), critical ethnography (Delgado-Gaitan 1990; LeCompte and deMarrais 1992), or critical pedagogy (Giroux 1988; McLaren 1989; Shor 1992). We can highlight these differences in ways that foreground issues for debate and dialogue among Discourses and reveal the values and ideological investments involved in particular constructions of empowerment. This may be done by reference to the kinds of processes and qualities seen to lead to empowerment, the ends or outcomes intended to result from empowerment, and the discursive parameters within which empowerment occurs.

In fast capitalist practices, employees are to be empowered to discover and implement 'the one best way' of meeting their organization's production and quality goals. Since the 'one best way' is always only the best way discovered to date, there are always *new* best ways to be discovered. Within those confines, employees are encouraged to seek, find, emulate and seek again. The *processes* through which empowerment occurs include the leader employing motivational strategies, applying positive reinforcement, and creating situations and structures within which employees can experience success. These processes result in employees experiencing *feelings* of confidence and being in control. The *qualities* that come with being empowered, and which constitute the 'springboard' for effective goal-pursuing action, are basically the experiences of feeling confident that one can 'do the job', and of having a sense of being in control over the processes involved in 'getting the job done'. The *ends* or *outcomes* of such empowerment include, most obviously, meeting the goals of the organization with optimal efficiency. They will also include, at the level of individual workers and work teams, experiences of intrinsic satisfaction and, possibly, some extrinsic rewards (praise, extended employment, promotion).

On the other hand, there are important silences in fast capitalist accounts of empowerment which are quite unacceptable from the standpoint of certain other Discourses and their inherent value positions. For example, while 'enchanted' employees who are empowered to find the 'one best way' to achieve organizational goals will experience 'feelings of being in control', greater confidence, and the satisfaction of 'winning', the parameters of these experiences are closely circumscribed. There is no notion of empowering employees to assess and (re)frame the goals of the organization, or to generate a more powerful role for themselves within decision-making structures and processes dealing with such matters as job tenure, whether or not to 'downsize' or 'go offshore', and so on. Similarly, from the perspective of other Discourses, the blurring of public and private domains and the assumed right by organizations to constant surveillance of employees under the aegis of corporate demand for 'over the edge loyalty' (Boyett and Conn 1992: 156) will be key targets for critique and change. So far as enchanted workplaces are concerned, however, the collapsing of public and private spaces around values and practices of 'loyalty' and ceaseless attention to duty are, quite simply, beyond question.

Under this kind of scrutiny, the central – and acknowledged – paradox of fast capitalism becomes explicit. In short, fast capitalism requires total and over the top commitment on the part of the worker, but this commitment will not be reciprocated in many of the ways that might seem necessary for engendering that commitment in the first place, such as genuine engagement with organizational goals and ends, and/or some degree of permanence or security of employment. An excerpt from the *Boston Globe* puts this in perspective:

> For those lucky enough to snag a job, permanence is a thing of the past. 'For the corporation I work with, at one point in time, they would talk about how "We promise our workers lifetime employment,"' says James Medoff, a Harvard economics professor. 'Now, they say with a big smile, "We want you to be eager to stay, but ready to leave."'
>
> (Carton: 1994)

It is worth noting here that states (of being) such as 'being eager to stay but ready to go' are not especially common. They appear, in fact, to be contradictory. To be sure, they require a very specific construal of 'identity', namely, an asocial identity for the worker as independent entrepreneur contracting out her or his own work, in the manner of someone working on a movie that is a well-bounded project from which one moves on for other projects with other studios. This identity may indeed be, in some sense, empowering, but one needs to be clear that the fast capitalist notion of empowerment is used in reference to such identities and social positionings. We may concede that such an identity is empowering, while nonetheless wanting to argue for quite different identities – i.e. more *social* ones that are empowering in quite different senses. More generally, we should note that the identity that goes along with the fast capitalist conception of empowerment is the same one that goes along with their notions of 'learning', 'self-direction', 'partnership', 'collaboration' and so on.

The paradoxical character of fast capitalist Discourse around empowerment can be extended in another direction. Fast capitalism is strong on encouraging and enabling 'critical reflection' on the part of employees at the level of understanding relations and processes *internal* to the organization's systems – its production and quality control/assurance system, the relationship of individual workers to the team system, the role of the team within the overall system, etc. Fast capitalists do not, however, want to promote critical reflection in the sense of questioning systems as wholes and in their political relations to other systems. On the contrary, they are keen to pre-empt this, as we have seen in the case of self-directed learning.

This, of course, is true of *all* social institutions with respect to their own systems. It is, indeed, true of Discourses *per se*. Discourses are resistant to internal criticism and self-scrutiny: entertaining and expressing/engaging viewpoints that seriously undermine them defines one as being outside them.

In other words, a Discourse involves a set of values and viewpoints in terms of which one must speak and act, otherwise one simply is not 'in' that Discourse. The Discourse itself defines what counts as acceptable criticism. The system of Discourses which collectively constitute the life of an institution – such as a business or manufacturing organization – necessarily imposes parameters on critical reflection and practice. To that extent it constrains the scope of the critical practice dimension of empowerment.

Making (fast capitalist) texts dealing with empowerment the object of critical language awareness enables us to identify points at which we would question or dispute the ways these accounts frame the processes and qualities, ends and outcomes, and the discursive parameters that define empowerment within their associated Discourses. This in turn challenges us to clarify the particular beliefs, values and purposes we would seek to enact in empowering practices. Bringing critical language awareness to bear on accounts of empowerment makes possible deeper understanding of the values and ideological investments of different Discourses, and reveals key questions and issues for debate and dialogue among Discourses. Such debate and dialogue is essential to democratic practices intended to protect us against intended and unintended consequences of changing economic and social systems and, more positively, to effect wider and deeper collaboration in 'humanizing' the world.

Critical engagement with accounts of empowerment also helps make explicit the inherent limits to critique and transformation within *any and all* Discourses. At this level of inquiry we can distinguish two very different *modes* of empowerment, developed in greater detail in Chapter 3. In one (treated as Modes A and B in Chapter 3), individuals and groups are empowered in the sense of being enabled to perform with mastery or excellence in relation to established ends and values – whether by following given procedures, or by discovering and implementing new and better ways of meeting prescribed ends. This is the mode envisaged in fast capitalist accounts of empowerment for enchanted workplaces.

The second mode (Mode C in Chapter 3) enables individuals and groups to contest and (re)define the very goals, purposes, and underlying beliefs and values of Discourses in which they are engaged or which otherwise impinge upon them. This calls for a critical 'meta-level' understanding of systems *per se* – those one is 'in' or 'subjected to', as well as others from the perspective of which critique of these former systems can be framed and waged, including critique of institutionalized conceptions and practices of empowerment.

Conclusion

As an enactive project, fast capitalism has made rapid and far-reaching progress. Its proponents have had considerable success in pulling other

Discourses 'into line': most notably, perhaps, such potentially significant competing Discourses as educational reform and cognitive science. In addition, fast capitalists have usurped key terms from the conceptual armament of critical pedagogy and critical literacy. They have redefined these terms and reframed the practices and procedures they denote within Discourses of critical practice, bringing them into closer alignment with fast capitalist values and goals. As a consequence, critical literacy and critical pedagogy are in danger of becoming impotent as oppositional practices of critique and transformation.

Fast capitalism will not – *cannot* – admit serious critique of its systems. Where fast capitalist texts are explicit about contradictions and dangers inherent in their underlying world-view and driving ethos, it is from a standpoint of genuine strength, and with a conviction that they will somehow either have to be lived with or else resolved as far as possible within the scope of the fast capitalist project.

This chapter is based on the conviction that enterprises like critical literacy/pedagogy and critical theory must be reframed as enactive projects, concerned with mobilizing reflection and action around informed awareness and evaluation of the complex and extended relations of systems as wholes. This kind of reframing needs to begin from acknowledging and acting upon the importance of critical language awareness for all who participate in the practices and texts of the fast capitalist world.

Appendix: a sample of fast capitalist books

Aguayo, R. (1990) *Dr. Deming: The American who Taught the Japanese about Quality*. New York: Carol Publishing Group.

Boyett, J. H. and Conn, H. P. (1992) *Workplace 2000: The Revolution Reshaping American Business*. New York: Plume/Penguin.

Crosby, P. B. (1994) *Completeness: Quality for the 21st Century*. New York: Plume.

Cross, K. F., Feather, J. J. and Lynch, R. L. (1994) *Corporate Renaissance: The Art of Reengineering*. Oxford: Basil Blackwell.

Davidow, W. H. and Malone, M. S. (1992) *The Virtual Corporation: Structuring and Revitalizing the Corporation for the 21st Century*. New York: Harper Business.

Deal, T. E. and Jenkins, W. A. (1994) *Managing the Hidden Organization: Strategies for Empowering Your Behind-the-Scenes Employees*. New York: Warner.

Dobyns, L. and Crawford-Mason, C. (1991) *Quality or Else: The Revolution in World Business*. Boston, MA: Houghton Mifflin.

Drucker, P. F. (1993) *Post-Capitalist Society*. New York: Harper.

Hamel, G. and Prahalad, C. K. (1994) *Competing for the Future: Breakthrough*

Strategies for Seizing Control of Your Industry and Creating the Markets of Tomorrow. Boston, MA: Harvard Business School Press.

Hammer, M. and Champy, J. (1993) *Reengineering the Corporation: a Manifesto for Business Revolution*. New York: Harper Business.

Handy, C. (1989) *The Age of Unreason*. London: Business Books.

Ishikawa, K. (1985) *What is Total Quality Control?: The Japanese Way*. Englewood Cliffs, NJ: Prentice Hall.

Lipnack, J. and Stamps, J. (1993) *The Team Net Factor: Bringing the Power of Boundary Crossing into the Heart of Your Business*. Essex Junction, VT: Oliver Wright.

Peters, T. (1992) *Liberation Management: Necessary Disorganization for the Nanosecond Nineties*. New York: Fawcett.

Peters, T. (1994) *The Tom Peters Seminar: Crazy Times Call for Crazy Organizations*. New York: Vintage Books.

Sashkin, M. and Kiser, K. J. (1993) *Putting Total Quality Management to Work*. San Francisco, CA: Berrett-Koehler.

Senge, P. M. (1991) *The Fifth Discipline: The Art and Practice of the Learning Organization*. New York: Doubleday.

Senge, P. M., Roberts, C., Ross, R. B., Smith, B. J. and Kleiner, A. (1994) *The Fifth-Discipline Fieldbook: Strategies and Tools for Building a Learning Organization*. New York: Doubleday.

Walton, M. (1990) *Deming Management at Work*. New York: Putnam.

five

LITERACY, WORK AND FUTURES: A VIEW FROM THE THIRD WORLD

Prelude: the San José Cooperative, Monte Fresco, Nicaragua – February 1995

Colin: Noél, why is there no work going on right now in the cooperative's factory, and why has there been almost no work at all during the past year?

Noél: It's the problem with the competitiveness of our products. We're manufacturing our products by hand, by comparison with other countries whose products are of better quality and are cheaper. It's been impossible for us to keep working because of that. Their products are cheaper and nicer. They look better. Because of that our products stopped selling. In the end we decided to stop producing.

    . . . The industrialization of other countries means that people like us in Nicaragua can make one unit whereas other countries can make 10 or 100. So theirs are cheaper. We couldn't go on because we'd be working for nothing – not making a profit, and not even able to make a wage, because to compete with the prices of industrialized goods we would have to work virtually for free.

(Interview, 16 February 1995)

Introduction: my primary and secondary worlds

In February 1990, the Sandinista National Liberation Front, which had spearheaded the Nicaraguan Revolution and had in effect governed the country between 1979 and 1990, was defeated at the polls by the Unified National Opposition coalition. Later that same year, Michael Best published an important and illuminating book called *The New Competition*. These two events, seemingly worlds apart, had – and continue to have – special significance for me. This chapter will attempt to explain this significance and to explore what I have come to see as a crucial global concern evoked by these events, which I view as symbolic enactments of much larger phenomena. First, however, we need to step back a little.

During the 1970s I became increasingly interested in the work of Paulo Freire, whose writings on the politics of literacy presented a signal challenge to the mainstream formal world of language and literacy education. Freire's work was appropriated by a number of revolutionary governments in Third World countries which, upon assuming power, instigated mass adult literacy campaigns. The Nicaraguan National Literacy Crusade, and the subsequent programme of Popular Basic Education for Adults in Nicaragua, was one such case. My interest in Freire's work led me to Nicaragua to investigate, over several years, literacy developments in that country – particularly as they related to wider programmes of social and economic reform. This work eventually led me, in 1989–90, to spend a year living and working in the San José manufacturing cooperative, located within the rural hamlet of Monte Fresco (population approximately 1000) some 30 kilometres from Managua on the old road to León.

The intensity and quality of my experience living in that community is such that I have come to regard it as my secondary world – a world to which I return most years and which is never far from my mind. In various ways, and on a daily basis, my consciousness of that world engages with my conscious lived experience of my primary world as a New Zealand citizen nowadays living and working as an academic in Australia.

Most of this chapter will be spent in my secondary world, exploring relationships among literacy, work and life chances. In order to set the scene, however, it is useful to introduce Best's notion of 'the new competition', which is integral to understanding and juxtaposing two very different forms of economic struggle which were taking place in these primary and secondary worlds during the 1980s, struggles which have come face to face with each other and whose resolution presents a major challenge confronting the new millennium.

'The new competition' and work in my primary world

Both of these economic struggles were integrally bound up with the world of work, and had important links to literacy education. As we will see, under the leadership of the Sandinistas daily life in Nicaragua was dominated by the struggle to bring about, in the face of increasing opposition from the US and its closest allies, a revolutionary social, economic and cultural programme based on broad social justice principles, with an emphasis on redistributing a greater proportion of benefits toward the traditionally impoverished sectors of the population, namely peasants and urban workers. One of the central planks in the change programme involved reorganizing the conditions, basis and availability of work.

Likewise, my primary world was deeply embroiled in a struggle which was very much one of economic restructuring. It was, however, a programme of economic restructuring designed to restructure First World economies as planned responses to 'the new competition'. Much of what we addressed in Chapter 4 is relevant here, since meeting the demands of the new competition has been very much a matter of trying to become part of the new work order on advantageous terms. I will briefly augment the account of the new capitalism and its new work order outlined in Chapter 4 by explicit reference to 'the new competition' as elaborated by people like Best himself and Lester Thurow.

Economic regions as otherwise different as Australasia, Britain and North America have undergone a broad shared experience during the past two or three decades: an awakening to new conditions, sources and forms of economic competition following severe blows to the economic advantage and privilege they had previously enjoyed on a world scale. Notwithstanding the relevant differences in detail between their respective economies, each of these regions has embraced the view that pursuing comparative economic advantage in the future calls for a new economic orientation: an orientation which emphasizes

> higher valued-added producing [presupposing] more manufacturing and marketing skills [and] more financial and other services, all of which would mean more use of high technology and more abstract thinking, and thus increased levels of education throughout the workforce.
>
> (Levett and Lankshear 1994: 28–9)

By the late 1970s there was an increasing sense among individuals and groups with influence over economic and corporate policies in these three regions that 'the economic game' was being won by players who were employing different ways of playing and succeeding from those long established in Anglo-American countries. At first this sense was largely inchoate. It was not until the 1980s that ideas about competition, with which we are now reasonably familiar, began to be articulated with much force, depth and precision. As they emerged, these ideas enjoyed wide currency and influence.

The modern world economy is dominated by three main trading blocks:

Europe, led by Germany; East Asia, led by Japan; and North America, led by the US. Europe and East Asia have developed a new approach to economic success, and nations who wish to 'keep up' will have to master these approaches. This is essentially a matter of understanding and participating within the rubric of a new kind of competition, calling for new technological, social and innovative/entrepreneurial emphases in work (Levett and Lankshear 1994).

Lester Thurow (1992) argues that the European and East Asian trading blocks employ a communitarian form of capitalism, which has successfully challenged the formerly dominant mode of individualistic capitalism employed in Anglo-American countries, and which had been mastered by the US in particular. Communitarian capitalism privileges producer over consumer economics and business groups over outstanding entrepreneurs (ch. 2). It emphasizes increased market share over short-term maximization of profit. Values like teamwork, strong loyalty to the firm, and social responsibility for skills are stressed, as opposed to quick and easy hiring and firing, large wage differentials, and individual responsibility for skills (hence national and regional training reform agendas and increasing business implication and involvement in education and training for work). Finally, communitarian capitalism promotes a characteristic range of industrial strategies and policies designed to promote growth (Levett and Lankshear 1994: 29).

Communitarian capitalism is seen as having important implications for workplace education and skill development. Attention is drawn to the fact that Japan (East Asia) has the world's highest 'bottom 50%' education level, and Germany the 'best educated workforce across a broad range of mid-level, non-college skills' (Thurow 1992: 52, cited in Levett and Lankshear 1994: 29). The purported implications include new technological and social requirements for work.

With regard to *technological* requirements, evidence from research in several countries indicates that office, factory, retail and repair operations work will increasingly draw on competence with high technology processes in addition to conventional practices of reading instructions. Workers need to be competent in diverse processes involving using computers and other high tech processes, interpreting symbols, and forms of monitoring. At its most rudimentary, the technological literacy characteristic of routine production work (Reich 1992), in food processing chains or in the production of mass-produced metal components, for example, entails the production and interpretation of spreadsheets and graphs, as well as reading from computerized displays in order to monitor and regulate the rate and quality of production.

Take quality assurance, for example. We are informed that in the past, quality control within manufacture was often simply 'a screening process, catching defects before they got out the door'. Likewise, when a machine malfunctioned, 'workers raised their hands, and a troubleshooter came to fix it'.

Under conditions of the new competition, however, things have changed. Ensuring quality, for example, is now an elaborate process – an entire Discourse – 'that prevents defects from occurring'. Quality has become a common new corporate language and literacy ('bell curves', 'probability functions', 'standard deviations', and a wholly new conception of quality) 'that pervades the company and applies to security guards and secretaries as well as manufacturing staff'. Similarly, workers are now expected routinely 'to know their equipment and begin any troubleshooting process themselves' (all quotations from Wiggenhorn 1990). This calls for conceptual understandings of this equipment and its role within a larger work process, as well as for forms of technological literacy, such as reading and translating 'manual-ese', interpreting the likely problem in a malfunction and, where specialist assistance is required, analysing the problem and communicating the malfunction in detail.

This, of course, lies behind much of what was described in Chapter 4, such as line workers having to understand their work as 'parts related to wholes' in increasingly sophisticated ways ('knowledge work'). Streamlining the workforce (in order to become competitive) has eliminated several layers of middle management. Maintaining a competitive edge means that change – innovation – must be continuous and participatory. If workers are to participate in innovation, they require a conceptual understanding of the entire work process, the ability to communicate ideas, and the capacity to glean relevant information from appropriate sources. Much of this work was previously done by management strata that have now disappeared, and much of it contains a demanding technological dimension.

The 'new competition' also entails a set of new *social* requirements for work, as contemporary factors like 'market fragmentation, global resource uncertainties, and microelectronic technology' combine to lend competitive advantage in many cases to 'small-scale flexible manufacturing' over 'large-scale mass production' (Levett and Lankshear 1994: 40). In this context,

> [M]ore and more of the world's goods require not standardisation and modest quality . . . but higher quality, continuous innovation, design and production changes. Flexible production and high quality in turn require different organisational structures and work practices . . .
>
> The new competition firm is entrepreneurial, as distinct from hierarchical, and has a strategic orientation, that is, chooses its terrain on which to compete. It achieves comparative advantage by continuous improvement in process and product. 'Innovation is not about abrupt changes (produced from time to time by research and development) but by the accretion of marginal adjustments in product, process and organization'. Working practices are seldom routinised.
>
> (p. 40)

In Best's words:

> Improvement is always possible and ideas can come from everyone including consumers, workers, suppliers, staff and managers. As a social process, innovation involves the interaction of people engaged in functionally distinct activities. It demands persistent and comprehensive re-examination of productive practices.
>
> (Best 1990: 12–13)

The 'new competition firm' aims to compete successfully by integrating thinking, judging and doing, emphasizing teamwork and, in team contexts, enhancing workers' capacities for 'perceptual discrimination, learning and inferring from experience, reasoning, making fine judgments, and coping with unforeseen events' (Levett and Lankshear 1994: 40).

It is against this kind of background that we must understand a good deal of recent and ongoing 'restructuring' within my primary world: administrative and organizational restructuring; economic restructuring; educational restructuring; award restructuring and workplace reform, and the like. For example, major changes to vocational education and training occurred in Britain from the late 1970s, with the creation of a Manpower Services Commission (MSC) which spearheaded a series of new training structures and programmes in England and Wales. Initially, the MSC's New Training Initiative spawned such programmes as the Youth Training Scheme, the Technical and Vocational Education Initiative (TVEI), and the Certificate of Pre-Vocational Training. Later, the MSC promoted a wholly revamped vocational education and training and certification strategy through the National Council for Vocational Qualifications. Separate but related initiatives unfolded in Scotland, with the Scottish Vocational Education Council (SCOTVEC). Since the late 1980s the Australian government has similarly instigated a range of comprehensive initiatives aimed at creating a 'clever country' of smart worker-citizens ready to take their places in the new world order and its highly competitive global economy. These initiatives include far-reaching programmes of industry and award restructuring and workplace change, backed by a national training reform agenda, negotiated and agreed between industry, government and unions. As with the British cases earlier, the Australian initiatives have included a heavy emphasis on outputs-driven, competency-based, best-practice approaches to education and training. Within this rubric, important emphasis has been given to adult and child literacy and numeracy. In Australia, the 1991 Language and Literacy Policy (DEET 1991a) generated an ambitious and ongoing programme of language and literacy projects and reforms, overseen by specially created offices. Many such projects focus on workplaces.

Within my primary world, then, the new competition has impacted powerfully on work in general, and its language and literacy requirements in particular. We are all well aware from our own experiences just how much this impact has changed our work lives and our preparation for work lives. Of course, in a global, interconnected world what happens in one place tends also to impact on what happens elsewhere. Sometimes this impact is dramatic. Often we do not notice these effects, or concern ourselves with them – especially when they occur far away, in contexts we cannot access empirically, where our knowledge is dependent upon what is reported, and when we already have major concerns of our own to deal with. Current trends suggest, however, that we ignore these wider effects at our moral, political and existential peril. With this said, it is time to enter my secondary world.

A background to San José

Following the defeat of the Somoza regime in July 1979, Nicaragua's revolutionary government launched a programme of social reform intended to address a historical legacy of underdevelopment compounded by a grossly unequal distribution of wealth, services and other resources. The complementary motifs of national development and social justice were evident across a rich array of entirely new (for Nicaragua) policy initiatives, laws and social programmes. Two are especially relevant to this chapter: first, the Nicaraguan National Literacy Crusade of 1980 and the subsequent programme of popular basic education for adults; second, policies designed to 'cooperativize' production.

Adult literacy and education initiatives in Nicaragua from 1980

At the time of the popular forces' challenge and overthrow of Somoza and his army, the country presented a classic case of Third World 'underdevelopment' and extremes of inequality. Typical assessments described malnutrition as routine among peasants and the urban poor, with infant mortality averaging 100–120 per 1000 and rising to 333 per 1000 in the poorest areas. Of rural homes, 80 per cent lacked any kind of sanitation facilities and the same proportion of homes in the capital city lacked running water. Almost half of all farmland – including the best land – was owned by less than 2 per cent of landowners, with 58 per cent of smallholders occupying 3.4 per cent of the total between them. Income was grossly uneven. In 1977 the per capita income of the top 5 per cent was US$5500. For the bottom 50 per cent it was $226, with the poorer half of the rural population existing on less than $40 per capita annually (Booth 1982; Weissberg 1982; Miller 1985). Just 5 per cent of the rural population had completed primary school, and 53 per cent of Nicaraguans over the age of 10 were estimated to be illiterate, with illiteracy topping 90 per cent in many rural areas. Only 18 per cent of those eligible for secondary education had access to it (Barndt 1985: 317. For an overview, see Lankshear and Lawler 1989: ch. 5). In the words of one moderate appraiser, 'Overall . . . Nicaragua distributed services and wealth very unequally and . . . living standards for the majority were poor, even in comparison to the rest of Central America' (Booth 1982: 10).

The Sandinista manifesto for radical social change included plans for a mass literacy campaign for adults, to be followed by a basic popular education programme intended to provide the equivalent of an elementary education for all adults who wanted it. While these were just two elements of an ambitious vision for a national development agenda, they were seen as absolutely central to the overall development strategy (FSLN 1969, 1982; Lankshear 1991: 98–9). The link between (adult) literacy and a national development agenda had crucial implications for what was to count as literacy and how it was to be pursued within popular education initiatives. Specifically, national development would require change on both international and internal dimensions. A long-established tradition of domination and economic exploitation by foreign colonial and neocolonial powers would have to give way to a more patriotic and dignified foreign policy, and economic, commercial and technical relationships with other countries would henceforth have to be conducive to Nicaragua's own economic and social development and growth.

On the internal dimension, political and economic structures which would permit the full participation of all Nicaraguans at national, regional and local levels were seen as necessary. A planned economy, agrarian reform, a labour code, redistribution of Somicista wealth, and policies designed to tackle unemployment and to guarantee the freedom of the worker-union movement were to be key components of economic restructuring. A raft of policies for structural change were proposed to address pressing issues related to ethnic, gender, cultural, health, housing and social security concerns.

This kind of social change and national development cannot simply be *donated* to a people, but must be created with and through the committed activity of marginalized groups, and be answerable to their needs and in tune with shifts in their social awareness and their capacity for informed and constructive social action. Consequently, a powerful literacy, capable of enlisting people in critically informed ways to projects of historical change, was seen as absolutely central.

The Sandinista perspective was that under Somoza, literacy had been irrelevant for most Nicaraguans precisely because Nicaragua was an underdeveloped and dependent country governed conspicuously in the interests of a few. By contrast, the very *meaning* of pursuing universal literacy within the revolutionary agenda was grounded in the quest for development and independence – of the people as individuals, groups and as a national community. Of course, there would be no great benefit for illiterate people in becoming literate unless the skills and understandings they acquired as a consequence played an integral role in enhancing their daily practice and their development as human beings. Consequently, the pursuit of rudimentary reading, writing and numeracy skills was seen from the outset as entailing wider educational and social aims, namely

> to encourage an integration and understanding among Nicaraguans of different classes and backgrounds; to increase political awareness and critical analysis of underdevelopment; to nurture attitudes and skills related to creativity, production, cooperation, discipline, and analytical thinking; to forge a sense of national consensus and of political responsibility; to strengthen channels of economic and political participation; to acquaint people with national development programs; to record oral histories and recover popular forms of culture; and to conduct research in health and agriculture for future development planning.
>
> (Cardenal and Miller 1981: 6)

During 1980 a five-month mass literacy campaign was undertaken in the dominant language, Spanish, with subsequent English and Miskitu language variants offered in the Atlantic Coast region. This involved the mass mobilization of almost 100,000 literacy teachers (many of them being school students), and well over 500,000 of the 722,000 Nicaraguans above 10 years of age identified as illiterate. The Literacy Crusade (CNA) was followed by an ongoing non-formal voluntary programme of popular basic education for adults (the EPB – see Torres 1983, 1985, 1986), which was designed to provide the equivalent of an elementary education for all adults who sought it. The CNA and EPB shared three distinctive features contrived to enable marginalized people to tackle the most pressing concerns of their daily lives:

1 A concerted effort was made to draw out and confront commonly held beliefs that contributed to oppressed people effectively accepting and consenting to their own domination: beliefs like 'we are powerless', 'we are nothing and don't count', 'we are ignorant', 'there is nothing we can do to change our conditions', 'things can't be changed, we must accept the world as it is.' Literacy lessons were designed to encourage a more critical and analytical understanding of local, national and international 'realities', consistent with adopting active roles in pursuit of just and democratic social change.

2 The task of becoming literate was tied as closely as possible to *acting* on the words and themes around which literacy lessons were built. Learners were encouraged to transcend beliefs they may have had about their inability to create a different history, within a literacy programme which was directly

linked to practical projects that objectively improved the quality of life. Furthermore, organizations for popular participation were being created and consolidated at the time, with teachers and learners alike being challenged by the lesson themes and discussions to join and to participate through them. As projects unfolded and were completed, participants actually *experienced* historical and cultural agency within the act of coming to see the possibility and importance of becoming literate historical agents.

3 The EPB programme which followed aimed to maintain a close link between educational content and realities of daily life. It also – largely from necessity – stressed a pedagogy which drew upon and enhanced the sense of historical agency and commitment to active involvement fostered within the CNA. Since it was impossible to provide formally trained teachers for the EPB, much of the teaching force had to be drawn from people who had only themselves become literate during the CNA. Hence the pedagogy had to be manageable by newly literate people. It also had to be self-motivating and self-sustaining, since the demands of the EPB teaching role could easily encourage 'dropping out', 'excuse-making' and 'backsliding'. (For fuller accounts of these initiatives, see Torres 1983, 1985, 1986; Miller 1985; Arnove 1986; Lankshear and Lawler 1989; Lankshear 1991.)

In the event, some 406,000 Nicaraguans were calculated to have either acquired or recovered a basic level of literacy via the mass campaigns, with thousands more subsequently doing so via the EPB programme. At its peak the EPB attracted almost 200,000 learners during one semester (at the time Nicaragua's total population was around 3 million), and three years after, the CNA had over 150,000 learners on the books. At the conclusion of the CNA, a youth newspaper reported to its membership that during the five-month campaign, besides learning and teaching basic literacy 'we held 2,398 political and cultural meetings and 1,620 rallies; harvested 17,134 manzanas (29,573) acres of coffee, beans, corn, rice and vegetables; constructed 5,195 latrines, 55 houses, 11 roads, 195 bridges, 271 schools, 14 communal baths, a canal, 55 health centres, 12 churches, 12 plazas and 28 parks' (Angus 1981: 14). In this simple but profound way, the 'building blocks' of learning to read and write simultaneously became invitations to enter materially into creating a new history. The spirit and logic of the CNA drew heavily on Paulo Freire's notion that 'the dead weight of history' bears down on those whose 'voices have been silenced', deadening them to the possibilities and relative ease of acting collectively to build a better life (see Freire 1972, 1973, 1985; Freire and Macedo 1987).

The encouragement of cooperative approaches to economic production

Among the major policy innovations intended to contribute to a socially just national development agenda were mechanisms and incentives for encouraging cooperative approaches to economic production. These were to some extent driven ideologically by extant conceptions of socialism and available exemplars of revolutionary economic, political and social programmes. In many cases, however, they simply made good economic sense – for example, by obviating the need to duplicate machinery and other infrastructure under conditions of extreme economic scarcity. Cooperatives were eligible for a range of incentives and means of support, ranging from credit advances to access to support structures available to assist their enterprises administratively, technically and educationally.

During the early 1980s agricultural and manufacturing cooperatives mushroomed, operating with varying degrees of success. Often they established opportunities for hitherto underemployed and impoverished Nicaraguans to obtain steady paid work, and to experience a sense of autonomy, ownership and control in the work process. Many members of these new cooperatives were newly and minimally literate 'graduates' of the 1980 Literacy Crusade and subsequent adult basic education programme.

During 1989–90 I lived in the San José light manufacturing cooperative in the rural neighbourhood of Monte Fresco, 30 kilometres south-west of the capital, Managua. San José had been established in 1985 by a group of peasants who had experienced grinding poverty, frequent periods of hunger and malnutrition, and insecure and irregular employment (always poorly paid) throughout their adult lives. While some among San José's *socios* (members) had been better off than many Nicaraguan peasants, others could fairly be ranked as having lived at the bottom of the Third World economic heap. In the event, nine men and six women pooled their meagre economic resources to establish the San José cooperative and begin production.

Literacy and production in San José

Most of the male *socios* were illiterate or semi-literate (able to read straightforward texts but having little or no writing competence). The women typically had at least a second-grade school level. Most could read (decode) newspapers, the Bible, magazines quite fluently, and could write (encode) messages, recipes and the like, albeit painstakingly. They lacked, however, the *generic* literate competencies associated with tasks integral to administering an enterprise like San José, negotiating deals at distance, and so on. In the early years of the cooperative, they depended on an accountant who lived locally to keep the books and maintain records. However, he was often away on business and eventually left Monte Fresco. During these periods the cooperative experienced real difficulties keeping abreast of administration. Isabel, San José's treasurer, found this created problems for her role, for when the accountant was away,

> I can't keep up to date and be sure if he's up to date. When I was asked how much money was in the bank I didn't know – because he was away at the time, and only he knew the figures then.
>
> (Interview, February 1989)

Isabel was acutely aware of the gap between the real demands of her role and her own competence:

> My task is to have control of all the finances, materials, what we buy and sell, what we bring in; to know how much is in the bank, how much has been spent. I have to see when the accountant does the balance – which is six-monthly – which cheques go out and which come in; what the money was spent on. Sometimes I need to make a statement of finances but can't because I only understand a little about numbers . . . Accountancy is based on numbers and one needs to be able to multiply and divide, and I'm lacking in that.
>
> (Interview, February 1989)

Valuing the fact that she had been given responsibility, Isabel nonetheless felt the burden of her position acutely:

> Sometimes when I can't do it I ask them to change me for another person, but they tell me I have to be there . . . there's no one else to do it. If I could understand numbers better I'd like the task a lot.
>
> (Interview, February 1989)

Isabel first learned to read and write in the CNA and continued in the EPB – completing the third level – until a fall-off in participants forced an end to the classes in Monte Fresco. As a child she never went to school.

> My parents never sent me . . . None of my brothers or sisters went. My mother had to work and we stayed home and helped with the housework . . . Not until I grew up, married, and had Nelson and Sandra. Nelson and Sandra began to go to school and at the parent meeting they said parents had to help their children at home, to make sure the homework's well done. They would come and ask me if I would help, but I couldn't because I didn't understand the letters. It was hard for me not to be able to help them. But when the Crusade came I thought this was my opportunity. Before the CNA I couldn't write my name. I didn't even know what letter my name began with. I had to be led by the

hand when I began – but the more I learned the more I could do on my own. When I couldn't write a sentence I worried, but when I started to be able to do it on my own I was pleased because I was learning . . . When I finished *Dawn of the People* [the CNA primer] I could read and in the second level [of the EPB] all seemed easy to me . . . Slowly I lost the fear. When I saw I could do it on my own I was thrilled. And in the end I learned.

(Interview, March 1989)

Isabel progressed through three levels of EPB before local classes ceased – at the very point where the curriculum would have been especially useful for her as San José's treasurer.

I learned to do small sums as from the first to third levels they taught adding and subtracting of small figures. In the fourth level they have much more and teach you to multiply, but as I didn't finish the fourth level I didn't learn all that . . . At the fourth level one learns accounting – it's in the textbook, but as I didn't finish I couldn't learn it well . . . I'd like to go on learning and finish sixth level.

(Interview, March 1989)

The San José cooperative began by producing a simple line of brooms. The bristles were made from a species of wheat, stitched into shape with wire – using a home-made device of hinged wood, like book covers that closed to flatten the wheat while it was stitched flat into its permanent shape – and wired to wooden handles that had been rounded laboriously by hand. These 'traditional' brooms were popular and sold well. Some of the profits were ploughed back into the enterprise to purchase equipment and materials and increase the scale and range of production.

By 1989 production had diversified. An all-weather concrete block factory had been built, and new machinery included a primitive lathe which would shape 25 mm by 25 mm timber stakes into wooden handles, a circular saw, arc welder, steel guillotine, electric drill and press, and an array of metal-working tools. In addition, the cooperative had obtained a machine that turned nylon pellets into nylon thread, under heat. Production, however, remained labour intensive. The product range now included: hand-plaited cotton mops (called *mechas*), similar to the wringer mops used in industrialized countries for large slab or tile floor surfaces; the attachments for holding *mechas* (called *lampazos*), which comprised a wooden handle and an intricate hand-made steel holding mechanism; and a range of nylon-bristled brushes and brooms which had taken over from the original wheat-bristled variety. With the assistance of funds from an international agency, a sub-group of the cooperative was funded to produce a hand-operated pump to be used on wells.

Their production processes and products as I observed them in 1989 bear further description.

Mecha production began by unpacking a large bale (one cubic metre) of unrefined cotton fibre which had been compressed into the bale. The women would draw out strands of fibre and pull them tight, using the full length of the factory floor (some 20 metres). These fibres were then wound around two nails some 60 cm apart and cut with a machete. This left 60 cm lengths of cotton fibre – by the tonne! These were kept orderly and gathered into 'lots' weighing half a kilo (using scales). The principle was half a kilo of cotton per *mecha*. Each 'lot' of cotton was laid out evenly in 15 cm widths, and held together by having a calico ribbon sewn flat through the middle of the cotton (that is, 30 cm in from each end. These hanks of cotton were then taken to a rectangular frame (like a table without its top). Women (mainly) and children sat around the frame on stools or forms. The hanks of cotton were tossed over the frame with the ribbon atop the frame, so that one side of the hank fell down the outside of the frame towards the seated person's lap. The worker then took several strands of fibre and rubbed them between the palms of her hands with an action that plaited the strands into a twist that stayed together. She then repeated this exercise all the way along the first half of the hank, resulting in 25–30 plaits of more or less equal 'body'. The hank was then flipped over the other way and the remaining side plaited.

The completed *mechas* were tossed on to a table. One worker (usually Gilberto) would inspect each *mecha* for evenness, give it a shake to get rid of loose fibres, and then put it into a plastic bag and heat seal the open end of the bag with a restored primitive (electrical wiring everywhere!) model of heat sealer. My field notes record that

> making *mechas* is a highly social process. It is flexible work, with the women coming and going in time to other routines (e.g. cooking). At the end of the day some of the men will come in after finishing work on the pumps or on *lampazos* and do some plaiting. Today husbands sat beside their wives and each partner took one side. They would meet in the middle and then flip the *mecha* and repeat the process. Children of 4 or 5 years showed great skill in plaiting. Payment is on the basis of quantity produced. The children's production is put on their parents' account. There is constant conversation during the day's work. Conditions are pleasant and there is no hint of pressure. One youth produced 55 mops in the day, which began casually at 8.20 and ended at 5.30, with meal breaks and other comings and goings. Some of the women could produce up to 75 *mechas* per day. The process is repetitive, but the skilled worker needn't watch closely. As a result there is plenty of scope for conversation, joking, etc. It also provides a built-in child care context for children of 2 and over – since they are either

working or else can play on the floor and immediate surroundings and be watched by parents, other workers, or siblings. The elasticity of the work makes for variety, because people come and go. Salvadora and Isabel get up for a break. Yamiled (12, female) comes and sits in Isabel's place and does some plaiting. Gilberto has bagged all the completed *mechas* and comes and sits between Yamiled and Milton (12, male), trying out Milton's sling shot. Alexis (male, 17) has returned to plait after playing with one of the infants. Chatting and plaiting go on, with Salvadora and Isabel now onlookers. Vilma comes in with her record book to record each person's production. Conversation shifts to the amount produced and how much longer they'll have to work today to meet quota. Cándida goes to the sewing machine to sew more hanks together. Javier (male, 20) arrives and plaits with Alexis where Cándida had been working. Elvis (male, 8) joins the workers, as does Gilberto. Conversation continues and production proceeds at the same pace and rhythm as before: except the actors have changed. This is how it goes on, hour by hour, day by day.

(Fieldnotes, March 1989)

Lampazo and nylon brush and broom production were similarly labour intensive. To hold the *mechas* securely, *lampazos* required nuts and bolts, as well as various types of brackets and movable parts. Producing the nuts and bolts is indicative of the production of *lampazos* as a whole. To produce nuts the men would mark out 12 mm by 12 mm squares on a piece of plate steel (3 mm thick) and drill a hole in the middle of each square, using an electric hand drill. These holes would then be threaded using a hand-held threading tap. When each square had been threaded, the squares would be cut out using a hacksaw. Bolts were made by threading steel rod using a hand-operated die and arc welding the bolt to the body of the *lampazo* at the appropriate spot. The nut, to be hand tightened, was completed by arc welding a horseshoe-shaped piece of plate steel to two edges of the nut, the top of the 'horseshoe' being above the hole in the nut. The nut could then be held, by the horseshoe, between thumb and index finger, and turned until it was hand tight on the bolt, holding the *mecha* firmly in place.

Nylon brush and broom products involved several processes. In one, a 'hole pattern' made from steel was slid over the piece of timber that was to contain the bristles. With the pattern in place, holes were drilled to the required depth in the timber, the bit being set to the correct depth in the drill chuck. Each hole was, then, hand drilled: one hand holding the pattern in place, the other operating the drill. Bristles were made by producing nylon thread from pellets under heat. The threads were wound on to a home-made mechanism similar to a garden hose reel, and then bundled like rope and taken to the factory. There one of the men, usually Gilberto, would cut bristles to length using a large pair of scissors. A cluster of bristles, more or less the same number, judged quickly by eye, would be held together by a twist of wire in the middle of each cluster and twisted on using a pair of pliers. Gilberto would make literally hundreds of bristle clusters while others were producing the brush or broom bodies outside the factory. When the bodies were delivered, Gilberto or one or more of the youths or younger children would grab a bristle cluster, poke the wire twist into a hole, then punch the wire to the bottom of the hole using a hammer and punch. The process was completed for each hole and each cluster of bristles. A small brush for scrubbing clothes might contain 30 holes, a broom head more than 50. Bristles were produced at different gauges for different types of products. Different coloured dyes were put into the pellets to make multicoloured bristle combinations to lend products an aesthetic dimension. With the bristles punched into the bodies, Gilberto would trim them off using scissors. These products, as you would expect, were never entirely precise.

Within these broad parameters of production, San José's workers pursued constant innovation, continual improvement and higher quality as organic principles. To take one very simple example, initially *mechas* had not been bagged. They were simply bundled together in lots of a dozen for buyers to purchase at the factory for resale in markets. In response to what they saw as the more professional finish of competitors who bagged their *mechas*, San José restored a primitive heat-sealing tool and hooked it up to electric current. At a different level the wheel and winding mechanism of the rope pumps underwent almost constant improvement and change.

The rope pump is a very simple hand pump technology. It works by means of a continuous nylon rope. The rope has washers held between two knots every one metre apart. Atop the well, the rope nestles in the V of a wheel rim which is turned by hand. The rope and washers travel to the bottom of the well and go through a guide. Once through the guide the rope and washers come back up through plastic tubing, the internal diameter of which is the same as the external diameter of the washers. As the handle on the wheel is turned, the rope draws water up through the tube in the space between the washers. Once clear of the well the water in the tube passes into a T joint and out through a secondary tube at right angles to the main tube, where it is collected in buckets. The pump makes water drawing (primarily women's and children's work) much easier, thereby ensuring more water is used – with scientifically demonstrated benefits for child health. Initially, the wheels were made from wood, with wooden spokes and a wooden wheel. They were heavy, cumbersome and resource intensive. By degrees the wheel was transformed to a light and very efficient mechanism using pairs of spokes made from steel rod opening out at the ends to house the walls of old car tyres (the walls being cut out of the tyres with a huge knife) in V formation. The rubber provided better traction and housing for the rope, less slippage meaning less wear on the rope. At the other end of the cycle, the guides went through continual refinement to reduce wear on the rope and prevent jamming at the bottom of the well. The steel handles were refined continually to make them more gentle on the hands, and to allow for easier oiling. Different tube diameters were experimented with in relation to different well depths since the weight of water in the tube was in proportion to the effort needed to turn the handles. Deep wells, therefore, called for narrower tube. At the height of rope pump production at San José, the men gave presentations at the 'Campesino University' (a non-formal learning institution for the peasant sector) on aspects of design and principles of hydraulics – as they understood them. As noted earlier, while some of these men could read elementary texts, most could not write, and some could neither read nor write. They understood acutely, however, the relationship between theory and practice, the significance of design, and the principles of competition, quality, innovation and improvement, and the relationships between them. These understandings informed their decisions to purchase better equipment from profits, to add colour to the nylon, bag *mechas*, move from hand-rounded broom handles to handles rounded by machine, and so on. They even went to the length of paying for an electricity transformer to guarantee regular current to drive their more sophisticated equipment (circular saw, drills, fluorescent lighting), and as a defence against power surges and cuts which could wreck their machines.

The examples that could be provided of trying to maximize market share through quality control and improvement are almost endless. They were, of course, proportionate to the level of technology being employed and the degree of labour intensity involved in the production processes. It is one thing to take great care trimming bristles with scissors, but another altogether to have machines that cut bristles to length in the first place and trim them at the end of the process.

Bearing in mind that production remained highly labour intensive, the scale and efficiency of activity was impressive. Vendors from city markets collected *lampazos* in lots of 500. On a good day 450 or more *mechas* were produced and bagged. These were a lucrative product. Most families associated with San José had built permanent material dwellings from income, purchasing materials as they could afford them and commencing construction once all the necessities had been acquired. These homes stand out in the wider community in terms of size, quality and amenities. The children were all in school, the older ones attending the *colégio* in Managua. Most intended to continue on to university or other tertiary institutions. Such factors indicated a quite remarkable change in life quality over a five-year period.

Two related factors came together in the period from 1985 to 1989 that contributed greatly to San José's success, in spite of the low educational level and strictly limited administrative capacity of its members (Lankshear 1994b). The first was the trade and economic blockade imposed on Nicaragua by the US government, where the US used its influence to coerce many other countries to refuse to trade with Nicaragua. This created a relative scarcity of imports in Nicaragua. Buttressing this was the policy of the Sandinista government itself to save on imports as much as possible. The government implemented policies which protected local products, such as those being produced at San José. As Noél said,

> In 1989 there was a Sandinista government and an economic blockade imposed by the US government, and there were no overseas products allowed in the country. The factory we operated was satisfying Nicaraguan customers and it was all they used to consume because there were no overseas products in the market. The ones that did come were very expensive because of the taxes, and the majority of the population had to use our own [Nicaraguan] products, and we made those products . . . Some people are happy now [in 1995] that their money now can be used to buy the things they want to buy, whereas before they couldn't buy what they wanted.
>
> (Interview, 16 February 1995)

Even so, producing successfully and profitably was always a challenge for the cooperative. As noted, the educational level of members was low, including the treasurer's, Isabel. Isabel had been a highly motivated adult learner during the early 1980s, convinced that the hard work of learning made sense in a context of social change which addressed the needs of the most vulnerable sectors of the population. By 1989, however, the cooperative's scale of production and commercial exchange, and the hyperinflation holding the economy in its grip, meant that the demands of her role far outstripped her capacities. It was possible, for example, to make huge losses as a result of inflation occurring between the purchase of raw materials and the sale of the final product – unless one had a grasp of inflation, pricing and the importance of keeping records and making adjustments.

At a timely moment, the Support Office for Small Enterprises (Pequeña Industria), established by the government to help cooperative producers, offered a week-long seminar on basic business administration and accountancy. Its content and pedagogy were designed precisely for people like Isabel, building on existing knowledge, experience and print skills, in order to open up highly relevant and effective new understandings and competencies.

The seminar was built around a 20-page (newsprint and staples) booklet, *Concepts of Accountancy*, produced by the Pequeña Industria. Its central theme was that the bases of good business administration are accurate records and the orderly handling of accounts. Key concepts were defined clearly and abundant everyday examples were provided in accessible language. A simple system of accounts was introduced, and information given on how to record transactions, make a stock inventory, distinguish direct from indirect costs. Participants were taught how to complete a statement of profits and losses, and why this is important. They were then taken through the process of producing a general balance for a small business.

The 'textbook' was supplemented with example sheets and problem sheets for group discussion and solution. Imagination games were a popular learning tool. Much of the work was done in small groups, and participants were drawn as far into the *teaching* process as possible, e.g. by having them work through their method and answer for the rest of the class, writing their procedure on the board or on paper displays, and by answering questions or responding to corrections posed by the class. A new point was not introduced until the previous one had been exhausted and the instructors were satisfied that everyone understood it as well as they were going to. In a key section the theme of 'the cooperative's doctor' was taken up. This was a troubleshooting exercise. The 'doctor' diagnoses ills in the operation of a small business – by checking records to locate losses and the likely source of these – and, having located causes of problems, prescribes a cure.

Isabel testified to the effectiveness of the seminar and the possibilities it opened for San José:

> When we were in a group the ones who understood would help me and explain how the income and expenditure worked; how the balance sheet is done; how you find out if the cooperative is losing money or has a profit . . . I found out what things were important for the cooperative or were damaging . . . I realized that here [in San José] we sometimes do things that are making a loss and we carry on anyway. I learned how to do the accounts and the balance, to keep the bank book, how to see the expenditure and income figures, all of that. For me this was important to learn because I didn't understand it before but it's my job. This seminar was very important for me . . . I've started to check our bank account. I was able to do that. One day I sat down to do it – what I learned in the seminar – and I did it well.
>
> (Interview, October 1989)

In the midst of all this, during 1989, San José was a bustling, thriving, energetic, optimistic centre of industry. Three images from that time stand out in particular. One is of the lively social scene of *mecha* production in the factory, where work was going on almost continually. The second is of the men involved in pump and *lampazo* production discussing possible improvements, defending their own suggestions for modification loudly and with enthusiasm, often sketching their ideas in the dust with a stick. The third is of Nelson (Isabel's 15-year-old son) and Milton driving the cattle during January and February to the stream by the main road to give them a long drink.

Watershed and downhill spiral – 1990–2

The Sandinista government was defeated in the February 1990 elections. The new government removed import restrictions, moving quickly toward a free market economy. The US government lifted the economic blockade with equal haste. These changes, not surprisingly, impacted strongly on San José's activity. The Nicaraguan consumer market was opened to imported lines that were cheaper and perceived to be of higher quality than local variants. San José's nylon brushes and brooms were early casualties here, followed quickly by *lampazos*. The rope pumps developed and produced as a pilot aid and development project proved highly popular nationwide, but project personnel found alternative local producers, who were using more sophisticated machinery and who had more efficient business administration than San José. These 'cheaper and higher quality' producers were subcontracted to do work previously done on the cooperative. *Mechas* remained a viable proposition, however.

Unfortunately for San José, availability of Nicaraguan cotton fell drastically, and imported cotton was relatively expensive. During 1991 and 1992 cotton supply for *mecha* production was irregular, sometimes with gaps of several months between supplies – which were never enough to provide for more than a week or two of work anyway.

Each of the income-earning activities of 1989 had disappeared by January 1992. By then production was restricted to two lines. First, a sophisticated imported lathe was being used to convert rough sawn timber stakes into high quality handles for brooms and mops. Profits on this line were good, although the local market was finite. Handles sold for twice the cost of the timber. The machine could, however, with the unskilled labour of one person produce more in a day than might be sold locally in a month.

The other line was especially interesting. The cooperative had returned to where it began, producing wheat-bristled brooms of the same original design and for which there remained a traditional market. Cooperative members were using land to grow the appropriate species of wheat, rather than cropping *yuca*, *trigo* (sorghum), rice and maize, as they had been in 1989. The original homemade 'machines', built in 1984 for shaping and holding bristles and for unwinding the wire for stitching, were in use again. In stunning juxtaposition, the imported lathe provided the technological complement, furnishing high quality handles for these homely brooms.

By the end of 1991, then, the women were effectively out of paid work and the men were on severely reduced work. Two men had left the cooperative: one to produce charcoal for sale in the city, the other to clean warehouses in another country.

The last post? February 1994 and February 1995

I returned briefly to Monte Fresco in February 1994, finding strictly limited paid work in evidence. Pedro had a contract to produce 13,000 *bolillos* (broom handles) by running wooden stakes through the lathe. This amounted to just a few short days of highly repetitive work. Our visit, however, coincided with the arrival of a small supply of cotton for producing *mechas*: a week's work. What we found was very interesting.

San José's quality agenda had moved *mecha* production on to a completely different footing from 1989. This time the cotton came as refined thread on large spools, not the large bales of unspun fibre. Plaiting had gone as a production process. Instead, several spools were set at one end of the factory, and thread from each was drawn to the other end and connected up to a hand drill. The drill was held like a pistol, toward the spools, and the trigger pressed, twisting the threads of cotton into compact regular twists. These twists of several strands of cotton, each corresponding to a single hand-made plait in the original process, were wound around a revolving purpose-built steel frame, and cut to length. Half a kilo of such plaits was then sewn together on the industrial sewing machine, using calico ribbon as before, producing a *mecha*.

This approach was highly ingenious, reflecting San José's appropriation of an approach they had heard about from an El Salvadorean who was visiting exiled compatriots now living on a nearby cooperative. It was also much more accurate than the hand-plaiting approach, and much less labour intensive. The plaiting frame was gone. Production rates were higher and the product was undeniably (in one sense) of a higher quality. Only three people, however, were required to produce what ten or more had previously been engaged in, and at a higher quality level. The factory was no longer a bustling lively social scene: just three people, one electric drill, five or so spools, a rotating steel frame, a sewing machine, and the redoubtable heat sealer.

Even that, however, was more than greeted our return in February 1995, and considerably less disturbing. In the year between visits the cooperative had purchased, for US$1200, a machine used in producing 'high quality *mechas*' from a factory that was closing down. As Pedro said,

> We need always to sit down and work out how to produce more appropriately and to win a market by achieving a better finish. In the case of *mechas* we were doing a good job and could compete with the El Salvadoreans because our product was good quality. The Salvadorean *mechas* contained dust. Ours didn't. When we got the cotton to make the *mechas* we used good cotton to make them dust-free. The dusty ones are not good. Ours are whiter. They look better.
>
> (Interview, 18 February 1995)

San José was hit by two compounding blows. The first was the closure of a local factory that produced good quality cotton at a price which allowed San José to be competitive. The second, contradictorily, was the fact that investing in the machine (which was a good deal, making good competitive sense) left the cooperative with few reserves for buying cotton. Little, but enough – other things being equal. They weren't, however. Imported cotton (the only quality cotton available for purchase) now cost more than the cooperative had available. With the cooperative hit first by lack of supply and then by absolute lack of finance for buying cotton when it *was* available, the *mecha*-producing machine had been lying idle so long it was covered in dust and cluttered with tools when we saw it. The loss of this potential opportunity was felt deeply. Isabel explained:

> The situation affects me greatly because I had a lot of wishes to work in this factory. My children were raised in there. The factory is close [50 metres] to my house. When I worked there I was close to my children. I could earn money. It wasn't much, but it was enough. Because I am older now I cannot go looking for domestic work. I want my children to be studying, to be wearing good clothes. Sometimes I can't buy a pair for one because I have to buy for another. I want them to be healthy. If I could work I could afford these things. If just my husband [Santiago] works there is only enough money for food. Obviously, every mother wants the best for her child.
>
> (Interview, 18 February 1995)

The other potential earner was *bolillos*. San José's high performance lathe produced very high quality handles: smooth, with a shiny surface, of exportable quality. The machine can produce up to 10,000 units per day, by one worker. According to Noél,

> We had an export market for *bolillos*. We found a channel to export to Mexico, but we couldn't produce because we couldn't get raw materials. The timber factory closed. There is timber in Nicaragua, but there is now a law against milling it. This is for conservation. We had the machine to make the *bolillos*, but we couldn't get the wood. So we lost the contract. In earlier times, Honduras, for example, didn't have timber to make *bolillos*, because of the need for conservation. But Nicaragua was still milling timber. Then the thing that happened to other countries started to happen to us. No raw materials!
>
> (Interview, 16 February 1995)

During February 1995 just two short-term earning activities were in operation. One member (Jorge) had put down a crop of wheat the previous season, the species of wheat used for making brooms. For the third successive year there had been poor rains, and Jorge's crop was minute. He had enough wheat to make just 180 brooms, at 5 córdobas (6.6 córdobas = $US1 at the time) per unit. There were enough wooden stakes left over from the previous year to make handles on the lathe. Even allowing for the handles as a cost-free component, this man's total crop production yielded less than two days of work and $140 worth of product.

In the second activity, one of the men had a contract to produce folding wooden chairs for sale to a church. He felled a laurel tree in the forest and brought it back piece by piece in a wheelbarrow to the factory. The timber was cut down to size with absolutely minimum waste, using the powerful circular saw and a joinery attachment which thicknesses the timber accurately. Any scraps of wood were used to fire the family's cooking oven.

I asked what the cooperative members were doing for economic survival, and whether the cooperative still existed; I was told that in principle there was still a cooperative because only three members had formally left (the two noted earlier, and Róger, aged 23, who is training in Peru to become a priest). But there was pessimism about the future, and pressure from some members to sell the machinery and divide up the spoils:

Isabel: Because we are doing nothing we decided to sell machinery. If we are not using it, it will deteriorate. It is very sad to have to sell what means so much to us – sad to think that everything has to go.

Colin: In your opinion, does the cooperative have a future?

Isabel: I have to say no, because there's not . . . like me . . . we don't have the energy, the enthusiasm we used to have – for example, the factory has closed many times, but because of our enthusiasm we used to find solutions and start up again. But now we don't have the enthusiasm we used to have and the men are working in other places. And that's why I feel there's no future.

(Interview, 18 February 1995)

Pedro reinforced this assessment, and explored the wider implications:

Colin: Are there markets for your products?

Pedro: There are markets for *bolillos, escobas* (brooms), *lampazos* and *mechas*. There's enough market for work, but we don't have raw materials.

Colin: What are the possibilities for getting the factory working?

Pedro: Asking for a loan, but we don't like to ask for a loan. We have to be very careful, because loans are things that can take you down. As a membership we don't want to do that. There are other things as well. The way banks lend you money, it's a matter of having an export contract with a client, and a guaranteed amount of work that will bring money into Nicaragua. The process of getting clients takes several steps. First, you need a contract with those who provide raw materials. Second, the people who are going to buy the product. Third, in order to make this contract serious we have to be sure that everyone is going to be doing their part well. For people like us it is very difficult to arrange all these things.

Colin: Does the cooperative still exist?

Pedro: Yes – because the members are still there, except the three who have gone. The other men are still here, and all the women.

Colin: Do you think there's a future for the cooperative?

Pedro: I don't see much now. It's very difficult.

Colin: Are the families surviving?

Pedro: More or less. In Cándida's house she doesn't work now, but her son, Alexis, is maintaining her. Santiago is working in Managua to maintain the house. Luisa isn't really getting by. She's making hand bread to sell in the neighbourhood, but it's not enough. She's surviving because God wants her to survive. If you're not working you're not getting money. Everyone is struggling to survive . . . Some of the members want to sell the machines, because we have nothing to do with the machines. But some of the women who worked here, for example, Luisa, if you asked her she would say 'don't sell the machines'; but others don't see any way out, and neither do I. If we improve our products, as we have and can, we can get into the market. But for that we need money. For example, the brooms that Jorge makes, they are everywhere. They're good for selling.

(Interview, 18 February 1995)

By one means or another each family was scraping by. The costs, however, seemed unacceptably high. Santiago, the illiterate refiner of rope pump wheels and 'lecturer' to fellow campesinos in the 'university', worked as security guard six and a half days a week in a city supermarket – leaving each morning at 5.30 a.m. by bus, and arriving back after 8 p.m. each night. Gilberto, also illiterate, was eking out a living cutting firewood by machete for sale locally. Edmundo was also working for some time in firewood and charcoal production (as was Reinaldo, who had left the cooperative to work for himself). Pedro and Noél worked irregularly in carpentry and joinery, work calling for using local timber resources. Rolando, illiterate refiner of *lampazos* and 'colour coordinator' for nylon brush and broom bristles, was cutting sugar cane by machete during the season, and raising some cattle with assistance from his wife's family. The women were confined to unpaid household work.

For me it was impossible to accept the displacement within economic and social life of human capacities I knew existed. Apart from the waste of Isabel's learning and Santiago's capacity to refine, and many other examples evident among the cooperative members, there was the unpalatable fact that some of the older children were able and obliged to work for youth rates in city supermarkets, to help maintain their families. Dulce and Erica worked full time in this capacity. Erica, top of her class in 1989, with the world seemingly in front of her, was stacking foodstuffs eight hours daily. The spark in her eyes, almost blinding in 1989, had gone, displaced by a look that bespoke a deep sense of futility. Alexis was working six or seven-hour shifts in a supermarket during the week, supporting his mother and siblings, and then beginning his daily studies for university. He said the work takes the edge off his energy for studying.

At San José, 'common sense' bears a strong familiar stamp. The *socios'* language is full of references to quality and competitive advantage. Besides Noél's observations, Pedro recognized San José's struggle to be 'competitive in a free market', adding that 'products from other countries are cheaper than ours, which are also of lower quality than theirs, for lack of resources to improve our production'. In Isabel's words: 'The imported products are of higher quality. They made our product go down. Ours was downgraded.' Within this world-view, competition is an inescapable fact of the given economic order. Quality is likewise a natural 'given'.

Besides the social and cultural cost of able children being forced prematurely into work that makes a mockery of the education they received and undertook with enthusiasm, and former 'teachers of hydraulics' being turned over to cane cutting, and skilled plaiters of *mechas* being reduced to dependence on children or on the paltry sale of hand bread, the ecological cost is horrendous. Five of the nine male members are depending at least partly for their livelihood on timber from nearby forests. The local forest is being stripped at an incredible rate, quite apart from former milling activity, and clear signs of 'desertification' are in evidence. The generous rains that made the spring and summer of 1989 and 1990 studies in rural splendour have stayed away since 1991. The stream where Nelson watered the cattle hasn't seen water in January or February since 1990.

Amidst all this I have one particular recurring thought. It concerns the meaning of quality and competitive advantage in relation to products like *mechas* and *lampazos*. All the talk of quality I heard in respect of products had to do with appearance, not function; with form, not substance. There are no dustier places anywhere than Monte Fresco, Nicaragua, in the dusty season. Yet in Monte Fresco the floors are as clean as any tiled floors to be found anywhere, and those who clean them are using the same *lampazos* I saw built there in 1989. And their own-produced *mechas*. Hence, I ponder what quality means, and whether its prevailing lived meaning can possibly compensate for the sorts of costs imposed by competitive edge and quality agendas on people like those in San José. I am *not* saying here simply that hand-made *lampazos* and *mechas* are 'good enough for Nicaraguans'. Rather, I am saying that from a functional point of view they – along with whole rafts of 'consumer goods' for which our *lampazos* and *mechas* may serve as symbolic representations – are good enough for *anyone*. And I am inviting a larger consideration of our economic languages and discursive practices as they bite at home as well as in more 'exotic' settings. After all, comparable stories of displaced labour, wasted talent, environmental distress and other casualties of rabid commodity and quality fetishism can be told drawing on experiences from our own milieux. In a global world, these stories are inextricably bound up with each other.

Reflections

Many important themes about the interfaces between literacy, social justice and work arise here. Jim Gee, Glynda Hull and I have addressed some of these at length in *The New Work Order* (Gee *et al.* 1996). The particular theme I want briefly to take up here concerns the potential of literacy and literacy education programmes to empower individuals and groups who seek social and economic justice and dignified lives, on their own behalf and on behalf of others.

The case of San José brings us face to face with the potential and the limits of literacy as 'an instrument for better times'. We see very clearly here the extent to which literacy is not an independent variable but, rather, is always some embedded social practice. Changing the nature and the contextual conditions of the larger social practices necessarily changes the nature and significance of the particular literacies that go with them. We see this with Isabel's literacy, which would surely have proved to be 'functional', so far as San José's economic prospects were concerned, had the policies and markets operating prior to 1990 continued, and had US foreign policy and international cooperation assisted the Nicaraguan government to get inflation under control prior to 1989 rather than contributing greatly to causing it. Indeed, even in a context of inflation there would have been every reason to expect Isabel to have coped with her administrative tasks given more practice at them and a few more seminars of the kind she experienced. Her literacy would have remained an integral dimension of larger social practices which underwrote an economically viable and dignified quality of life for her and her associates – with spillover effects into Monte Fresco at large.

Under the mere impact of transnational competition from such otherwise comparatively 'underdeveloped' economies as those of Honduras, El Salvador, Guatemala and Costa Rica, however, Isabel's literacy has no significant functional significance for her own economic viability or that of her family and her cooperative. At the same time, her literacy remains perfectly adequate for the demands of other social practices which do *not* fall under the principle of (the new) competition. For example, Isabel's spiritual life remains enriched by her ability to access the word of her God in daily Bible reading and devotions, and by her ability to handle the texts that mediate the preparation of the neighbourhood children for Easter each year during their Lent observances. But 'skills' that remain adequate within one social practice – religious observance – are no longer adequate for another – viable economic production.

It is worth remembering here also that San José actively pursued and enunciated an economic D/discourse of quality and competitive edge. Furthermore, for all its 'traditional' character, their enterprise shared features identified in fast capitalist texts as indicative of paradigmatic new capitalist workplaces. San José's *socios* constituted a 'community of practice', and distributed their knowledge and work within a flat hierarchy. There was no strong border (or delineation) between their work lives and their 'private' lives. To a person the *socios* exhibited 'total commitment' to their enterprise. Their work patterns were flexible and highly adaptive, and they established links to outside providers. In many ways they 'read' and 'wrote' the code/text of the new work order and the new competition, literally and metaphorically (see Freire and Macedo 1987). They got the 'micro-setting' of work relations, attitudes and organization pretty much 'right'. While they had not read the books or attended the seminars, they could scarcely have followed fast capitalist advice more closely. San José's workers thought in terms of processes rather than isolated tasks; they engaged in flexible production; they adopted the most sophisticated technologies available to them; they thought in terms of 'wholes' and not just 'parts'; they engaged in both 'incremental improvement' and 'radical change'; they asked the tough questions: 'Why are we doing this at all?', 'Why not think of doing or producing something else altogether?', 'What's our real business?'; they engaged in 'flat structures', 'shared collective responsibility', 'every worker a decision-maker', and 'worker empowerment'; they had high motivation, full commitment and loyalty, and full identification with 'the mission', 'core values' and 'vision' of the enterprise.

What disempowered San José was the 'bigger picture' – the larger frame – of global and nation-state politics, historical exploitation, access to information and education, the complex workings of technology, and the 'winner-take-all' nature of contemporary capitalism (Gee *et al.* 1996: 145). Their familiarity with and conformity to the dictates of the new capitalism – with its new work order and conditions of competition – could not offset the fact that larger and, ultimately, insuperable conditions were against them.

In this respect, the circumstances facing San José's *socios* are analogous to those facing peripheral and excluded workers within our own countries (within my primary world), and for essentially the same reasons. In a game where winners take all, where winners are few, and where competition for jobs is increasingly global and the jobs themselves polarized in terms of rewards and conditions, we have to inquire into the prospects of our own literacy policies and programmes to empower students and citizens in accordance with the ideals of economic and social justice. This is as true of policies and programmes that stress 'basics' and 'core competencies' in accordance with national curricula as it is of more high sounding policies and programmes inspired by visions of 'smart workers' and 'clever countries'.

The arguments and cases addressed in this and the previous chapter suggest additional dimensions and foci for the development and practice of critical literacy to those explored in Chapter 2. The language and practices of the new capitalism and the new work order must be taken up as central themes in our practices of critical literacy. As we have argued elsewhere (Gee *et al.* 1996: ch. 1), a sociocultural approach to literacy insists that language and literacy must always be understood in their social, cultural and political contexts. One of these contexts is the globally interconnected space of the new capitalism, with its new competition and its new work order, *and in all its ramifications*. For

> language – indeed, our very humanity – is in danger of losing meaning if we do not carefully reflect on this context and its attempts to make *us* into 'new kinds' of people . . . e.g., people who are 'smart' because they buy the highest 'quality' brushes [videos, communications technologies], but do not care about – or even see – the legacies of their greed writ large on the world.
>
> (pp. 150–1)

The world on which these legacies are writ large is an interconnected global world. The victims of our reconstitution as new kinds of people increasingly include our fellow citizens at home as well as our fellow citizens in the Third and Fourth Worlds (Cardoso 1993; Castells 1993). Increasingly, they (will) include our own children. Ethics, critical literacy and sociological imagination (Mills 1959) with a global perspective intersect at this point, and call us to embrace what Cardoso (1993: 158–9) calls a 'new humanism': an ethical perspective which 'owns' the humanity of all who are beset by legacies of dependence and deprivation – a humanity which indeed risks being lost when people merit recognition only as 'consumers' or 'value adders' (Gee *et al.* 1996: 151). If the case for making critical literacy a central plank in the curriculum rested on no more than the insights afforded by cases like San José, this would surely be sufficient foundation.

part 3

LITERACY, NEW TECHNOLOGIES AND OLD PATTERNS

six

LITERACIES, TEXTS AND DIFFERENCE IN THE ELECTRONIC AGE

Colin Lankshear and Michele Knobel

Introduction

This chapter explores a pressing challenge facing classroom teachers and conventional classroom literacy practices right now. It stems from our immediate sociocultural context in the late 1990s – a context of rapid technological change centred particularly on constant developments in microelectronic technologies. Increasingly, claims are made of growing gaps between the experiences and values investments of teacher and student 'generations' respectively, and allegations persist that schools are not performing well enough; specifically, we hear claims that schools are not in touch with emergent technological literacies. We offer here a working definition of technological literacies, and identify examples of technological literacies that may usefully be incorporated within classroom learning. Several important dimensions of 'difference' that cluster around technology-mediated language and literacy practices are described, and some of their implications for classroom learning identified. The chapter concludes by suggesting how technological literacies might be integrated into 'critical' forms of classroom inquiry.

A contemporary challenge

Since the late 1950s schools in Australasia, Britain and North America have faced seemingly endless allegations of failure to perform at acceptable levels. These include charges that schools have failed to produce leading-edge scientists and mathematicians; that since the mid-1970s schools have failed to prepare students adequately for the world of work; and that schools currently are not yet up to speed in technology education. These allegations span two different agendas. One is a school *reform* agenda: i.e. to restructure and reorient schools so that they (can) do their job properly. The other is much more radical: 'deschooling', or abolish school altogether.

Interestingly, we find elements of both surfacing at present around the theme of technology and its social and educational roles. Very much in the reform vein, writers like Seymour Papert (1993) advance constructive suggestions about how classroom teachers might transform their classroom practices by integrating new technologies – notably (micro)computers – into pedagogy in ways that engage the interests and prior experiences of students and, at the same time, place them within reach of envisaged communicative competencies of the future. Papert observes that children around the globe have 'entered an enduring and passionate love affair with the computer' (p. ix). To a large extent video games have provided the conduit to this affair. Whatever its origins, an affair it is, says Papert, and educators must address the question of how the relationship between children and computers affects learning. Indeed, he observes, 'understanding this relationship will be crucial to our ability to shape the future' (p. ix). Beyond *understanding* lies, of course, the imperative to *act* upon it pedagogically.

From the standpoint of the competing agenda, hardline opponents of schools *per se*, like Lewis Perelman (1992), would not be at all impressed by calls to improve the performance of teachers and school-based learning. Perelman's book, *School's Out*, is subtitled 'a radical new formula for the revitalization of America's educational system'. It is, however, a formula in which school has no place. According to Perelman, we are in the throes of a process of economic transformation being driven along 'by an implacable technological revolution' (p. 7). Within this revolution there is simply no point in searching for ways to save, improve, reform or even reinvent schools. Rather, says Perelman, there is a need to remove altogether 'the increasingly costly barrier schooling poses to economic and social progress' (p. 7).

Perelman argues that we have entered a new historical era: the knowledge age. Knowledge has become 'the steel of the modern economy': a consequence of the rapid development and proliferation of new electronic technologies. In the process of generating a veritable knowledge 'explosion', new technologies have necessitated a whole new appreciation of, and emphasis upon, *learning*. He claims that those countries which 'stop trying to "reform" their education and training institutions', and decide rather 'to totally replace them with a brand-new, high-tech learning system', will be the next century's 'economic powerhouses' (p. 20). According to Perelman, knowledge is increasing at such a rate that expertise 'now has a shelf life measured in days' (p. 22). Old notions of learning in youth for the needs of one's life, and of entrusting learning to the care of teachers who knew what needed to be learned and who would transmit this through *instruction* are, for Perelman, *passé*. Learning that is relevant for life has gone beyond the teacher-learner relationship. 'For what piano lessons would cost, you now can buy an electronic piano that will teach you how to play it' (p. 22). The fact that school education is predicated on instruction and, in turn, on expertise and finite and relatively abiding essential knowledge, renders school obsolete and expensively counterproductive, in Perelman's view.

In place of school, he envisages 'hyperlearning': the 'transformation of knowledge and behavior through experience' – as opposed to teacher-based transmission of the 'world' through 'words' – by means of diverse information technologies in which 'knowledge, experience, media, and brains . . . both human and non human' are connected 'to an unprecedented degree' (p. 23). Perelman claims that whereas instruction is the essence of school education,

> the essence of the coming integrated, universal, multimedia, digital network is *discovery* – the empowerment of human minds to learn spontaneously, without coercion, both independently and cooperatively. The focus is on learning as an action that is 'done by', not 'done to,' the actor.
>
> (p. 23)

Against such views, Steven Hodas (1993) rejects as naive claims by people like Perelman that schools will become redundant simply because they are no longer the primary modellers of information processing and knowledge transmission. Schools, says Hodas, have other and larger functions: notably, functions relating to reproducing 'the values and processes of the society in which they are situated'. Hodas's argument points toward what we see as a worthy challenge facing classroom teachers with regard to new technologies and pedagogy within electronic classrooms.

Hodas claims that attempts during the last century to introduce a range of technologies to classrooms have impacted very little on the *structure* of teaching practice. The technologies have been more or less ignored, or else they have been assimilated into existing modes and routines of classroom activity and interchange, such that 'the look-and-feel of school' remains essentially the same as it was previously:

> Textbooks, paperbacks, blackboards, radio, film . . . television, satellite systems and telecommunications have all in their time been hailed as modernizers of American education (Cuban, 1986). Cohen . . . demonstrates how, with the exception of the blackboard, none of these much vaunted exemplars of modern efficiency have had any significant effect on school organization or practice (Cohen, 1987). They have not made

schools more modern, more efficient [or] more congruent with the world outside school.

(Hodas 1993: 9)

The fate, thus far, of computers in schools has mainly followed this trend. Many classroom teachers have been denied, or have otherwise refused, opportunities to implement computers into their pedagogies in anything other than the most 'domesticated' ways (e.g. as substitutes for pens and pencils, typewriters, etc.). In other cases, computer use has been limited to the arid 'computer lab' approach where, at its worst,

> kids are brought en masse to a . . . room presided over by a man with no other function than to administer the machines. There they work for between 30 and 50 minutes on drill-and-practice software . . . until they reach a preset level of proficiency, at which time they are started on new tasks.

(p. 14)

Of course, it's not simply in computer labs where unimaginative and counterproductive 'domesticated' uses of new technologies abound. The case of Nicholas, observed and recorded in a Year 7 classroom in Brisbane, Australia, is far from isolated.

> Nicholas is 12 years old. He is a proficient 'touch keyboarder'. There are both Apple and IBM-type computers in his home. He and his older siblings spend time on the home computers daily, in a range of activities including school work. By contrast, there is no permanant computer in his classroom. Rather, two classrooms and the library share a single computer of limited capacity and with limited software. The classroom 'houses' the computer for one-third of the school year. The students are rostered to use the computer, in pairs, for half an hour per week. The pairs go to the computer when it is their rostered time to do so, regardless of what's going on in class. They have their set time and that's it. Most students spend their weekly half hours playing educational games, like 'Where in the world is Carmen Sandiego?', or 'publishing' work they have already written in class, using a beginner-level desktop publishing program. The teacher rarely intervenes, and when he does it is usually to restore discipline.
>
> The episode in question sees Nicholas seated at the computer. He has to produce a short recount of Athletics Day for the school magazine. As a competent keyboarder and a proficient computer user since reaching school age, Nicholas's preferred mode is to compose directly on to a machine. This is more than a matter of his 'skills' alone. He thinks better on the computer.
>
> Earlier in the day he and a friend had had a strong debate with the

teacher (male, 24 years) over the need for pen-and-paper first drafts. Nicholas had stated the case for composing directly on to the computer, but the teacher had said 'you will always need to be able to write with pen and paper', adding 'what about your brothers and sisters at high school doing their assignments? Don't they use pen and paper for drafts?' Nicholas replied that, on the contrary, they always use computers: there is a very sophisticated word processing program on their Apple home computer.

Meanwhile, seated at the school computer, Nicholas tries to start his story. He quickly becomes frustrated and complains. 'I hate this computer' he says, rolling his eyes. The program was too basic for his skills and knowledge. It was a lockstepped, linear program which was not at all flexible. It began with commands for inputting 'the heading', then for moving to 'the first paragraph', and so on. The default font on the screen was – for someone like Nicholas – insultingly large. He wants to go directly to composing text, and does so – only to find his text has gone into the heading space. He tries to select a different function, but cannot break easily out of the lockstep.

He gets frustrated – 'Can you believe this stuff?' – gives up on composing, and spends the next half hour keying 'Athletics Day' into the heading space, in an Old English font, alternately enlarging and reducing it. His friend, Robert, stops by and says that he personally 'can't stand Apples'. He prefers his home IBM, which is equipped with Word Perfect – but 'Word Perfect with Windows. Not DOS. Windows is much better'. At the end of his half hour, with the story not written, Nicholas asks for an extension. The teacher is not impressed, but agrees. Nicholas takes the assignment home and produces it inside ten minutes.

Papert provides an interesting and important angle on matters here. He claims that the current generation of students, who have grown up in a cultural milieu in which video games have a prominent place, have already learned what computers are beginning to teach adults:

> that some forms of learning are fast-paced, immensely compelling, and rewarding. The fact that they are enormously demanding of one's time and require new ways of thinking remains a small price to pay . . . to be vaulted into the future. Not surprisingly, by comparison School strikes many young people as slow, boring, and frankly out of touch.
>
> (1993: 5)

Schools indeed face a serious challenge here. Besides facing serious attacks on their legitimation from business interests, politicians and people like Perelman who speak on behalf of widespread adult disaffection (whether justified or otherwise) with school performances, schools and teachers are now experiencing negative responses by unprecedented numbers of students. Papert observes that while students may not actually have *enjoyed* school in the past, they could at least be persuaded that it provided a passport to later success in life. To the extent that students reject school 'as being out of touch with contemporary life', schools risk losing their legitimation among their direct clientele. Like any social structure, schools need to be accepted by their participants (Howe and Strauss 1993; Papert 1993: 6).

Added to the general clamour from 'the outside world' that schools get up to speed with the demands of 'a new work order', a burgeoning knowledge society and a whole new orientation toward learning – all of which emanate from developments in electronic technologies – student perceptions and experiences of school as 'out of touch' place strong pressure on schools to engage new technologies in appropriate ways. Indeed, this would seem to be a requirement of those 'larger functions' of school – which, according to Hodas, underwrite their future – of reproducing 'the values and processes of the society in which they are situated' (1993: 17).

Before hurtling headlong into the digital fray, however, we do well to heed Chris Bigum and Bill Green's (1992: 4) reminder that 'technologizing literacy [is] a matter par excellence of the nexus of profit and reason, as the central organizing principles of contemporary social life', and that we should, consequently, approach the whole area from an appropriately sceptical and socially critical perspective.

Furthermore, the reasons and grounds for technology refusal by teachers and other educators and educationists are complex, and some of them emanate from 'educationally worthy' spaces. Hodas identifies a range of factors contributing to technology refusal on the part of educators. These include structural factors, such as inbuilt organizational dispositions and acquired means to self-perpetuation; teacher fears that computers might displace them; contradictory messages received by teachers about the reasons for and advantages of introducing computers;[1] teacher concerns about the time and energies needed to get up to speed technologically and in relevant aspects of theory; and teacher perceptions of their authority potentially being undermined – or at least threatened – in contexts where students will often be much more *au fait* with technologies than they are. In an important addition, however, Hodas recognizes grounds and reasons for technology refusal that stem from legitimate and abiding educational values and concerns. He claims that teachers who have experienced the worst excesses of 'computer lab' pedagogy and/or the 'techno-rationalist' drive for standardization, conclude on the basis of their experiences that 'computers in schools are anathema to their notions of what schools ought to do with and for children' (Hodas 1993: 14). He speaks of the frustration many teachers feel when rationalism runs amok in education, as with many applications of behaviourist theory, positivist reductions of assessment and measurement, along with curricular and administrative forms of standardization in general. After all, he says,

> teachers . . . are witness and partner to human development in a richer and more complex sense than educational technologists will ever be. Schools are where children grow up . . . The violence that technologists do to our only public children's space by reducing it to an 'instructional delivery vehicle' is enormous, and teachers know that . . . Many simply prefer not to collaborate with [processes] they experience as fundamentally disrespectful to kids and teachers alike.
>
> (Hodas 1993: 15)

Bearing in mind such considerations, we must frame the contemporary challenge teachers face in relation to technology and literacy in a way that preserves cardinal educational and social values, like respect for persons, and the development of reflective and critically informed approaches to the world. As a contribution to this end we will address the question of how teachers might integrate electronic technologies into 'critical' practices of language and literacy.

Clarifying 'technological literacies': some conceptual distinctions

The question of what counts as 'technological literacies' is complex. If we think of technological literacies as socially constructed conceptions and practices of engaging semiotic texts in processes where some kind of technology is integrally involved, then (virtually) all literacies have to be seen as 'technological'. Scripts themselves (alphabetic, logographic, etc.) comprise technologies, in the sense of being culturally constructed systematic means for achieving goals and purposes; as are the various instruments used in encoding, decoding and making meaning with them (such as pens, printing presses, dictionaries, translators, eyes and brains).

Talk of *technological* literacies seems to arise from the fact that the technologies integral to conventional or 'normal' literacy practices have become 'invisible', as a result of their always having 'been there' in our practice. Hence, we take them for granted and they do not stand out as *technologies*. When *new* technologies come along, however, they stand out in relief from our conventional practice, and notions of applying them to and incorporating them into literacy practices strikes us as introducing a technological dimension, as constituting 'technological literacies'. As Bigum and Green note, we are currently witnessing the enactment of a project (see Gee 1994a) to technologize literacy, in the sense of applying 'computer-based technologies in literacy practices' (Bigum and Green 1992: 4). Not surprisingly, 'technological literacies' refers primarily to practices in which computers and, perhaps, closely related or similarly 'exotic' technologies (like video applications, compact discs and satellite communications) are integral. To move toward a working definition of technological literacies two complicating factors must be negotiated.

The first is covered nicely by Bigum and Green (p. 5), who distinguish four ways in which the terms 'technology' and 'literacy' might be combined under the general idea of technologizing literacy:

- technology *for* literacy
- literacy *for* technology
- literacy *as* technology
- technology *as* literacy.

By 'technology for literacy' they mean applying various information technologies to literacy pedagogy. 'Literacy for technology' refers to text-mediated practices that enable people to operate particular technologies. Reading a manual to tune a television set, program a VCR, tune a vehicle engine and so on, provide examples here. To speak of 'literacy as technology' is to recognize that the various socially constructed and maintained practices and conceptions of reading and writing that exist (Street 1984) comprise so many social technologies: ways of applying means to ends, tools/techniques to purposes, or applying modes of knowing to goals. The notion of 'technology as literacy' is involved in talk of people being 'computer literate', 'information literate', 'audiovisually literate', and so on. In such uses, 'literacy' stands in for a body of knowledge or know-how (Bigum and Green 1992: 6), such that to be literate is to possess an acceptable amount of the knowledge or know-how in question. The first issue to be resolved, then, is which of these ideas contribute most usefully to a working concept of technological literacies.

The second complication has to do with the fact that *literacies themselves* vary enormously. Some of this variation is captured in broad qualitative categories and distinctions, such as 'functional literacy' vs. 'cultural literacy' vs. 'critical literacy'. So whatever we include under the umbrella of 'technological literacies', we may wish to distinguish those technological literacies that are more or less *functional* in quality and *raison d'être*, from those technological literacies which are better thought of in terms of being *cultural*, or *critical*, etc.

This complication goes still deeper. 'Functional', 'cultural' and 'critical' literacies are themselves multiple: i.e. there are many of each of them. For example, conceptions and practices of critical literacy include variants which draw on Freirean critical pedagogy, feminist theories, functional systemic linguistics, discourse analytic approaches of various types, linguistic analysis, speech act theories, reader response theory, conversation analysis, and so on (see Australian Reading Association 1993; Lankshear and McLaren 1993; Luke and Walton 1993; Lankshear 1994a). Likewise, very different conceptions and practices of functional and cultural literacy are apparent. Some of these differences turn on quantitative matters, such as what equivalent reading age constitutes being functionally literate in this or that society/ context, or how many 'great books'/'great authors' are required for an adequate cultural literacy syllabus. Other sources of variation may be more qualitative – e.g. what kinds of texts are integral to functionality (timetables? enterprise bargaining documents? insurance policies?) or to being culturally literate (e.g. Shakespeare's plays? Toni Morrison's novels? Plato's dialogues?).

Consequently, once we move beyond such naive conceptions of literacy as 'reading and writing', 'encoding and decoding' and others that Brian Street (1984, 1993) has subsumed within 'the autonomous model of literacy', we may expect to find as much variety among literacies within the realm of technological literacies as we find in the realm of more conventional types of texts. This suggests that the best approach to producing a working definition of technological literacies is probably to advance a generic definition that captures the broad scope of our interest, and then to draw on the kinds of distinctions and categories noted here (as well as others not noted here) to identify more or less specific and discrete technological literacies within the overall web.

For present purposes 'technological literacies' may be defined as social practices in which texts (i.e. meaningful stretches of language) are constructed, transmitted, received, modified, shared (and otherwise engaged), within processes employing codes which are digitized electronically, primarily, though not exclusively, by means of (micro)computers. This definition can encompass practices involving hand-held games, video games, electronic translators, electronic organizers, compact disc players, and the like.

In addition, a range of secondary (or supporting) practices of technological literacy exist which include such examples as: reading or writing manuals for the purposes of operating, repairing or modifying particular forms of hardware or software (a form of 'literacy *for* technology'); reading, writing, discussing and swapping Nintendo or Sega magazines which show key moves for playing games (another example of literacy *for* technology or, perhaps, of technology *as* literacy); studying texts to learn about ways of applying electronic technology to literacy pedagogy (an example of literacy supporting 'technology *for* literacy').

Our main interest in this chapter is with extant conceptions and practices of reading, writing, viewing, manipulating, communicating, etc. *digital* texts, and their potential integration into *critical* forms of literate practice. Within these parameters it is easy to identify and distinguish a wide array of

Table 6.1

(Examples of) generic practices	(Examples of) aspects/activities	(Examples of) procedures/techniques
Word, sound and image processing	• data entry • essay, article, book writing • emailing • desktop publishing • posting messages on bulletin boards • illustrating texts • operating a computer-based organizer	• keyboarding • manipulating text, sounds, images • importing/exporting graphics • formatting documents • entering memos • morphing • ray tracing • solving equations • preparing texts as Web pages (HTML codes)
Emailing	• letters to friends • academic interchanges • doing email interviews for publication • writing joint articles • obtaining information • distance education • supervising at distance • on-line conference participation	• getting an account • logging on/off • keyboarding • attaching text, sound and graphic files • organizing one's mail • deleting old mail • up/downloading • subscribing/unsubscribing to discussion lists and journals
Netting	• participating in user/news groups • searching for information on the World Wide Web (WWW) • TELNETing • FTPing • perusing distant library catalogues 'on line' • HTTPing	• logging on • connecting to the WWW using Netscape, Lynx, Mosaic, etc. • observing news group protocols and norms • sharing resource locations on the WWW • reading on-line journal, newspaper, etc. articles • purchasing from on-line catalogues
Gaming	• classroom activity around 'Where in the world is Carmen Sandiego?' • playing Nintendo/Sega • playing 'Dr Brain', 'Super Mario Brothers', etc. • playing hand-held games	• speeding up or down • reading up on moves, swapping information • swapping gamesware • operating joysticks • operating cursors • keyboarding • loading software

technological literacies. We will identify and name some examples here and describe them in the next section. The short list provided below is in no way exhaustive. Indeed, other people might classify and distinguish technological literacies by reference to quite different taxonomies and purposes. We have chosen a set of practices with which we are reasonably familiar *and* which we think can usefully and quite easily be integrated into *critical* literacy practices, along lines argued in the final section.

Typical examples of technological literacies include what we call 'word, sound and image processing', 'emailing', 'netting', and 'gaming'.

Technological literacies as practice

In this section we develop a basic taxonomy which is sensitive to the multiplicity and complexities of *literacies*, yet allows us to make some practical points. It has three components:

- broad or generic forms of literate practice;
- particular aspects of those practices and more specific activities falling within them;
- procedures or techniques involved in those practices.

Of course, things are not as linear or compartmentalized as our taxonomy (elaborated in Table 6.1) suggests. For example, emailing can be seen both as an activity falling within the broad ambit of word processing *and* as a 'generic' technological literacy in its own right. In addition, emailing can afford us access to information held on 'servers' comprising parts of the Internet computer network. When we use email to subscribe to an ejournal such as *Postmodern Culture* (pmc@jefferson.village.virginia.edu) we can then use email to retrieve copies of articles from whatever volumes we wish to read. This provides an efficient alternative to accessing the Internet site for *Postmodern Culture* by means of Netscape (or some other Internet browser) and the relevant site address (its URL).[2]

Processing

'Word, sound and image processing' refers to the whole gamut of activities clustering around generating, manipulating and communicating *digitally coded texts*. Word processing started out as a somewhat mechanistic phenomenon: in many cases word processing was simply a more effective means of 'getting typing done'. You could correct on the screen, move text around ('cutting and pasting' became metaphorical), and so on. These days, of course, processing is endlessly complex and diverse. We still word process in the 'old ways' – keying in essays, memos, letters, etc. But we also process a lot of other kinds of texts, using machines we don't call or think of as word processors. We enter memos, accounts, addresses, phone and fax numbers in electronic organizers; do all manner of desktop publishing; email friends, colleagues, experts (having hooked up our computer to a modem and installed the appropriate software); cut and paste sounds; add sound to 'written' text using CD-ROM, sound cards, video cards; send and receive faxes, and so on.

Things are more complex still. Nicholas's 'word processing as composition' is a radically different technological literacy from that envisaged by his teacher, viz. 'word processing as keying in what you have already written with pen and paper'. Indeed, the technology itself is made into different things in these two instances. For Nicholas, the computer is an accomplice to the creative/composing act. It is a kind of prosthesis integrated with his creative faculties. For a person who uses the computer like a typewriter in order to 'present the final copy', the 'technology itself' is different. It is not a 'prosthetic accomplice' to the creative activity so much as scribing instrument to set in type what has *already been created*. Indeed, coming to be able to compose on the screen takes a lot of doing and learning. This is sometimes described for people of older generations (who did not 'grow up with computers') by analogy with learning a second language as an adult. When we learn a second language having mastered a first, we initially think in our first language and translate to the second, and then speak or write. After some time we automatically do it all in the second language.

> I cannot compose what is difficult for me directly on to the screen. I still have to use pencil and paper. After several years of working daily with computers I can now compose more, and 'more-difficult-for-me', material on the screen than I once could. But when the stakes are high and the going tough I revert to the technology that I became apprenticed to 'thinking beyond myself' with. I learned to 'think-write' with pencil and paper. Apart from anything else, this involves double labour, and is wasteful of material resources. Nicholas needn't 'suffer' this (although most of his peers probably still do). He has learned/taught himself/ become accustomed to 'think-write' with a computer from the very outset. In that way, among others, Nicholas and I are 'differently literate' as word processing beings.
>
> (Colin)

The technological literacies involved around processing as a generic literacy are many:

> For example, I can call up one or other of three talking heads on my computer's daily organizer program – to make a diary entry, as one would in a conventional diary or by setting an alarm on a hand-held

electronic organizer, enter a reminder for a meeting which will activate before the event and (other things being equal) allow me to get there on time. Using Igor (or Simon, or Perkins) is entertaining (albeit a bit frivolous), has a definite and quirky aesthetic and humorous aspect, and draws on a somewhat wider array of techniques, procedures and technological componentry that are integral to other increasingly important and interesting literacies. I use the mouse to scroll through the calendars and choose the right day, month and year. I set the clock to my appointment time; key in who I'm meeting, where and why; and choose the best talking head for the job – either Igor, Perkins or Simon (each has his own personality) – abetted by the sound and video cards installed in the computer. Near the appointed time, Igor (or Perkins or Simon) breaks into whatever I'm working on and reminds me I have an engagement in 15 minutes (or in whatever time leeway I choose to set). These same kinds of hardware and software components, procedures and techniques are used in such practices as interacting with CD-ROM 'living books' or hypertext encyclopedias, and engaging in a range of other multimedia applications.

(Michele)

Emailing

Email is a facility for sending messages to other computer users. We can contact local users via local network systems, and contact people in many overseas countries using networked computers via the Internet.

> Email is fast – messages to anywhere in the world are usually delivered within minutes. The computer system of the person you are contacting will accept and store the email message in a mail file, so the person does not have to be using the computer at the time the message is sent . . .
> . . . You can exchange many sorts of information via email – including memos, letters, data and programs. People working on a paper together can exchange drafts. You can send messages to multiple users, making email a useable means of contacting all the students enrolled for a particular course, or any group of people needing the same information.
>
> (Goldstein and Heard 1991: 10)

Email programs are part word processor, part mailbox, and part file organizer (Kurland 1996: 51). Email enables us to:

● send messages to other people, reply to messages, forward messages;
● read messages sent to us;
● print messages;

- delete messages;
- organize and manipulate the messages stored in our mail file;
- attach files;
- include portions of the original message in our replies to help clarify responses.

(see Goldstein and Heard 1991: 10; Warschauer 1995)

The software requirements and procedures for operating email vary. The important point, however, is that as a generic practice emailing is quite straightforward. Indeed, programs like Eudora make the process almost absurdly simple, including sending and receiving documents as attachments, organizing them in files, moving files around, joining files, and so on. There are two key points about email. First, the medium is very powerful for obtaining information and engaging in other forms of communication like transmitting messages, writing with other people, etc. Once you have addresses and contacts you can interact with anyone anywhere who is linked up to the Internet. You can access (and communicate) many kinds of information, points of view, attitudes, perspectives, experiences, beliefs, etc., from many points on the globe and very quickly – given the willingness of others to interact.

Second, *emailing* is made into diverse *literacies* by different users. In our own cases, our emailing will in the course of a typical day move across several (more or less) distinct literacies, characterized by different purposes, different social contexts, different audiences, different 'voices' being involved in composing the messages, etc. These include sending and receiving memos, writing more or less informal letters, responding to chunks of thesis emailed in by students, sending information to or receiving it from some list server on the Internet, and sending or receiving chunks of composition for books or articles from co-authors. Other literacies are negotiated as well. Early in 1995 one particular message reached us several times from different people involved in different networks. It originated with a networked anthropologist in Chiapas, Southern Mexico. The message stated that contrary to official Mexican government information and mainstream media despatches, the Mexican army had been shooting and otherwise bringing violence to *Indio* communities (believed to be) associated with the Zapatista National Liberation Front. This was a form of political or activist or mobilizing literacy – different in tone, purpose and other features from a friendly letter or a memo.

Thus email is not the same *one* social practice and conception of giving and receiving meanings via digital text. Like 'literacy', 'email' is an umbrella term for a diverse and ever growing array of technological literacies. The practices we have mentioned here are substantively different and discrete literate practices mediated by electronic texts.

Netting

'Netting' refers to activities involving electronic networks ranging from purpose-built local area networks (e.g. between classrooms in a school, faculties within a university, across a web of schools or universities), all the way to the worldwide 'network of networks': the Internet. Almost innumerable tomes have been written during the past few years about communicative practices in 'cyberspace' (e.g. Stone 1992; Heim 1993; Branwyn 1994; Dery 1994), especially about activity using the Internet, and it would be folly to attempt any kind of general coverage here. Rather, we will merely provide some examples, definitions and illustrations that help to reiterate the main points we have been driving at in this section.

- Like word, sound and image processing and emailing, 'netting' has certain hardware and software implications. The aspect we will focus on here is that these are less complicated and costly than might be imagined by the uninitiated.
- Netting activities are basically quite simple.
- They are, nonetheless, pedagogically very powerful and fruitful.
- 'Netting' is an umbrella term which covers multifarious more or less discrete technological literacies.

Let us take these briefly in turn.

As with email, the basic infrastructural needs for netting comprise a computer with a medium to high speed modem, telephone line access, and software that enables the computer to link into the telecommunications network via the computer. The most basic of these facilities will enable users to receive and read simple text, i.e. straight prose. At the opposite extreme, the most sophisticated facilities permit such activities as accessing museums and galleries overseas, browsing high resolution images in full colour (e.g. the Mona Lisa), and printing them out. To perform these feats calls for machines sufficiently powerful to take Windows software (or equivalent), modems with fast baud rates and, of course, a high resolution computer monitor, up-to-date graphics-based 'Internet browser' software, and sophisticated printers – if you really want the Mona Lisa.

The interesting point, however, is that most of this can now be done *relatively* cheaply in countries like Australia, Britain and the United States. Of course, we do not want to downplay the fact that what is relatively cheap for one person, group or school may be relatively expensive for others. Neither do we wish to appear insensitive to many schools' genuine economic deprivation. On the other hand, we *do* want to stress the importance in this context of grasping certain *concepts*: of having a *conceptual* understanding of netting in relation to hardware and software needs; and of how and when netting might become an important *educative* component of classroom language and literacy practice. This is a matter of having relevant 'meta-level knowledge and awareness'. You have to know at a conceptual level how netting operates in order to make intelligent and optimal pedagogical and economic decisions (Landow 1994). This, of course, is not simply about being an economic optimizer. It is, profoundly, about teacher professional development. Pursuing this kind of awareness is the very stuff of developing professionally for the present – let alone the future. This holds for the technological sphere specifically, but also for the pedagogic domain in general. Being an effective teacher is crucially about having meta-level knowledge and understanding of the fields one teaches within (Gee 1990, 1991, 1992).

Fortunately, it is not especially difficult to come by this meta-level knowledge. Interestingly, much of it is already available in many classrooms from middle school level onwards, via the students themselves. Students like Nicholas, and many others we have met in the course of our classroom research at all grade levels have grown up with this technology. They have 'organically' acquired knowledge of how nets and webs and systems are put together (Taylor and Saarinen 1994; Wark 1995). They may not, however, have made this knowledge explicit. The teacher can draw on this knowledge and help make it explicit for all, by addressing practical issues like how to get the best netting arrangement going for the classroom.

Over an 18-month period, without intense effort, by very casual means and with the generous assistance of friends and colleagues, we learned enough to locate and employ a wide range of resources on the Internet. There is much more to learn, but none of what we are ever likely to need as educational theorists, researchers and language and literacy educators is unduly difficult conceptually or technically. There are abundant user-friendly materials available. More importantly, there are always people close to hand who are generous with their knowledge. In many areas with which we are familiar, expertise is something we are encouraged to keep to ourselves, because the rewards associated with it are directly proportional to limiting the number of people who possess it. A good deal of netting, however, is dependent on having *large* communities of participants (Branwyn 1994; Landow 1994). Hence there is a principle operating to draw people in rather than exclude them.

So, what sorts of things can be done in netting, how easy is it, and how useful or fruitful is it? One simple example will suffice here.

> At the time we started getting serious about technological literacies we were doing coursework towards an MEd (TESOL) degree and during 1995 mentioned this casually to a friend while in the US. We arrived home to find that he had emailed us details of the TESL-L discussion list and instructions for subscribing – which we did. Each morning when I checked my email I would find up to 50 messages of varying quality and

usefulness, all part of a rich, ongoing discussion between ESL academics, teachers and students, covering everything from pronunciation drills through to requests for research data. The TESL-L Internet site is good value as well. Here, I can browse through the main menu choosing different hyperlinks to follow, leading to articles on classroom teaching and hints, computers in ESL, software archives and much more. If I want to brush up on my Spanish or German, I can (and do) HTTP to Tyler Jones's Human Languages Page and download some lesson software (which includes sound and images), browse through the on-line language dictionaries and vocabulary lists, or follow links that take me to that day's foreign language newspapers and magazines.

(Michele)

Finally, there is a 'literacy *for* technology' (Bigum and Green 1992) dimension within the generic space of netting:

When we began teaching ourselves some basics in our attempt to get up to speed with emergent technological literacies we would browse publications like the *Internet Yellow Pages* (Hahn and Stout 1994) to locate addresses for user groups, home pages, bulletin boards and the like. There is also the 'support literacy' involved in reading manuals and other 'how to do it' texts, in order to get access in the first instance. In the days before Netscape (and before we had access at work to relevant seminars and effective computing services back up), Michele got one of our work-based machines 'on to Mosaic' by reading Gareth Branwyn's do-it-yourself book, *Mosaic Quick Tour for Windows: Accessing and Navigating the Internet's World Wide Web* (1994). We then spent a couple of hours following the directions – made easier by our having actively sought a meta-level grasp of key operative concepts, knowing it was there to be had.

(Colin)

Gaming

'Gaming' spans the wide spectrum from playing with hand-held machines, through Nintendo and Sega-type games (which involve units connected to the TV) and arcade-type games (including virtual reality set-ups), to engaging games loaded on to the hard drives of computers. Games are of diverse types and can be categorized in many ways. Some call for combinations of rapid and precise hand-eye-brain coordination, as well as knowledge and memory of moves that can be made and of what is likely to happen in this or that kind of situation. Others – like the 'Dr Brain' series – may call for sophisticated prediction and problem solving. Some games are of the action (and, not infrequently, violence) variety; others have sporting motifs; some tend toward the pornographic; some are simulations of real life constructs (e.g. 'SimCity'); some are incarnations of popular toys (e.g. Barbie); others are intentionally educational. Many teachers will be familiar here with variants like the Carmen Sandiego series: 'Where in the world is Carmen Sandiego?' or 'Where in space is Carmen Sandiego?'

Two points are noteworthy here. First, we do well to heed Papert's observations concerning the interfaces between the culture of school and that of gaming. Papert comments:

> Schools would have parents – who honestly don't know how to interpret their children's obvious love affair with video games – believe that children love them and dislike homework because the first is easy and the second hard. In reality, the reverse is more often true. Any adult who thinks these games are easy need only sit down and try to master one. Most are hard, with complex information – as well as techniques – to be mastered, the information often much more difficult and time consuming to master than the technique.
>
> ... [V]ideo games, being the first example of computer technology applied to toy making, have nonetheless been the entryway for children into the world of computers. These toys, by empowering children to test out ideas about working within prefixed rules and structures in a way few other toys are capable of doing, have proved capable of teaching students about the possibilities and drawbacks of a newly presented system in ways many adults should envy.
>
> (1993: 4)

In the light of Papert's remarks and our experience of 'educational' games like 'Where in the world is Carmen Sandiego?', it is apparent that gaming has *educative/educational* significance both overtly and covertly, and both aspects are important.

Overtly, the form(s) of technological literacy inherent in playing 'Where in the world is Carmen Sandiego?' encourage acquisition of problem-solving and prediction skills, and draw upon and develop a range of 'higher order capacities' such as cognitive processes of analysis and synthesis. These are important, and gaming – like netting and emailing – provides new opportunities for applying educational principles like building on existing interests, experiences and forms of mastery in order to enable and enhance classroom learning.

Covertly, it is important to attend to the hidden curriculum of games: namely, that in learning the game, one is being apprenticed to rule-governed activities and, more importantly, to testing ideas about how to work within rule-governed settings. This is what any form of disciplined engagement – theoretical, practical and praxical – is about. Furthermore, as Papert has already reminded us, video games – and wider involvements with computers

– teach young people that some forms of *learning* are fast-paced, compelling and rewarding. It is the emphasis on learning that is important here. The hidden curriculum of gaming is an initiation into modes of practice that are characterized much more by learning, and self/collaborative direction and discovery than about wholesale exposure to teaching and instruction. We have entered a period when the pace of learning and relearning will necessarily be rapid, and where didactic teaching will have strict limits to its effectiveness. Teachers are going to have to become adept at enabling students' learning, particularly evaluative and analytical forms of learning that enable students to make explicit what the rules and structures are that permit and limit the social practices that collectively make us what we are and are not. These forms of learning include those that are fast-paced, wide-ranging and short-lived. This is the very logic of 'technological literacies', where details of technique and content are forever changing, and new parameters and purposes are constantly evolving. It is, in Papert's words, 'a culture of learning'.

Some dimensions of difference

The theme of technological literacies raises some interesting dimensions of difference. We will deal here with just four of the many that impinge on education.

Technology-rich and -poor

First, there is the important difference between 'technology-rich' and 'technology-poor'. Differences operate here at each level, from individuals and homes, to schools, regions and nations. Two recent Australian reports released in 1995 found a similar trend emerging here to that previously reported in the US and Britain (McIntosh 1995). A significant gap already exists between white and blue collar workers with respect to home computer ownership: 52 per cent to 40 per cent respectively, with PC ownership estimated at that time to stand at 40 per cent of Australian households. Hence rates of ownership in 'non-working' homes were considerably lower than blue collar rates. Furthermore, whereas in 1995 69 per cent of Australian workers earning above $50,000 per year used computers at work, the figure fell to 50 per cent for workers earning $30,000–$50,000, and to 28 per cent for those earning less than $30,000 (p. 45). It was reported that approximately 7 per cent of Australia's households had access to the Internet in mid-1995, with the rate increasing rapidly.

These are quantitative rather than qualitative figures. From what we know about literate practices and cultural practices generally, however, it is a safe bet that significant qualitative differences exist between the technological literacy practices enacted across different homes and worksites: these differences will have inevitable consequences for patterns of scholastic success and failure, other things being equal. This means that once again schools and teachers inevitably become instrumental in equity agendas, being called on to make access to technological literacies as equitable as possible. This is partly a quantitative matter – which may call for positive funding discrimination in favour of classrooms populated by children from 'technology-poor' backgrounds. It is very largely, however, a qualitative agenda, of ensuring so far as possible that electronic technology in classrooms is integrated into practices of 'powerful technological literacies'. This is what was *not* happening, for example, in Nicholas's classroom.

Digital and conventional texts

Second, there are some important differences between what we call 'the digital (or virtual or electronic) text of cyberspace' and the conventional 'printed text of bookspace' (see Lankshear *et al.* 1996; Peters and Lankshear 1996).

The digital text exists only as code. Unlike print, it has a radical convertibility. It can be transmitted in different mediums and reconstituted at various points of arrival. The code as electronic impulses exists not as a physical object in itself – as a closed system of text delivery, such as with the conventional book – but as flows and relays of digital information, infinitely plastic, continuously available, and able to be recycled. The digital text is radically interactive. It breaks down the reader–writer distinction in dramatic ways. The electronic text is, in Richard Lanham's words (1993: 4), both 'creator-controlled and reader-controlled'. Thus, practices of reading and writing undergo major transformation. The reader can control the size, shape and scale of screen-print, altering its typography, its readability, its illumination. The reader can add or delete, incorporate textual scribbles as part of the text, rearrange paragraphs before saving and printing it. Lanham (p. 6) suggests that 'the interactive reader of the electronic word incarnates the responsive reader of whom we make so much'. With digital text we shift from an author-controlled textual environment where words are fixed on the page in a top–down, left–right, beginning–end materiality to a reader-controlled environment, infinitely flexible and open to manipulation.

Moreover, the digital text realigns alphabetic, graphic and sound components into a single common denominator allowing simultaneously the processing of word, image and sound. This presents serious challenges to notions and demarcations of 'disciplinarity', i.e. of separate, distinct subjects each with its own textual time-space – its separate learning-teaching space and its own canon. The space between subject specialities becomes eroded and conventional roles for experts and teachers as subject specialists are open to redefinition. Broad-band, multimedia digital 'texts' already permit the reader opportunities for experimentation to design and rearrange sequences, and produce custom-tailored endings. When traditional print-based texts are rearranged in this fashion, re-created and supplemented with image- and sound-processing, questions of curriculum are also thereby open to reordering.

Digital text makes possible new reconfigurations of discourse, particularly at intersections between informal modes of communication and more traditional, scholarly/academic forms. Within cyberspace, the emergence of new forms of discourse is especially evident in such forums as electronic journals, email, news groups, and a diverse array of MOOs, Web pages, message boards and the like. Some of these, according to Anne Okerson (1994: 10), 'are not like anything we have experienced in the print world'. On-line user groups and bulletin boards, and specific cyberspace genres like 'flaming' and 'ranting' (see Rucker *et al.* 1992; Dery 1994), have been described as 'high tech universal graffiti'. Social practices based on digital text have given new scope to experimentation and creativity evident in the development of new vocabularies, signs and codes by participants. These testify anew to the human will to activity, invention and transformative practice (Peters and Lankshear 1996).

New forms of student subjectivity

Third, increasing attention is being paid to the possibility that distinctively new forms of student subjectivity are upon us: that 'today's student is quite different [from] students of previous eras' (Green and Bigum 1992: 119), different in important ways from their teachers, and different from constructions of the 'ideal student' which underlie current curricula. For some, like Green and Bigum, the focus is on the emergence of 'the postmodern student-subject' and the intriguing possibility that we may have 'aliens in our classroom' (p. 119). For others, the demarcation is drawn between the 'baby boomer' generation and the 'baby buster' (known variously as Generation X, Generation Doom, 13th Gen, etc.) generation. The two generations are allegedly distinguished by radically different world-views, expectations, and personal and collective goals (see Rucker *et al.* 1992; Howe and Strauss 1993; Rushkoff 1994). At a more specific level, and of particular relevance here, many teachers identify 'technological competence' as a key line of difference between their students and themselves. In some, though not all, cases this acts as a disincentive to enter the domain of technological literacies wholeheartedly. Papert (author of the renowned Logo software program) describes an illuminating case of a fifth-grade teacher, Joe, talking about being faced with employing Logo in the classroom:

From the time the computers came I began to be afraid of the day my students would know more about programming than I ever will. Of course, at the beginning I had a big advantage. I came fresh from a summer workshop on Logo, and the students were just beginning. But during the year they were catching up. They were spending more time on it than I could. Actually, they didn't catch up the first year. But I knew that each year the children would know more because they would have had experience in previous grades. Besides, children are more in tune with computers than we grown-ups.

The first few times I noticed that the students had problems I couldn't even understand, let alone solve, I struggled to avoid facing the fact that I could not keep up my stance of knowing more than they did. I was afraid that giving it up would undermine my authority as a teacher. But the situation became worse. Eventually I broke down and said I didn't understand the problem – go discuss it with some of the others in the class who might be able to help. Which they did. And it turned out that together the kids could figure out a solution. Now the amazing thing is that what I was afraid of turned out to be a liberation. I no longer had to fear being exposed. I was. I no longer had to pretend. And the wonderful thing was that I realized that my bluff was called for more than computers. I felt I could no longer pretend to know everything in other subjects as well. What a relief! It has changed my relationship with the children and with myself. My class has become much more of a collaborative community where we are all learning together.

(Papert 1993: 65–6)

Multiple subjectivity/ies

Fourth, technological literacies offer students information about and experience of multiple forms of difference played out in important ways within everyday life. 'Cyberspace' environments provide almost unlimited access to the complexity, diversity and sheer multiplicity of human subjectivities and cultural forms of life, together with the highly fluid nature of identity and the extensive possibilities for constructing personal identity. Electronic networks abound with 'spaces' in which people communicate freely – typically from the safety of anonymity or pseudonymity – about aspects of subjectivity and identity, and their associated implications, consequences and challenges (Haraway 1991; Stone 1991; Taylor and Saarinen 1994). They also make available information on how different individuals and groups respond to issues and concerns that transcend local, regional and national confines.

Meeting the challenge of technological literacies: possibilities for critical practice

> To resist electronic technology is as futile as trying to turn back the tides. It has already swept over us in ways we have yet to realize. It is not a question of whether to accept or reject this new world but of who is going to use it and how.
>
> > (Taylor and Saarinen 1994: Net Effects 1)

Much has been written about critical (approaches) to pedagogy and inquiry generally, and to literacy more specifically (see Chapter 2). We will briefly recall some features we associate with critical practices and indicate how electronic technologies and technological literacies might be integrated into the pursuit and achievement of these critical ends.

First, critical practices involve two generic components: analysis and evaluation. A 'critical orientation' implies judging, comparing or evaluating on the basis of careful analysis. To critique X – i.e. to judge X (positively, negatively, etc.) – is to comment on the qualities and merits of X. This requires knowing what these are, through some kind of analysis. It is to know X 'for what it is', and to judge or evaluate accordingly.

Second, critical pedagogy and critical literacy engage students and teachers collaboratively in making explicit the socially constructed character of knowledge, language and literacy, and asking in whose interests particular 'knowledges' and textual practices are constructed, legitimated and given privileged status within education. From this perspective, education is approached not simply in terms of being able to know and do things, but also in terms of being able to know these things for what they are and for their social consequences. We see this as implying four related goals for classroom learning:

1 Enabling learners to render explicit the relationship between 'word' and 'world'. Textual practices (or 'word') – i.e. making, transmitting, giving and receiving meanings in and through *language* – are embedded within and co-constitutive of larger, embodied and enacted meanings that comprise social-cultural practices *per se*. Our daily practices of encoding and decoding meanings from literal texts (i.e. language and literacy practices) are part and parcel of the myriad webs of social practice that comprise our social-cultural reality ('world') – the world of biological humans made and remade discursively as social and cultural beings. Language is (a) social practice; although it is by no means *all* of social practice (see Kress 1985, 1988b). Coming to understand this relationship in concrete everyday terms is a hallmark of the critically literate person, and assisting students toward such understanding is central to the role of teachers who wish to promote critical literacy.

2 Providing learners with opportunities to explore the extent to which social practices, ways of doing and being, and forms of knowledge are historical, contingent and transformable, rather than natural, fixed and immutable.
3 Encouraging learners to explore the social implications, for various individuals and groups, of (particular) discursive practices and values being the way they are, and to consider how different forms of practice and different values might produce different outcomes for the individuals and groups in question.
4 Providing learners with opportunities to enhance their appreciation of the vast range of actual and possible ways of doing and being.

Let us consider some possibilities for pursuing these goals by integrating electronic technologies and 'technological literacies' into mainstream classroom practice. Our ideas are directed mainly at middle school years, but teachers at all levels will be able to produce their own adaptations and improvements. Our suggestions presuppose a certain level of infrastructure and access to some kind of network – the more global the better.

Regarding infrastructure, accessing the 'critical' potential of literacies like emailing, netting, and processing words, images and sounds, calls for a minimum 486 DX processor speed (or equivalent), Windows-type applications, quad speed CD-ROM and 16-bit sound and video cards, and a modem with at least a 2400 baud rate. The practical imperative is to invest available funds wisely. It is likely many classes will contain students whose knowledge of such matters outstrips their teacher's. This provides an excellent basis from which to explore alternative knowledge and authority relations, allowing 'organic' student knowledge to assume high ground in important decision-making processes pertaining to resourcing critical pedagogy. This does not mean simply accepting student knowledge on face value but, when appropriate, taking advice from learners and extending them responsibility for checking (and pricing) options. Moreover, inviting students to justify their ideas and preferences provides pedagogical opportunities for making explicit the relationship between particular forms of hardware and software and the technological literacies to which they are integral, thus encouraging the development of important meta-level understandings.

Access to global email and cyberspace networks – such as the Internet and its myriad nets – through a modem is also optimal. Where schools are not networked as part of their regular resourcing, it may be necessary for teachers and students to explore ways of obtaining at least some degree of access. Various forms of strategic or entrepreneurial activity might be employed here. For example, teachers who are involved in graduate programmes may be able to obtain dial-in facilities through their institution, or else they might seek to have their classroom integrated into research and development projects through which access is made available. Alternatively, the class might pursue entrepreneurial methods, such as negotiating partnerships with networked corporations, or with telecommunications and/or electronics companies. In addition, classes might subscribe to bulletin board servers, rather than to Vax/Unix servers directly. As noted above, a wide range of servers are available at very reasonable rates, and others are free.

The important principle is to network the classroom to a range of local, regional, national and worldwide virtual communities which provide variety in terms of social practices, subjectivity and identity. At its most straight-forward, this might be done by establishing email connections with students in other schools, near and far. More ambitious options could include using cyberspace to develop collaborative learning across contexts of cultural and social difference and diversity, along the lines described by Taylor and Saarinen, where the authors jointly developed and 'taught' a course involving their respective students in a North American and a Finnish university. Other options are to post messages relevant to classroom learning themes to existing user groups, or to generate a new user group or discussion list with its own particular purposes, values and modes of interaction, as an experiment in creating a space of discursive practice and production. Alternatively, a class might create interactive Web pages that present information about the school community, local issues, etc., and invite feedback, discussion and appropriate contributions from other Internet users. Within these virtual communities, students and teachers together can engage in dialogue across difference, seeking out commonalities, experimenting with identities, tracing borders and moving in and out of different discourse communities.

As a variation on such *active* forms of participation, a class might simply log into a range of cyberspaces and collect interactions over a period of time as hard copy (having obtained permission to do so from the original writers). These could be used in the manner of Freirean 'codifications' (Freire 1974) to interrogate how information and knowledge are constructed, controlled and legitimated, and to undertake 'anatomies' of the various social practices within which these texts were produced. In each case the aim will be to arrive at *explicit* understandings: e.g. of the social practices themselves; how they are regulated; who engages in them and for what purposes; and the relationship between particular texts (the hard copies) and their larger discursive contexts (the discursive practices on the Net).

The superabundance of information available in cyberspace frees the teacher considerably from having to provide content. Consequently, electronic technologies can be employed by teachers to provide contexts in which they can devote their energies and understandings principally to maintaining processes where the emphasis is on rendering the implicit explicit. In this role the teacher keeps in front of students the task of interrogating what they encounter in cyberspace. What is this practice? Where does it come from? What are its purposes? What does it make of participants? What forms of subjectivity and what kinds of identities are associated with it? What alternative forms of practice exist here, or might exist? Who benefits from the practice as currently constituted? Who controls and regulates knowledge and information within this practice, and by what means? What counts as knowledge and information here, and why? Which practices 'go together' and which do not? Why not? What sorts of combinations of practices might be possible, interesting, challenging? What patterns are evident between patterns of values and beliefs and discursive histories, across time and place?

Let us consider in a little more detail how this might work. Take the case of participating in a user group. This involves acknowledging the norms and etiquette of appropriate use, as an individual member of a self-monitoring and self-regulating community. It is common, for example, to find segments of 'conversation' among participants in cyberspace activities suggesting that it is time to move to a new 'venue', because the conversation is moving into purposes or activities that fall outside the bounds of the current 'space'. Failure to do so risks censure, of varying degrees of severity. At the other extreme, users quickly learn recognized 'counter' forms of involvement, like 'flaming' and 'ranting' (see Dery 1994: 1, 5) which have their own names and are explicitly known and understood as distinctive practices and genres. In such ways, members of virtual communities are involved in forms of social interaction in which 'words' are always manifestly components of purpose-related and value-laden social practices associated with roles, identities and forms of production (i.e. aspects of 'world'). Idiosyncratic vocabularies of cyberspace are integral to this general phenomenon. Users have to master specialized vocabularies that go along with doing and being in certain ways. This calls for explicit knowledge which helps, in turn, to make explicit the relationship between language, forms of engagement in social practices, and the taking up of particular types or elements of identity.

The historical and contingent nature of discursive practice becomes readily apparent within cyberspaces. To experience oneself as engaged with others in constructing, refining and monitoring social practices which comprise amalgamations of reading-writing-imaging, values, purposes, theories, roles, identities, etc., is necessarily to envisage one's activity as simply so many representations of what social practice(s) *might* be, and to be aware of alternative possibilities within and outside cyberspace. It is to realize there is nothing *necessary* about inhabiting any particular discursive space or spaces: all such spaces are contingent and historical. This insight is central to meta-level awareness of discursive practice and the possibilities for trans-formative praxis predicated upon it.

The same insight is enabled by the immediacy available in icon-assisted Windows-type applications, and CD-ROM, hypertext, hypercard stacks and morphing facilities, which can convey the vast sweep and transitoriness of discourses and entire discursive formations at the click of a mouse. The electronic processes that make almost endless human variety accessible in visual and textual forms instantaneously convey overtly the 'message' that social practices come and go: they emerge and evolve in particular contexts, under given conditions, for certain purposes and in association with specific values, beliefs and theories; they give way to other practices under different constellations of purposes, beliefs, values and conditions. While this awareness is in principle available in similar ways via engagement with more conventional text forms, it is nonetheless much more *readily* apparent and, indeed, is practically unavoidable, where electronic hardware and relevant software is employed.

Finally and, perhaps, more contentiously, practising technological literacies within cyberspace environments provides valuable opportunities for learners to explore the social implications for various groups and individuals of particular discursive practices and orders of discourse (Fairclough 1989). From such vantage points learners can make informed evaluations of social practices and envisage possibilities for transformative action. (Here we might also consider, for example, how the kind of approach to critical literacy across the curriculum outlined in Chapter 2 could be augmented by using electronic texts – including graphics, sound, video clips, etc. – as well as, or in place of, conventional texts.) The anonymity of network 'spaces' offers rich possibilities in 'safe places' for people to 'speak out' and 'talk back' about experiences of oppression or marginality (Ellsworth 1989). Net users can form or join affinity groups within which experiences may be analysed and shared, responses framed and actions organized. They can access people on a global scale who have encountered shared or similar issues and experiences, and who have framed and addressed these in various ways. The information and accounts of experience thereby available provide bases for reflective evaluation/judgement and ideas for possible action, as well as access to support and solidarity that can be vital in mobilizing and sustaining efforts to bring about social and cultural change.

Our knowledge of children as young as 5 establishing Web sites, bulletin boards and user groups, and collaborating in their ongoing development, indicates something of the potential for integrating electronic technologies and technological literacies into 'critical' forms of classroom learning. Acting on this potential will, at the very least, bring classroom learning into closer contact with developments and forces operating in the world beyond the school gates. At best, it will contribute to the ideal of educating for active and informed citizens committed to the pursuit of 'difference with dignity'.

It is, of course, one thing to state possibilities and ideals to be pursued in classrooms, and quite another for them to be realized in practice. It is yet another thing for them to be realized (or actualized) in ways that give all learners a more or less equal shot at being apprenticed to effective and powerful control of technological literacies. In the next chapter we explore some of the ways in which schools currently serve as brokers of radically uneven and unequal proficiencies and prospects with respect to technological literacies.

Notes

1 Hodas says here that 'the introduction of computers is hailed in one discourse (directed towards the public and towards policy makers) as a process which will radically change the nature of what goes on in the classroom, give students entirely new sets of skills, and permanently shift the terrain of learning and schools. In other discourse (directed towards administrators and teachers) computers are sold as straightforward tools to assist them in carrying out pre-existing tasks and fulfilling pre-existing roles, not as Trojan Horses whose acceptance will ultimately require the acquisition of an entirely new set of skills and world outlook' (Hodas 1993: 10).

2 For definitions of the technical terms in this paragraph and in other parts of this chapter, see the following Appendix.

Appendix: glossary of technical terms

16-bit
'Bit' is short for 'binary digit', 'a single unit of data' (Kurland 1996: 204). A 16-bit sound card can process bits twice as fast as an 8-bit card.

account
'When you are registered to use a particular computer system, you are given an account. Associated with the account are a unique user name and a password. You must enter these to show you are authorised to use the system' (Goldstein and Heard 1991: 48).

baud
A unit of data transmission speed, usually equivalent to bits per second. The baud rate of a modem denotes 'the maximum speed at which data can be sent down a channel, such as a telephone line' (Frasse 1994: 319). Hence a 9600 baud modem has a lower maximum transferral speed than a 14,400 baud modem.

BBS
(Bulletin Board System) 'A computerized version of the bulletin boards frequently found in grocery stores – places to leave messages and to advertise things you want to buy or sell. One thing you can get from a computerized bulletin board that you can't get from a cork board is free software' (Frasse 1994: 319); 'A conferencing system where a number of people with similar interests can post information which can then be read by any member of the group' (Goldstein and Heard 1991: 48).

browser
Software that enables the user to access Internet servers (e.g. Mosaic, Netscape, etc.).

CD-ROM

(Compact Disc, Read-Only Memory) Used for storage of computer text or programs. Typically, a CD-ROM can store in excess of 500 megabytes (millions of bytes) of data, as compared with the capacity of hard disks for home computers, whose storage capacity is about 120 megabytes (Feldman 1993).

cyberspace

'Word coined by sci-fi writer William Gibson to refer to a near-future computer network where users can mentally travel through matrices of data. The term is now often used to describe today's Internet' (Branwyn 1994: 176).

DOS

(Disk Operating System) This usually refers to 'the operating system in IBM-compatible PCs' (Kurland 1996: 206).

ejournal

Electronic journal.

email

(Electronic mail) 'A network service that enables users to send and receive messages via computer' (Frasse 1994: 322).

flaming

'Exchanging insults electronically' (White 1994: 322).

FTP

(File Transfer Protocol) *noun*: 'A commonly used protocol for transferring files from one computer to another. [*verb*:] The action of transferring files' [sometimes known as 'FTPing'] (Branwyn 1994: 177).

Gopher

'A menu-driven system for searching online information' (Branwyn 1994: 177).

HTML

(HyperText Markup Language) A 'system for tagging the various parts of a Web document that tells the browsing software how to display the document's text, links, graphics, and attached media' (Branwyn 1994: 178). For example, the coloured 'click on' words in a Web text show up because the text has been written in HTML.

HTTP

(HyperText Transport Protocol) 'A server computer that uses the communication protocol for [World Wide] Web document transfer' (Branwyn 1994: 178).

home page

'commonly used to refer to the first document you come to in a collection of documents on a [World Wide] Web site' (Branwyn 1994: 178).

hypercard stacks

See: hypertext.

hypertext

'The idea of hypertext is that one has an electronic document in which each page might have buttons leading not to one single next page but to many possible next pages. Hypertext can include sounds, images, film clips, and computer demonstrations as well as words. Some writers have attempted creating written forms of hypertext, and a wide variety of software "stacks" for the [Apple] HyperCard program are available – a recent example is the *Beyond Cyberpunk* stack' (Rucker *et al.* 1992: 148).

Internet

A worldwide interconnected group of networks. Internally the Internet is composed of similar networks that use different protocols. 'Gateway' programs are used to convert protocols between networks so that, externally, the Internet appears to be a single network (see Frasse 1994: 325).

log on/log off	'To indicate to a system or network that you are starting your work and are beginning interaction'. *Log off* means to terminate interaction (Frasse 1994: 326).
Logo	A language developed by Seymour Papert, designed to teach children basic computer programming logic.
Lynx	A text-based World Wide Web browser with limited hypertext capacities.
modem	'Short for modulator/demodulator; a peripheral device that links your computer to other computers and information services using telephone lines' (Frasse 1994: 327).
MOO	(MUD, Object-Oriented) 'A sub-species of MUD' (Dibbell 1994: 240).
morphing	'Morphing is a technique used to give the illusion of one image melting into another. It is accomplished by defining areas on the first image (the source) that will be reshaped to match corresponding areas on the second image (the destination)' (Chmiel 1993).
Mosaic	'A World Wide Web multimedia browser developed at the National Center for Supercomputing Applications at the University of Illinois, Urbana-Champaign. Mosaic is made available free of charge to the Internet community' (Branwyn 1994: 179).
MUD	(Multi-User Domain) 'Semi-fictional digital otherworlds [on the Internet] . . . a kind of data base especially designed to give users the vivid impression of moving through a physical space that in reality exists only as descriptive data [i.e. narrative text] filed away on a hard drive' (Dibbell 1994: 238, 240–1).
Netscape	Another World Wide Web multimedia browser, successor to Mosaic.
on-line	When a user is connected via computer to the Internet (or a sub-network).
platform	A software program that 'supports' a particular 'function' (e.g. Windows is a platform for word-processing software, etc.).
protocol	Protocols determine the nature of a telecommunications network (e.g. TCP/IP or Transmission Control Protocol/Internet Protocol). They set programming 'rules' and 'syntax' for network platforms; 'the rules determine, amongst other things, how the data is interpreted, what sort of message has been received, and what the contents of the message may be' (Goldstein and Heard 1991: 5).
rant	'On-line demagoguery in which users give themselves over to inspired hyperbole and wild, zany capitalization and punctuation' (White 1994: 324).
server	'A computer that provides a particular service across a network. The service might be file access, log in access, file transfer, printing and so on. Computers from which users initiate the service are called *clients*' (Frasse 1994: 331).

soundcard	Hardware installed inside your computer that enables your computer system to produce high quality sounds using appropriate software (music, voices, special effects, etc.).
TELNET	'A terminal emulation protocol that enables you to log in remotely to other computers on the Internet' (Frasse 1994: 332).
terminal emulation	'Software that enables a personal computer to communicate with a host computer by transmitting in the form [i.e. protocol] used by the host's terminals' (Frasse 1994: 332).
URL	(Uniform Resource Locator) The 'format for indicating the protocol and address for accessing information on the Internet' (Kurland 1996: 212). Each URL begins 'http:// . . .'
user groups/news groups	Groups of users interacting within specially designated 'spaces' on the Internet. 'Think of network news [and news groups] as a worldwide collection of automatically updated electronic bulletin boards [used by millions of people every day]' (Frasse 1994: 148).
videocard	Hardware installed inside your computer that enables it to produce high quality images using appropriate software (e.g. graphic pictures, photographs, film clips, video clips, etc.).
WWW	'A hypertext-based Internet service used for organizing and browsing Internet resources' (Frasse 1994: 332).

seven

DIFFERENT WORLDS? TECHNOLOGY-MEDIATED CLASSROOM LEARNING AND STUDENTS' SOCIAL PRACTICES WITH NEW TECHNOLOGIES IN HOME AND COMMUNITY SETTINGS

Colin Lankshear and Michele Knobel

Introduction

This final chapter provides theory-based 'snapshots' involving seven Australian school students of different ages and backgrounds as they engage in social practices mediated by electronic technologies in school and out-of-school settings. It is based on research loosely organized as an investigation of the claim that commodified technology amplifies difference. Our theoretical frame takes in larger social, economic, cultural and policy contexts and processes beyond the classroom, home and immediate community. We hope to indicate some of the complexities facing educators who are seriously concerned with issues of equitable education in the electronic age. The study has focused mainly on language and literacy learning, with particular reference to subject English, and has grown out of a wider investigation into elementary school students' understandings and uses of language for social purposes.

Our original pilot study population comprised 275 Year 6 students from 12 Queensland primary schools, representing an urban socio-economic mix, and drawing equally on state, Catholic and Lutheran education systems. Of these students, 36 were chosen for intensive observation and interview, providing the main data for a study funded by the National Language and Literacy Institute of Australia (Knobel and Lankshear 1995). As an extension to this project, one of the authors identified four students to serve as case study subjects for a Ph.D. research project. The students chosen to participate in the Ph.D. study have provided the focus for four of our following 'snapshots'. They are Nicholas, Hannah, Jacques and Layla. All were Year 7 students when the data we draw on here was collected.

The original study and Michele's Ph.D. investigation aim in different ways to examine and compare these students' understandings and uses of language in school and out-of-school settings with particular reference to the six key genres foregrounded in Queensland's P-10 English syllabus (Department of Education, Queensland 1994). Although it was obvious from the outset that electronic game-playing and a range of other language uses and purposes mediated by new technologies would surface in the research, there was no intention to make this a specific focus in either investigation. During 1994–5, however, a combination of institutional, professional and personal factors came together to change our minds on this: notably, the fact that 'technology and literacy' – including 'technological literacies' – was increasingly becoming a curriculum and professional development issue for Australian teachers, education administrators and policymakers. Also we were involved in a federally funded research project to investigate the interface between new technologies and learning language and literacy within classroom settings. Such factors prompted us to broaden the scope of investigation of these four case study subjects to include an additional explicit focus on electronic technologies, and to expand this dimension into a separate, self-contained study. Besides retaining the theme of comparing the students' in-school and out-of-school understandings and uses of language mediated by 'new technologies', we focused increasingly on significant aspects of difference between the four subjects. At the same time we added a new study site by including a Year 11 English class whose teacher was committed to integrating electronic technologies into language and literacy learning as expertly as possible. This addition has provided a further 'snapshot' (Stephen and Nohman).

Finally, we have recently begun adding opportunistically to our research by following up 'interesting' cases of school students engaging with new technologies as they come to our attention. This approach has provided our final 'snapshot' (Alex, with Scott).

So, while we remain interested in the relationship (or lack of it) between new technologies and language and literacy learning both inside and outside classroom settings, we are also increasingly interested in aspects of difference and linkages between (on the one hand) formal policy and syllabus statements pertaining to the development of technological literacies and related 'competencies', and (on the other) actual classroom learning programmes and pedagogies.

President Clinton's Technology Literacy Challenge announcement of 15

February 1996 provided a timely backdrop to this account of our current work. The $2 billion five-year package challenges 'the private sector, schools, teachers, parents, students, community groups, state and local governments, and the federal government' to meet the goal of making all US children 'technologically literate' by 'the dawn of the 21st century'. The strategy comprises four 'pillars' that will ensure all teachers receive the necessary training and support 'to help students learn via computers and the information superhighway', develop 'effective and engaging software and on-line learning resources' as integral elements of school curricula, provide all teachers and students with access to modern computers, and connect every US classroom to the information superhighway (Winters 1996). Without in any way seeking to impugn the presidential initiative – indeed, a proportionate investment by our own federal government would be widely welcomed in Australia – or to suggest there is any direct translation of experience from Australian 'realities' to other national scenes, we believe studies like our own indicate something of the depth and complexity of 'the challenge,' and caution against unrealistic expectations of significantly more equitable opportunities flowing organically from fiscal genuflections at technological fixes.

Data collection

The Year 7 students

The four Year 7 students (aged 12–13) were selected with a view to getting as much diversity as possible among them on the dimensions of socio-economic status, gender, type of family, community, religion, school type and location, and teacher-rated language competence. Two female and two male students were subsequently selected for in-depth study.

Each was observed intensively over a two-week period in school settings (classrooms, playground, assembly hall and library, etc.) and out-of-school settings (home, rollerskating-drome, music lessons, drama club, church, parties, Saturday basketball competition, etc.). Methods and tools used to collect information included observation, written fieldnotes, audiotaped events, interviews, artefact collection (including texts produced by students, plus samples of English textbooks or worksheets used in class), language journals maintained by participants (written and/or audiotaped records of significant language events encountered over the course of one week), and enlisting each participant as a 'researcher' and providing them with personal cassette recorders and audiotapes for recording self-selected language events, and engaging in informal conversations with each participant, their parents and other family members, teachers and other school personnel, friends and classmates. Using a number of standard ethnographic and sociolinguistic methods and tools in data collection allowed optimal access to 'insider' views of classroom literacy learning.

The 'best practice' classroom students

Following a day of in-class observations, student interviews and teacher consultation in a 'best practice' classroom, two male students (aged 14 and 16) in their penultimate year of secondary schooling (Year 11) were selected for more in-depth study. Apart from holding technological expertise constant, our selection emphasized difference as far as possible. Both students were recognized and valued by teachers and peers alike as 'computer experts', and were called on regularly to troubleshoot software glitches or to repair hardware.

Initial observations and fieldnotes were supplemented during subsequent visits by observing these two students at work in class, interacting with teachers, peers and computers, documenting their personal technological histories and aspirations, collecting computer-generated texts they had produced, and interviewing them about their out-of-school practices. Their class teacher (Doug) and members of the school-based computer club to which both belonged were also interviewed about school technology politics and practices.

A second phase of data collection occurred at Queensland University of Technology. Along with Doug and two other members of the school computer club, the two students were videoed over a seven-hour period of use of the Internet (i.e. Netscape browser). Until then they had known about the Internet but had never had a chance to 'surf' it. Besides the video recording, we collected further information by means of observations and fieldnotes, the 'bookmark' feature of the Netscape browsers, a log of the Internet sites the students visited, the software they copied, plus text and graphics they downloaded. A semistructured *group* interview was held at the end of the day.

The 5-year-old 'outlier'

Alex (aged 5), the remaining student in our study, has recently been hailed as 'The World's Youngest Web Builder' (*The Australian*, 6 February 1996). Data was collected about Alex and his father, Scott, a commercial Website designer. Data collection included making visits to Alex's Web pages (http://peg.apc.org/~balson/story), analysing his pages and other postings displayed there, and conducting informal face-to-face and email interviews with Alex and his parents. Newspaper and television stories featuring Alex also were analysed, to identify their public 'construction' of Alex and his technological expertise.

Approach to analysis and interpretation

Mapping events and identifying discourses

Analytic techniques and 'tools' were based on widely reported studies conducted at the intersection of ethnographic study, classroom literacy research, and sociocultural literacy theory (e.g. Heath 1983; Gee 1990; Green and Meyer 1991). To address our research questions it was necessary to identify and describe technological literacy events, and their associated discourses and communities of practice, that occur in the everyday lives of young people, inside and outside the classroom.

Event mapping was used to organize and interpret data (Green and Meyer 1991). An *event* is a set of social practices (including roles and props) and language uses demarcated by shifts in activity, time, location, physical presence or absence, and/or language (Santa Barbara Classroom Discourse Group 1995). Marking boundaries around literacy events recorded in our fieldnotes and transcripts (supported by artefacts, headnotes, etc.) enabled us to examine literacy practices and discourses both in detail and in relation to patterns of technological literacy events across time and context.

Event mapping was also used to identify membership in communities of practice (i.e. patterned and shared ways of talking, dressing, being literate, acting, gesturing, valuing, etc. in particular contexts or around particular objects). We drew on Gee's (1990) notion of Discourses as social practices which amount to 'ways of being in the world' (such as being a teacher, being a student, being a home boy, being a mate, being a computer geek or netgrrl) to further analyse the technological literacy events being mapped.

Using these analytic tools, we were able to identify and examine more or less discrete speech and literacy events within larger social practices and contexts, and to compare classroom events and patterns of events with those occurring in wider settings.

The interpretive frame

This section assembles several ideas and trends as a basis for framing specific 'snapshots' drawing on our data collection and analysis. These are but a small sample of factors and variables that would need to be taken into account in any truly comprehensive study of the present topic.

Contemporary work and life chances

We have seen that working life has changed in 'new times', and that the 'middle' of the old work order has largely disappeared, tending to polarize work quite dramatically. Despite the widespread talk of 'enchanted workplaces' and the increased sophistication of contemporary postindustrial/post-Fordist work over the earlier industrial order with its Taylorist and Fordist modes of control, hierarchy and routinization, the reality is that 'enchanted work' and well-remunerated work is the exception rather than the rule.

We observe here Reich's three broad categories of work that are emerging in modern economies: 'routine production services', 'in-person services' and 'symbolic-analytic services'. (There is, in addition, the large sector of unemployed and underemployed labour.) Symbolic-analytic work involves services which are delivered in the form of data, words and oral and visual representations. It comprises diverse problem-identifying, problem-solving and strategic brokering activities (see Reich 1992: 177). As such, symbolic-analytic services span the work of research scientists, all manner of engineers (from civil to sound), management consultants, investment bankers, systems analysts, authors, editors, art directors, video and film producers, musicians and so on (Gee *et al.* 1996: 47).

This is what is commonly referred to as 'value-adding' work. By contrast, much 'routine production' and 'in-person' service work is not regarded as adding substantial value. The 'collapsed middle' in the new work order is evident in the fact that beyond demands for basic literacy and numeracy (and, often, not even that), such work calls largely for 'reliability, loyalty, and the capacity to take direction, and, in the case of in-person workers, "a pleasant demeanour" ' (p. 47).

The obvious implication, given instantaneous global communications and the proliferation of multinational corporate activity, is that the labour pool for routine service work has become global. Supply and demand logistics, coupled with perceptions of routine work as 'non-value-adding', result in this work being poorly rewarded in comparison with symbolic-analytic work, as well as being generally more peripheral, temporary and insecure. With respect to economies in societies like our own, Reich speaks of a rising one-fifth and a falling four-fifths of earners, calculating that on present trends 'the top fifth of American earners will account for more than 60 per cent of all the income earned by Americans; the bottom fifth 2 per cent' by 2020 (1992: 302). This rising one-fifth is composed largely of symbolic analysts – many of whom, like much of the remainder of the high income bracket, are self-employed. Moreover, indications are that a strictly finite proportion of a modern workforce will be engaged in symbolic-analytic work, and that current levels are at or close to saturation level.

Symbolic-analytic work is closely associated with new technologies and the capacity to integrate them into 'adding value'. This does *not* mean, of course, that *all* work involving dexterity and technical know-how with new technologies is symbolic-analytic work. Much of it is routine. This has important implications for different kinds of acquired and learned abilities

(Krashen 1982; Gee 1991) mediated by and centred around new technologies – whether these acquisitions and learnings occur in school, via the formal curriculum, or out of school.

Combined and uneven curricular guidelines

Two factors are especially relevant to the Queensland context from which our snapshots are drawn. First, so far as technological literacies are concerned, there are important 'silences' in national level curriculum policy statements, and some notable variations between national level statements and state level syllabus guidelines within key learning areas. Second, some troublesome anomalies emerge at the Queensland state level from tensions between syllabus goals and emerging diagnostic assessment procedures.

The following themes are indicative and will almost certainly resonate with 'realities' far beyond their local context.

Australia's National Curriculum Statement for the English key learning area (Curriculum Corporation 1994) is characterized by a near total lack of reference to computer-mediated communications and closely allied technologies, as sources and media of text production, distribution and exchange. A sole reference to computer programs and video games, occurring at the end of a long list of items, is the only indication in the document that sophisticated technologies – already fundamental to vast tracts of economic, leisure, aesthetic and intellectual production worldwide – even exist, let alone that they will increasingly become central to many routine language and literacy events in students' future lives, including many of the most vital. The section on 'Literacy' in the English statement makes no mention whatsoever of electronic media and technological literacies.

In partial – by no means *stark* – contrast, the Queensland English Syllabus for Years 1 to 10 makes several explicit references to the nature and role of new technologies within the social practices and discourses of contemporary life, to which Subject English must respond and be accountable (Department of Education, Queensland 1994: 19, 31, 34, 46, 48). Despite these references, the Queensland Syllabus cannot be said to foreground – or even really to reflect – the extent to which new technologies permeate daily life. The syllabus as a whole is strongly dominated by literary and grammar overtones that maintain an emphasis on conventional print texts and on 'media texts' (read film, print and TV advertisements) over digitally coded texts. Moreover, in the syllabus support materials no explicit references are made to resources, examples, activities or outcomes involving electronic/computer-mediated communications technologies. Hence, the Syllabus does not alert uninitiated teachers to the prevalence and centrality of technological literacies in daily social practices, and it certainly does not send a *strong* message that classroom programmes, school planning, teacher education for prospective language teachers, and in-service professional development should be expanding their horizons in this direction.

The important point here is that whether we focus on the near-silence of the National Curriculum Statement, or on the explicit but still relatively marginal references to language and literacy practices mediated by new technologies in the Queensland English Syllabus, classroom learning opportunities concerning new technologies are likely to be highly uneven, and based on teacher preferences, prior experience and zones of comfort. Those teachers who are inclined to avoid 'the technologies challenge' find endorsement for their stance in the at best marginal acknowledgement of new technologically mediated language and literacy forms; on the other hand, those teachers and schools who want to move in this direction can also feel vindicated. The issue of the new literacies has been consigned to individual teachers and/or school policies. In a context where students' out-of-school lives are increasingly impacted by new technologies, and where student interests, experiences and preferred activities are often centred around new technologies, such unevenness becomes important in terms of equity considerations and pedagogical principles; such principles advocate relating formal learning in productive ways to students' prior experiences and interests.

In Queensland the government has responded to evidence that significant numbers of children experience literacy learning difficulties by introducing a Diagnostic Net in Year 2, designed to catch children 'at risk' and provide them with remedial assistance (Department of Education, Queensland 1995). The conceptions of language and literacy underlying the diagnostic procedures emphasize traditional mechanical encoding and decoding skills, in direct contrast to the meta-linguistic/genre-based ethos of the English Syllabus. It is only to be expected that teachers will increasingly direct their teaching toward the diagnostic procedures – especially in schools serving communities perceived as having large numbers of 'at risk' students. Classroom learning opportunities which integrate new technologies into language and literacy learning seem likely to be further marginalized, especially for those students who least have alternative access to relevant experiences of potentially powerful new literacies.

Syllabus ideals and classroom realities

The Queensland English Syllabus is based on ideas that are, in principle, conducive to developing symbolic-analytic competence. One guiding motif is that if learners are to become powerful language users and controllers of powerful genres, they must develop a meta-level awareness of language: they need to know genres for what they are, and to master those genres which underlie effective participation in everyday life. Teachers are exhorted to make the purposes, generic structures, linguistic features and cultural contexts of text production and functions explicit (Department of Education, Queensland 1994: especially 2, 6, 11, 27–36).

Unfortunately, early assessments of classroom realities – in both New South Wales (where a new state government has axed the genre-based components of the English syllabus) and Queensland – suggest that attainment of the desired meta-level grasp of language is highly uneven, and that much of what teachers are trying to teach is being 'mis-learned'. Our own research (Knobel and Lankshear 1995) indicates that teachers themselves have not been adequately prepared in theoretical and pedagogical terms for handling a genre/meta-type syllabus, and that where students manifest meta-level understandings of language purposes and generic forms, in many cases it probably has less to do with *learning* derived from classroom *teaching*, and more to do with what they have *acquired* from their out-of-school milieux (their 'habitus') (see Bourdieu 1991; Gee 1991: 10).

In-school versus out-of-school practices

Educationists have long observed that what goes on in classroom learning is often very different from what goes on in the lives and learning of children outside school. Moreover, they stress the extent to which school-based learning approximates much more to the discourse universes of some social groups than to others. This impacts powerfully on the extent to which different students can 'make productive or effective use' of school learning and credentialling opportunities.

On the other hand, discrepancies between school learning opportunities and wider social practices may positively advantage groups and individuals who have outside access to highly rewarded practices that are not available via school.

Six 'snapshots'

Nicholas

We met Nicholas (aged 12) in the previous chapter. He attended a large Lutheran primary school. His literacy competence was rated as 'advanced' by his teacher. He belongs to a two-income family: his father is a project manager who coordinates interior designers and his mother teaches business principles at a private secondary school. The family lives in a predominantly white upper-middle-class suburb. As in each of the Year 7 classrooms observed, technological literacies were marginal in Nicholas's class. His classroom (32 students) housed one computer for half the year, and students were rostered in pairs to play educational games. They took their time slots regardless of what else was happening in the wider learning context. The teacher's involvement was confined largely to reprimanding students who were 'mucking around' or who were too noisy while working at the computer.

Nicholas's experience described in the previous chapter highlights what we see as rapidly increasing tensions between technological practices occurring in the classroom and those in students' own 'communities of practice' outside school. Nicholas has much more expertise with computers than his teacher. The teacher freely conceded this in a follow-up interview, but was nonetheless reluctant to give his role as teacher in this area over to Nicholas and other students (female and male), who were obviously more comfortable with using computers and a range of software applications, and who had gained this expertise in practices outside the classroom. Our observations in numerous classrooms beyond this study suggest that Nicholas's situation is by no means unusual. In such cases, students' access to expert performance through which to acquire and learn the bases for competence in technology-mediated social practices is entirely dependent on what they have available to them within home and community settings. This is a potent source of difference and inequality among young people.

Nicholas was especially advantaged in terms of access to expert performance learning opportunities across a range of practices and computing facilities. He was part of a complex computer gaming network that spanned age peers from school and church youth groups, his older siblings and their friends. They exchanged software and gaming tips, and members travelling abroad were charged with bringing back information about recent releases and software not available locally. By participating in this informal network Nicholas acquired a specialized language for understanding and talking about electronic technologies and particular computer-mediated practices, an understanding of technical aspects of different forms of hardware and software, knowledge of diverse relevant information sources, and considerable finesse in using a range of these. A typical exchange between Nicholas and his older brother, while playing an electronic sports game, covered discussion of computer processing speeds, modem types and speeds, disk capacities and quality, bulletin boards and Web browsers.

In addition, his parents were sophisticated mentors of high status technology-mediated practices, and enthusiastic and generous providers of electronic wherewithal. His father used a state-of-the-art Apple computer at home in his interior design and engineering work, although it was the powerful word processing program that Nicholas used most once he had negotiated his way past other family members to access it. His mother modelled expert performance in key aspects of text production across a range of school genres. During one event observed at home in the study she addressed matters of formatting and layout (font choice, indenting), grammar, organization of ideas (use of sub-headings, some of which she would actually identify and key in to help Nicholas structure his information as a text), academic conventions (glossary and use of multiple reference sources) and generic structure.

Debra: Why don't you just make that a direct quote?
Nicholas: What's that?
Debra: Where you copy something straight from the book.
Nicholas: Is that what you call it? How do you do that?
Debra: Just put it in quotation marks. Just put that [pointing to text on screen] in quotation marks.
Nicholas: Do I write where it's from?
Debra: Mm-hm [pause]. Do you use the Harvard method of bibliography, or not? Where you've got to put the brackets around it?
Nicholas: Yeah, that's it. Yep.

Debra's conviction that computer literacies are crucial for Nicholas's generation was nowhere more evident than in the fact that during his first year at school she would give him a few cents every time he practised touch typing. He mastered this early and is now highly proficient.

Hannah

Hannah (aged 12) attended a large state primary school. Her literacy competence was rated by her teacher as 'above average'. She belonged to a single-income family. Her father was in charge of delivery rosters for a soft drink company and drove delivery trucks. Her mother administered the household and did a lot of voluntary work at Hannah's school. They lived in a strongly working-class suburb whose general locale is renowned as being one of the toughest areas in the city. Hannah was in a double classroom (54 students and two teachers) which shared a lab of eight computers with another Year 7 class. The computer lab was used in part for gender-segregated classes on 'sensitive subjects', as well as for other purposes and subjects in which the computers were invisible. When the computers were used it was mainly for word processing, playing educational games (e.g. 'Where in the world is Carmen Sandiego?', and for publishing student texts as part of 'process writing'. Hence, the computer as a curriculum and pedagogical 'add-on' prevailed. During the data collection period, the lab was used mainly by one of Hannah's two teachers (male) to compose, collate and lay out the school magazine. Occasionally, he was assisted by two female students who scanned students' photographs into computer files for the teacher to later manipulate and reprint.

There was no computer in Hannah's home, and despite Hannah's eagerness there was not going to be one until her (non-scholastic) older brother's grades improved. Furthermore, Hannah's abhorrence of her brother's infatuation with violent video/computer games meant that, unlike Layla (see below), she did not engage new technologies outside of class. Hannah presents a 'snapshot' of an above-average student in a working-class school, who uses spoken and written language well, having no effective access to technologically mediated language and literacy practices beyond the minimal 'add-on' varieties available in her classroom.

Jacques

Jacques (aged 13) attended a large state primary school. His teacher described him as experiencing much difficulty with literacy at school. He belongs to a self-employed single-income family. Jacques' father runs an earth-moving business, while his mother administers the home and is heavily involved in volunteer church work. The family lives in a predominantly white executive neighbourhood.

There was no computer in Jacques' classroom. His teacher lamented 'poor decision making' (prior to the time she began working at the school) which established a computing lab stocked with little-known machines for which no up-to-date software was available, and which broke down regularly, requiring costly and time-consuming repairs. She had given up trying to use them. All but three of her 30 students had computer access at home, and she occasionally set word processing tasks for homework.

Jacques loathed school, and was patiently 'doing time' until he could leave in Year 10 and work with his father. He found the world of adult work far more compelling than school. He insisted he was 'not a pen man', and could not see any point in going to school. During class, Jacques would engineer elaborate strategies and ruses for evading school work, particularly where there was any writing involved. Indeed, his teacher bemoaned his treatment of the 'Writers' Centre', in the corner of the classroom, where Jacques had recently spent two hours stapling together a miniature book on which he subsequently wrote two or three words per page – effectively 'sending up' the process-writing approach adopted in this classroom.

There was a computer at home, which was mainly used by Jacques' father for keeping records and accounts. Jacques, too, used it for business purposes. With some editorial help from his mother and brother, he designed and published a flier advertising 'JPs Mowing Service'. The flier was remarkable for its business-like language and practices: 'efficient reliable service', 'all edging done', and 'for free quote phone . . .' It was printed, photocopied and dropped in neighbourhood letterboxes, and Jacques had soon established a thriving mowing business over the summer holidays.

This 'snapshot' juxtaposes Jacques' home literacy practice against his classroom practice. At home he integrates a computer into a discourse to which he has been apprenticed and with which he feels an affinity. This is a business discourse, which was certainly marginal to the point of being invisible in class during the period of data collection, yet which is a powerful discourse so far as adult life is concerned. The technology-mediated literacy which Jacques engaged at home, although he finds typing laborious, is likewise a potentially powerful literacy, assuming an enterprise (sub)culture. This contrasts markedly with his response to school literacy practices where, if computers were employed, he would probably reject them in the same way that he rejected the technologies (pen and paper) of conventional print.

Layla

Layla (aged 12) attended a very large Catholic school. Her literacy competence was rated 'average' by her teacher. She belongs to a two-income family (her father ran his own tiling business, and her mother worked part-time as a medical secretary) living in a predominantly white lower-middle/middle-class suburb. Layla and her brother, Jason, rented Nintendo games each week. Jason also had a close group of friends who played Nintendo regularly and swapped 'cheats' garnered from their magazine reading. At the time of the study, Layla's family intended buying a computer for Christmas.

Although there was a computer in Layla's classroom it was not used during the period of observation. The Year 7 class next door had a computer with a modem connection, and Layla was observed using this computer during a session intended to formally introduce students to email. During this session Layla sat in front of the computer, with two female and two male classmates grouped in a semicircle around her. The computer was attached to an external modem, and Layla's teacher, Mr Wills, gave the group instructions about how to switch on the modem and dial up Keylink headquarters, using the computer software and keyboard.

Keylink is an Australian 'technology in education' initiative designed to introduce students to computer-mediated communication. Keylink runs these programmes regularly. During the first email session the task was for the group to collect and decipher a cryptic clue sent by another school as their first step in making their way around Australia to track down a (virtual) criminal. In subsequent sessions they used email to send and gain further clues about the gradually unfolding trail mapped out for each participating school by headquarters. Students used an atlas and did other research work in the course of composing their cryptic email messages and deciphering clues that were in turn sent to them.

Mr Wills pointed to a list of instructions he had written on sheets of paper that morning and stuck to the wall above the computer terminal. He talked the students through each step, instructing Layla what to key in, as the others looked on, increasingly offering advice or corrections. At times Layla hesitated or looked confused, until someone helped her out, then she laughed and continued. Mr Wills explained passwords and usernames, sending and receiving mail, organizing mailboxes, session menus, file capturing, creating files, scroll bars, the mouse, printing in 'economy' mode, and closing down connections, all the while reminding the group that they needed to work quickly because 'time is money'. The telephone line was shared with the school administration, and the students were told that administrative staff always had 'right of way' on this line. The log-on process was repeated, this time with a different keyboarder. Mr Wills talked about 'agreeing to pretend' they were detectives following a trail of clues, using non-sexist language in their messages, and about managing information.

They opened their electronic mailbox and found their first clue: 'Criminal was overheard talking about travelling north to gamble'. They began discussing possible answers, then moved to tables to look through descriptions sent in earlier by participating schools and downloaded that morning by Mr Wills. At different times they used atlases to check a 'suspected' school's location. Everybody made notes as they went, and discussed possibilities with each other, before finally agreeing that the message referred to a school in Townsville (where there is a casino). Using pen and paper, they drafted an email message, or as Mr Wills called it, a 'letter' . The group logged on again, and keyed in their edited letter. Mr Wills demonstrated how to send messages, and drew their attention again to the instructions pinned to the wall.

During the next four weeks this group logged in and checked their mailbox during non-lesson times (e.g. before school, lunchtime, etc.), decoded clues, and passed on information to other participating schools. None of this work was otherwise linked to classroom work or events. Layla said she enjoyed participating, although she didn't quite understand why she was doing it, or how it all worked.

While schools are coming under increasing pressure to introduce new technologies into their curriculum, teachers are very often poorly prepared for doing this in any integrated way. Often, the result is just one more 'add-on'. Students engage in established learning activities, except that computers are added on – as, for example, where students write a narrative and then key it in using a computer and a word processing package. While this contributes to students acquiring keyboard skills and, perhaps, operating spelling and grammar checkers, it does not constitute an initiation into full-fledged forms of computer-mediated composition and communication. Entirely new social practices with their characteristic embedded languages and literacies are emerging apace around new technologies. Many of these are tomorrow's powerful literacies: for example, Web pages as commercial advertising and information ventures, infotainment genres, conducting business by email, etc.

Effective integration of new technologies into worthwhile and engaging forms of learning presupposes theoretical finesse and knowledge of authentic social practices associated with these technologies, which many teachers currently lack. Mastery, fruitful experimentation, testing the borders of contemporary usages, inventing new social practices and technology-mediated literacies, etc., call for knowledge and a good theoretical grasp of authentic practices every bit as much here as they do in other pursuits (e.g. to be a good postmodern theorist one must have mastered modernist theory). Unfortunately, the necessary theoretical grasp and knowledge of authentic social practices in which new technologies are embedded cannot be acquired merely by means of 'quick fix' in-service and professional development packages.

Even though a range of technology-mediated literacy practices operated in the Year 7 classrooms, including Layla's, they were typically of an 'add-on' nature, such as Nicholas producing his sports report. When potential opportunities arose to use technologies in 'real-world' ways within classrooms – such as email, which has become an organic part of academic and economic production in many countries – they were reduced to 'school' exercises, preventing students making ready links between what they were learning in the way of technological literacies at school, and what they might need in their (future) lives beyond school.

Stephen and Nohman

Stephen and Nohman were students in Doug's Year 11 English classroom, which we identify as a 'best practice' classroom so far as integrating new technologies (video, film, graphics as well as computer-mediated communications) into English teaching is concerned. Doug had designed a unit of work, 'Investigating Social Issues', which called for teams of students to use the Microsoft Publisher program to produce texts using a range of genres to be addressed in Year 11, and which approximated as closely as possible to texts which would be produced within the corresponding authentic social practices in the world beyond the classroom, e.g. an invitation, newsletter, TV report, radio interview, etc. The social issues and problems from which a topic theme was to be selected and researched as a focus for producing and presenting the texts included youth homelessness, drug abuse, discrimination (race, age, gender), social violence, unemployment, and the like. This unit of work came with a unit outline which identified the main steps in the text production process: defining the area, planning, structuring, and researching (including framing key questions, and suggestions for information sources).

The school was heavily technologized by local standards, having 350 new computers for 1200 students. A bank of specialized machines had been installed in a simulated Business Learning Centre. In addition, four computer labs, each with 20–26 computers had been linked in a local area network, and some access to a server was available via a nearby university. Doug had Internet access at home and had organized his teaching around the (to that time unfulfilled) expectation that classes would be linking to the Internet. (The fear of students accessing pornography had delayed this up to the time of data collection.) His students used computers in a range of other school subjects, and some of them were adept at programming.

Doug's English class used a computer lab comprising 15 machines arranged down two walls with a line of three machines in the middle of the room. There was a computer-free area of desks and benches, and space for video and other equipment to be used. Doug's desk was set apart from the machines. Students had been organized into work teams of three or four. In the classes we observed, Doug alternately moved around the class observing practice, and sat at his desk to 'consult' with team members on tasks and processes involved in their work. His consultation focused very much on providing explicit links between the meta-language of the genres involved in the tasks – making explicit the purposes, linguistic features, social context, structure, etc. of the particular genres (invitations, reports, etc.) – and the concrete tasks in which the students were engaged, the stage of the task they were at, and the degree of expertise (or lack of it) they were demonstrating thus far. In this way he could add substance to and explain the guidelines provided in the unit outline.

The students did relevant research (e.g. about racism) using school and community-based resources, in class time and for homework, and used class time for working together as a production and refinement team – especially, using the computers and printers to do what they might not be able to do out of class. (Of course, Doug's plan to use the Internet as a main information source could not happen.)

Stephen was 14 years old, having skipped two grades of school along the way. His parents had separated five years previously; his father lived in New South Wales, and Stephen stayed with his mother in Queensland during the school year. He was very articulate, as well as having sophisticated computer knowledge and technical expertise. His main hobby was ray tracing, which draws heavily on fractal mathematics principles. There had been computers in his home for several years, and as a 12-year-old he had taken apart and reassembled his father's modem, to understand how it worked and to assess the chances of making one for himself. He belonged to the school computer club, and was a trusted 'troubleshooter and fixer' of school computer glitches. From the age of 7 he had received 'passed down' computers from his father, a systems programmer with Telstra (Telecom), who upgraded his home computer regularly. Stephen's father gave him books to read on computer programming, and Stephen began teaching himself Basic at the age of 7. While his father provided books and hardware, Stephen did not recall receiving any direct explicit computer-related teaching from his father. At the time of the study Stephen had an enhanced 386 PC-type machine which ran Windows 95.

Nohman was a 'new Australian', who had arrived in Australia from Iran three years previously. He knew practically no English (other than greetings) when he arrived in Australia. After a brief period of immersion in an English-learning centre for migrants, Nohman moved into the 9th grade of high school. After three years he spoke fluent, though accented, English. He claimed he could not always express his ideas fully in English, but said this applied to technical pursuits in school, not to our interviews and conversations. His father had been a qualified mechanic and electrician in Iran, his mother a grade 1 teacher. In Australia they were marginally employed, by friends, for whom they painted Aboriginal icons on to souvenir boomerangs. Nohman worked from 4 p.m. until 8 or 8.30 p.m., seven evenings a week all year round as a kitchen hand in a local restaurant. His first serious engagement with electronic technologies was upon arrival in Australia through his cousin who had emigrated earlier. After a year in Australia Nohman bought the 386 PC computer he still had at the time of the study, but which he hoped to upgrade since it cannot run Windows efficiently. Nohman had acquired his knowledge and competence with electronic technologies largely through learning by doing, on his own and with peers. Outside of school he mainly used his computer 'to design pictures', often for school assignments, and to play games. While his father had some computer training in Iran, it was 'only for typing and spreadsheets' involved in his work. Like Stephen, Nohman was a computer club member and a trusted 'troubleshooter and fixer' around the school. He spent as much time as possible during breaks and immediately after school using the school computers in activities as varied as producing school work and engaging in harmless elementary 'hacking'.

The 'snapshot' of Stephen and Nohman is drawn from a day spent using equipment at the Queensland University of Technology. On this day Doug brought four students with him to take up an invitation to 'have a day on the Internet'. These students shared Doug's frustration that school access to the Internet had been delayed. They had planned to establish an on-line bulletin board and had raised money for that through the computer club. It now seemed that the money would be spent purchasing a scanner. We were happy to provide an opportunity for them to spend a sustained period of time on the Net – during which time, needless to say, they would contribute to our own research purposes (which were also of interest to Doug). The students spent seven hours exploring the Internet around their personal interests, with information and suggestions from Doug and ourselves being available on request. As noted above, the students kept a log of where they went and what they did on the Net, and much of their activity was video recorded. We also showed them how to use Netscape's bookmark function, to provide a further record of trails taken.

Stephen and Nohman's self-directed activities were significantly different. Nohman's exploration emphasized technique and the search for information. Much of his time was spent gathering information – browsing Playboy pages, visiting President Clinton, etc. The rest of his time was mainly taken up in MOOs where he engaged in a series of short-lived 'conversations' with partners from around the globe. He was less interested in mastering the full gamut of the MOO – learning the moves and exploring all the available spaces – than with 'making the technology work' enough to establish that it was in fact possible to 'talk' with someone in New York in a MOO and download chunks of information from an Internet site in Finland. Stephen, by contrast, spent most of his time downloading utilities that could be used in ray tracing. He combined his theoretical and conceptual understanding of ray tracing with his technical skills and knowledge that the Internet was a source of useful resources for his hobby. He went home with a disk full of utilities to use with a powerful ray tracing program that creates the effect of things moving. He also downloaded examples of other people's ray tracing products to learn from and to integrate into his own home-based activities.

Our interest in these differences was sharpened by the semistructured interview conducted at the end of the day involving Stephen, Nohman, ourselves, one of our colleagues (Paul), Doug, and the other two students. In the sub-event in question, only Stephen and Nohman of the students participated. The topic concerned how they would organize material garnered from the Internet for use in a school assignment.

Transcript

Large event:	Four students spend a day at the university using the Internet
Smaller event:	Discussing their experiences on the Internet
This event:	Stephen and Nohman (ESL) describing how they would organize material garnered from the Internet to complete a school assignment
Site:	University classroom
Date:	July 1995

01	*Paul*:	I was just wondering, you've got all this information, how are you going to decide what's useful?
02	*Stephen*:	It depends what sort of information it is.
03	*Nohman*:	And then you just go through it again at home using your own computer. Just take out all the ones you don't need.
04	*Paul*:	What are you using to decide what you're going to keep?

05	*Stephen*:	Well it depends what you're intending it to be used for. Like if it was pictures and you decide you just want to have them sit there you just gotta have something that you want – like if you want to use them in Windows you don't want something that you desperately hate, and so anything like that would be useless for you.
06	*Paul*:	So if you were using . . . if you found lots and lots of stuff for an assignment, how are you going to decide what to keep?
07	*Stephen*:	Well, probably which is more – most relevant.
08	*Nohman*:	Which has more information.
09	*Stephen*:	No, which is more relevant – it doesn't matter how much there is.
10	*Paul*:	Yeah . . . to what?
11	*Stephen*:	Oh . . . to the topic that you're researching.
12	*Paul*:	Okay.
13	*Colin*:	So how do you decide that?
14	*Stephen*:	Oh well you have to look at the question and analyse what . . . yeah what this information's about and then see if it will be useful and keep on thinking about it.
15	*Nohman*:	Or exactly what you need.
16	*Paul*:	So now you've decided 'I'm going to keep this information because it's relevant to the topic', what are you going to do with it?
17	*Stephen*:	Ah well . . .
18	*Nohman*:	Use it.
19	*Stephen*:	Yeah, use it . . . well you have to . . . extract bits from it, and rewrite it and sort of go to other sources and look up things.
20	*Nohman*:	A bit of this and a bit of that and put it all together.
21	*Paul*:	How would the teacher know which was yours and which was the Internet material?
22	*Stephen*:	If you put footnotes in . . . or you could put bibliographies in like obtained from this part of the Internet, from this area, this file etc., or footnotes and then he knows.
23	*Paul*:	Yep.
[Interrupted]		
24	*Paul*:	So, can I get you to think forward now, you've got an assignment topic. Would you like to describe how you'd use – and you can all chip in here – how do you think you'd use the Internet to get a finished product? What do you think would be the steps you'd go through?
25	*Stephen*:	Well first, you'd probably do a search, until you get some very broad criteria about what you were searching for, then

after that you'd just have to sift through what the search had come up with, and sort of pick out things that have anything to do with the topic, and just sort of put them aside, and then you can go through it really detailed and cut out bits that you want . . . then probably –

26 *Nohman*: Any pictures that you think are [part of the topic]

27 *Stephen*: Then you get information from other places like books and things.

28 *Nohman*: Well, if you really couldn't find . . . if you've got like – well that's what I do, if I couldn't find much I'd look in the books . . . there's so much choice there.

29 *Stephen*: And then you sort of all just compile it together and hand it in.

While both had equal speaking rights and ample opportunity to articulate their views, only Stephen provided evidence of an analytic, meta-level grasp of the operations involved in the assignment writing discourse. Their respective responses parallel in an interesting way the differences between their respective activities during the day. For all their similarities – both are bright, technologically adept, share an exemplary teacher, and are passionately interested in new technologies and their associated social practices – their interview responses indicated a very significant difference. In Stephen, we believe, we encounter the emerging symbolic analyst of true aptitude. He seems already to have been well apprenticed to social practices and theoretical understandings of symbolic analysis.

Alex (and Scott)

Alex is 5 years old. He began school recently. He reads and writes conventional texts, but much of his text production is computer mediated. As mentioned earlier, Alex has his own Website, 'Alex's Scribbles – Koala Trouble' (Balson and Balson 1996), which he produces with the assistance of his father, Scott. Alex creates the images for stories featuring Max, a young koala bear. To date eight Max stories have been published on the site, with more in process. All employ a simple hypertext format, with instructions (typically in the form of clues) about where to click to move to the next page. Alex produces the drawings by hand as a story sequence in the manner of a 'storyboard' and, with help from Scott, scans them into a PC and colours them using a graphics program, 'Animator Pro'. The page includes a feedback link enlisting active involvement of other children from around the world. Their collaboration takes two main forms. Many send email messages to Alex's page responding to the stories. Others also 'host' Max on his new 'round the world trip' – by sending back to Alex and Scott pictures, stories and ideas about Max visiting and having adventures in their part of the world, to be added to the page.

The idea behind the page is to promote cooperative activity by children who are stimulated by material designed and drawn by their peers (beginning with Alex): the page is a global classroom as seen through the eyes of children, based on information delivered by children for children in a format they can relate to. Alex is described by Scott as 'a mean Net surfer' who finds most of the material on the Net 'boring' – hence the 'Alex's Scribbles – Koala Trouble' Web, 'a page for kids (of all ages)'. Alex's page registered more than 60,000 'hits' – national and international – during January and February 1996. Among the accolades for 'Koala Trouble' are included an 'awesome page' rating from *Kids on the Net* author, Brendan Kehoe, a 'must see' rating from *Yahoo*, and a 'wonderful' from *Berit's Best Sites for Children*. Alex replies personally to all his email, often by typing 'Alex', leaving the message to Scott, and hitting the 'send' button. With so many messages to reply to, there is a risk – which Scott is keen to avoid – of Alex becoming bored with and alienated from the medium. At 5, there are other things to do!

Scott completed Year 12 aged 15, but never went on to tertiary education. He admits to hating conventional study with a passion. After being retrenched from a computer-related sales position, Scott began a computer-based marketing industry in his tool shed in 1990. By 1994 he had formed four companies involved in all areas of multimedia (touch screen kiosks to floppy disk-based presentations). His clients have included some major national, international, and multinational companies in areas as diverse as air transportation, banking and newspapers, as well as government departments. After doing a computer-based presentation of his 'vision for the electronic community of the future' to a city council in Queensland, Scott was contracted to set up that city's electronic network. At the end of his contract, Scott established Global Web Builders (GWB), a company which builds commercial Webs for clients. GWB's home page is called 'The Definitive Lifestyle Guide to Australian Webs' (DLG) (Balson/Global Web Builders 1996), and is found at http://www.gwb.com.au/gwb/guide.html. It attracts an enormous amount of global traffic and is today the Australian gateway on the Internet, registering more than 360,000 national and international hits in the week 5–12 February 1996.

The DLG concept is now being franchised globally through a multinational company called GLOBE (Global Online Business Enterprises) International. GLOBE International have sites in New Zealand and are in the process of signing up GLOBE Asia, with nine Asian countries participating. 'Koala Trouble' is a specific niche market (i.e. families and kids) on the DLG and is one of a number of niche market content-based Webs generating traffic for it.

Scott laments the fact that at school 'they play silly games on computers', adding 'that's fine for a start', but maximum use of the Internet 'within a controlled project-based environment must be part of the very early curriculum' if children's education for life in the information age is not to be stunted. According to Scott, Alex's 'Scribbles' site is much more than just a Web: 'it's a major educational "lifestyle" opportunity for Alex', comprising the hub of an electronic community of Internet users who receive monthly email newsletters on what's up at 'Alex's Scribbles – Koala Trouble', and who reciprocate with email correspondence, much of it from school classes in the US.

The company was approached by the Australian Koala Foundation (AKF), and the two have collaborated to produce a line of T-shirts which carry Alex's pictures of Max as well as the Alex's Scribbles URL. Sale of the T-shirts provides funds for the AKF, and Alex's Scribbles receives a share of the profits. 'With our email list we have a ready market and credibility through the AKF. Alex at 5 has a business. I registered Alex's Scribbles last week. I (on Alex's behalf) have entered into preliminary arrangements on a profit share of the Koala Trouble T-shirts' (Scott in email interview, 29 February 1996). Looking beyond schooling to Alex's education for his later years, Scott emphasizes the relevance of the discursive logic which is integral to their joint activity, namely, 'global contacts, global perspective, product line, business based on his [i.e. Alex's] work, and new opportunities as he embraces the technology' (email interview, 29 February 1996). The joint venture was launched publicly on 19 April 1996, and in September 1996 'Alex's Scribbles – Koala Trouble' won Best Web Site for Children up to 15 years in the Inaugural Australian Internet Awards.

Conclusions/implications

These snapshots are, of course, radically incomplete. Even as highly partial windows on the educational experiences and circumstances of the students involved, they merit considerably more detailed development than is possible here. Nonetheless, we believe they reflect specific *new* aspects of important trends and processes with which educators who are on the lookout for such things are generally familiar. Certainly, they give us cause to be cautious in our expectations of outcomes when we consider initiatives as bold as President Clinton's Technology Literacy Challenge, or even their 'country cousin' equivalents – such as one Australian state government's plan to put 90,000 new laptop computers in classrooms during the next three years and to give in-service training to 30,000 teachers in the curricular applications of new technologies.

The snapshots exemplify at least some of the following considerations:

• Highly uneven practices associated with new technologies are evident from classroom to classroom. Even allowing for the gap between Year 7 and

Year 11 we found nothing in our twelve Year 7 classrooms that approximated in equivalent terms to Doug's classroom so far as computer-mediated communication technologies are concerned. The Year 7 teacher (Mr Wills) whose capacity to handle the meta-level aspects of the Queensland English syllabus via conventional print media most closely approximated Doug's pedagogy in sophistication, was quite out of his depth (and was poorly served in terms of resources and curricular suggestions) when it came to new technology-mediated literacies.

● Out-of-school access to expert performance and mentoring in respect of literacy practices mediated by new technologies is grossly uneven (Alex, Stephen and Nicholas vs. the rest).

● These days Jacques would probably have been caught in the Diagnostic Net at Year 2 level and subjected to years of some packaged remedial nightmare or other – of which several are currently in contention in the different Australian states – which would doubtless have alienated him even beyond the level we observed. What school-based literacy remediation could offer him in terms of life chances by comparison with the benefits conveyed by his home-based apprenticeship to an entrepreneurial discourse that adds enormous value to his reluctant and modest (technologically mediated) literacy practices probably does not bear serious contemplation. Certainly, Jacques' parents are not at all concerned about his school performance, being convinced that he is going to be a successful owner and operator of a business. Interestingly, as a teenage entrepreneur running an in-person service enterprise, Jacques has analysed many of its core language and literacy elements (symbols) and put them to effective use. The relationship between being able to analyse symbols effectively (in some sense) and functioning as a symbolic analyst is not straightforward. Nor is the relationship between language and literacy education, symbolic analysis, and economic life chances. These complexities will almost certainly repay serious investigation.

● To what extent do/can schools on their own prepare students for excellence as symbolic analysts in the electronic age? Many can doubtless do better than they manage at present, given improved appropriate preservice and in-service teacher preparation. Other things being equal, however, the Stephens and Alexes have a clear head start. The situation is especially confounded at present in places where renewed 'back to basics' policies are evident.

● There are massive differences between teachers' understanding of 'new literacies and technologies' and their interrelatedness. Such differences prevent students experiencing continuity in their experiences of (new) technology-mediated classroom learning. It is common to hear of students who have had extensive exposure to new literacies and technologies in one school, or school level, moving to another whereupon their progress in this area is promptly arrested.

- Teachers who have not 'grown up around contemporary technologies' would require prolonged professional development opportunities to acquire anything approximating genuine mastery of/expertise in technology-mediated social practices which are assuming increased power and significance in daily life. Those who have a good meta-level understanding of language and literacy as social practices – which are always to a greater or lesser extent mediated by some technology or another – have a head start on those who do not. They may also have a head start on teachers who have 'technique' but who nonetheless lack the meta-knowledge to 'add value' to that technique.
- Since several of the teachers in our overall study population were relatively young, it is a reasonable guess that teacher education programmes are out of date as far as new literacies and technologies are concerned.

This is, in multiple senses, a partial study. Our cases are not necessarily typical or representative, although we believe they are reasonably indicative of much that goes on in classroom, home and community settings. Certainly, our theoretical and normative selections here have been partial. There is, for instance, an 'economic' motif evident in this chapter that we have not questioned, and which surely does not comprise the only – or even the primary – guiding value for school education. Neither is it an educational value to which are we especially wedded. We are, however, mindful that we state this from the standpoint of individuals who *are* economically advantaged, and who are economically advantaged precisely because we perform symbolic analytic work that is mediated in crucial ways by new technologies and draws on our relative mastery of some new literacies.

Moreover, we are mindful that for many parents much of the time, the contribution education can make to the future economic viability and security of their children ranks high in their perceptions of school legitimacy and of the capacity of schooling to promote equitable outcomes for learners. What is more, very many school age learners voice precisely these perceptions. These same parents and students are also often aware of social, economic and cultural changes that add up to the growth and consolidation of 'an information society'. Their calculations of a 'good and equal education' do, and probably *should*, assume that good quality curricular and pedagogical encounters with new technologies and literacies are an important element of such an education.

Taken together, our implications and 'conclusions' strongly suggest that any hopes for 'quick fixes' of existing inequities in respect of opportunities to master new technologies and literacies are misplaced. Our prediction is that we are facing considerably more problems than the $2 billion provided for the US Technology Literacy Challenge will solve. While welcoming presidential initiatives we must also look to larger and wider aspects of the situation, many of which are not addressed simply, or even significantly, by throwing money, technology, or technique at visible symptoms.

CONCLUSION

In the preceding pages I have tried to traverse a wide spread of existential, experiential and geographic terrain, in the course of interrogating what are for me some landmark features of changing literacies in recent times.

At some steps removed – and here I commend readers to the inspiring original accounts – we have acknowledged the Trackton and Roadville folk described by Shirley Brice Heath, Patricia Irvine's freshmen students in the Virgin Islands, and a 7-year-old storyteller, Leona, together with the Discourses they operated out of respectively, and those they had to negotiate within their secondary settings. We have likewise acknowledged the students of 5M and 5S in Alison Jones's study, and have encountered at closer range the worlds of folk manufacturers in San José, high school students in Brisbane classrooms, and a father and son engaged in building and bridging worlds on the Internet. These discursive worlds span bedtime storybook reading, pen and paper-based activities within school class-rooms, special-purpose seminars for peasant producers, electronic game-playing in out-of-school settings, computer technology-mediated text productions in and out of school, and global interchanges on the World Wide Web.

In each case we find literacies – whether more or less 'traditional' or (post)modern – always embedded in social practices/Discourses, and we find these same literacies 'brokering' opportunities and outcomes. We see people coordinating elements within Discourses, and being coordinated in turn within Discourses. We see difference and diversity. And we find difference and diversity being channelled into hierarchies of outcomes and life chances, according to orders of dominant and subordinate Discourses;

these are in turn ordered through the discursive 'work' of human agents as bearers of roles (coordinators of elements) within Discourses, and brokers of power produced within the play of these Discourses. We have found little evidence of fairly distributed rewards for effort and other investments in social practices. On the contrary, we find differential 'legacies' contingent upon being apprenticed to some Discourses rather than others. In all, we have seen a range of consequences of social productions of power, the fickle contingencies attending these productions, and their impact on the prospects of individuals and groups. In the case of San José, we have seen functional powers of literacy obliterated at the stroke of a policy pen, and with that the devastation of futures: analogous, perhaps, to the fears of disempowerment currently facing 'maestros' of conventional print literacies as digital texts move imperialistically to usurp 'text space'.

In many ways it is a disheartening story, not least because we seem to have entered an age when belief has waned in the efficacy of 'big projects', like the Sandinista Revolution, or even a planned economy that ensures dignified paid work for all. With that waning we face the loss of our most familiar vision of how to pursue a more just and expansive world.

We do well to avoid the deleterious effects of political and moral subordination to those modernist enactments of grand narratives which end up 'forcing people to be free and (more) equal'. It is equally clear, however, that we face grave risks to prospects of human dignity and fulfilment by blindly worshipping at the altar of 'fast capitalism' and trusting to the vicissitudes of labour markets finding their 'natural' levels in the new work order. And, as the case of San José reveals all too clearly, attending to the micro setting on its own is not enough.

Where, then, lies a better path? There are no easy answers, quick fixes or magic bullets here. We certainly cannot expect 'Education' alone to do the job. History has been a long time in the making, and building new and more expansive human (and humanizing) histories is a long-term task. Amid the successes and defeats and the 'long odds' depicted in earlier pages we find, I believe, some clues as to where some likely paths may lie – at least so far as educators are concerned.

Although teachers, schools and education generally cannot make it 'all right', there are nonetheless crucial things educators can and should be doing in quest of better times. These begin with engaging in, and engaging learners in, practices of critical literacy. In particular, to use Jim Gee's idea from the Foreword, we need to develop proficiency in 'juxtaposing Discourses'; in identifying competing Discourses and observing how they 'frame' and 're-frame' various elements; and in sorting out those Discourses that 'cut off context' and thereby 'cut off meaning' before meaning 'gets social and political'. The larger, long-term project – to which this book hopefully contributes a share – is to create a new Discourse, with a new community of human elements, that has as its goal the re-framing of elements, human and otherwise, in the name of social justice and more humane treatment for all, human and non-human, as well.

(Gee, this volume: xviii)

AFTERWORD
Chris Searle

There is much to learn and give cause for intense reflection in the preceding pages. Colin Lankshear and his cooperators, Jim Gee and Michele Knobel, have crossed many a landscape in their labours. I found myself repeatedly stopping in my pursuit of them by reading, applying them to my own situation as a British inner city teacher, and considering the import of their insights for my own practice and that of my students. For there is nothing finite in the ideas and imaginings of literacy in this book. Exemplars and lessons from Australia, Nicaragua and Britain spark a process of powerful meaning and value for teachers and learners, and those who form a part of the community of education everywhere.

As I read *Changing Literacies* I wrote down theme phrases and sentences that stayed in my mind for direct application to my own work: 'Human beings are literally born into cultural participation'; 'Literacies are myriad'; 'Language is deeply and inescapably bound up with producing, reproducing and maintaining arrangements for power which are unequal'; the new responsibilities for teachers to ensure that they and their students 'interrogate what they encounter in cyberspace'. These conceptualizations and the meanings they carry are profound and vital: around them centre the future of language, its critical significance as a tool for learning and the uses that we and our children make of it. To these ends, Lankshear and his friends have pioneered and articulated many questions and issues to which we shall constantly return during the remaining years of this century and beyond. They have suggested an agenda for literacy and learning to help us in the relentless search for strategies and answers.

But I must respond to the book in my own way, as all other readers will do in theirs, letting – as the Grenadian calypsoian The Flying Turkey once sang –

'our consciousness be our guide' through its pages. In 1971 I edited an anthology of poems by my students at a secondary school in east London. From among these *Stepney Words*, an anonymous 12-year-old wrote of his expectations:

> I am just a boy
> with a lot of dreams
> but what's the point
> I won't get nowhere
> I'm just ordinary
> nothing special just
> ordinary
> Got no chance in this
> world unless you're
> clever
> which I'm not[1]

This poem has haunted me this last quarter-century, ever since it was left on a nameless sheet of paper in a Stepney classroom. The act of publishing such a message of despair filled me with doubt and worry, despite the pertinence of the young poet's anguish. Should we not be setting down in print only statements of hope, of unambiguous commitment and combative will to learn? Should we be exposing such testimonies of distraught loss and oppression? But where would truth be then? For within that same 25 years of a teaching life I have also seen much writing that was determined, wilful, hopeful and sure of success and confident to learn and progress from other writers I have encountered in my classes in Mozambique, Grenada and Sheffield, as well as east London. Yet I felt also that at the heart of my consciousness I was a literacy and literature teacher *because* of this poem and what lay behind it – and others thematically akin to it which I kept meeting along the way, up to the point of my work in the school of Fir Vale, Sheffield, where I found myself a headteacher and where a boy of the same age as the earlier poet, called Haneef, wrote, in 1995:

> One day I went to the fortune tellers'
> And I asked them, 'what's the future lying for Fir Vale?'
> There are going to be a few good fellers
> There are going to be a lot of drug sellers.
> A person in prison
> A person on bail
> Many school children are going to fail –
> That was the fortune tellers' tale.[2]

During these intervening decades, in my own country a welter of backward education legislation has built up a market system of education and a narrow, uniform and racist National Curriculum; yet also multiple technological development has created opportunities for 'hyperlearning' and such digital texts and networks that make possible the 'virtual communities' that would bring Nicaraguan broom-makers and rope pump manufacturers together with Australian workers and the sons and daughters of redundant Sheffield steelworkers. So I quote these two inner city verses, with two great cities and so many years between them, not to sow discouragement among readers and teachers but to mark a reminder that most young people in the schools of the world still struggle with pencil, pen and paper in 'technology-poor' situations, to make sense of a language which is a 'secondary discourse', often having their own first language, their 'primary discourse', deemed irrelevant (beyond an 'interference'), rubbished or ripped away from them as an expression of 'linguistic deprivation'.

In such contexts of official contempt for their own communities' cultures, languages and ways of learning, contexts of the educational alienation, distrust and demotivation being institutionalized within their schools, these students and many of their teachers still work towards giving full respect and value for both 'discourses' and the common objectives of learning for the betterment of all life and futures, for as Amber imagines:

> The school of the world is in the valley
> The school of the world has different cultures
> Its people have different languages
> Its people have different life stories
> The children all get along together in peace
> The school of the world has children that come
> From all different places in the world
> The school of the world is a friendly school
> The school of the world has taught me everything I know
> The school of the world has taught me how to love others[3]

Such young people in the hearts of our cities, believing with Farooq that

> if you want more of a life
> then build unity in the community![4]

still retain a faith in the teachers who reach them, and who in reaching them change them as they change themselves, for,

> Nothing can stop us knowing each other
> as day by day we increase our knowledge.
> Without the word *know*, the world is a disaster.[5]

These are wise words from Shahid, but he knows, as we know, it is not easy for the teacher as it is not easy for the student. The effects of 'fast capitalism' poison our language and bring coups on our curriculum, as *Changing*

Literacies shows us; they also threaten, at their most integral parts, the very structure and ethos of our schools. As an ex-headteacher, I was struck hard by Lankshear and Gee's joint-written chapter on this theme, expressing as it does the ugly truth of the blight of a new 'management culture' tyrannizing British schools and their organization. 'Enchanted workplaces' of 'performance indicators', 'benchmarking', 'quality assurance', 'total quality management', 'downsizing exercises' and the bald and ubiquitous 'value for money' criteria are all contributing to create a disenchanted workforce of teachers and a disaffected student body of whom thousands are being excluded from their schools and thousands more taking the way of truancy in every major city in Britain. When I was asked by OFSTED (Office for Standards in Education) inspectors how I saw my post, I naively did not realize it at the time but I virtually committed professional suicide by denying that I was essentially a manager and affirming that I was a 'teacher with extended responsibilities'. What an admission for a headteacher in mid-1990s Britain! – as I later discovered. And to assert, too, that the local community, democratic structures and the imagination were my three preferred tools for progress! 'No! You are not a teacher. You are a manager.' That was the riposte, spoken as if in absolute and unerring truth by the bearers of a new culture. But such 'enchantment' is a new slavery for teachers – who must now become the deliverers of pre-hashed and state-licensed curriculum, and certainly not the creators of shared knowledge and dialogue in the classroom, unless we create our own new literacies with our students and their communities which will break up this new hegemony of management control and culture that threatens to overcome our schools and crush the human future that they embrace.

But let us return to a literacy that itself struggles and overcomes, that in the words of Paulo Freire, teaches us: 'As humans relate to their world by responding to the challenges of the environment, they begin to dynamize . . . and to humanize reality. They add to it something of their own making . . . by creating culture.'⁶ And what else do they use beyond the tools of their language and literacy to make that extra, unique contribution, to forge that 'addition'? They use their imagination. For it is within the concept of imaginings, of empathies, of becoming the other, of creating newly-realized meanings through combinations of words and images that our students, the new 'meaning makers', take up the challenge of Freire and 'add something of their own making', thus creating culture in the classroom before our eyes and inside our minds.

Here are two examples of this process at work. In the first, 11-year-old Sarah looks around her at the waste ground, alleyways, sidewalks and playgrounds around her school and sees danger. She has heard how deadly diseases can be spread by the careless dropping of syringes by drug users. They are like venomous snakes on the rare earth and common tarmac of her inner city world. She wants to warn her schoolmates and neighbours, and by doing so she adds her voice and insight to their knowledge and vigilance by becoming the menace herself – and by an act of empathy humanizing the danger around her, creating a new moment of culture as a result:

The syringe

I am the syringe
that you find in the street.
I am the syringe
that attacks you on the waste ground.
I am the syringe
that pricks you and kills you.
I am the syringe
that you should stay away from!

I am like a live snake
that gives you a bite.
I am like a live wire
that gives you a shock.
Stay away!
Or else you will have
a very short time to live.

What does it feel like
When you leave your child
standing on the waste ground?
and I prick her?
What would you do
When your child is infected?
What would you do?[7]

A short time before Sarah wrote her poem, a local toddler had found a discarded syringe on a vacant plot and had lifted it to her mouth, while her horrified mother looked on, 20 yards away. The cautionary message of the poem, distributed and read widely in the school – and later published and recited at assemblies – became imprinted in the minds of students and community; in short, a part of the culture.

Wiel's poem which follows has a very specific context. In December 1995 the 13-year-old poet from a refugee family had just heard that his family home in Yemen, the house where he had grown to boyhood, had been torn down, razed to the ground, by government soldiers. At the same time, the British government was in the midst of introducing a draconian law against refugee families and asylum seekers in Britain. This Bill would not only make sanctuary in Britain much more precarious and difficult, but it would also remove essential benefits for the most vulnerable families: the rights to income support, housing benefit, and free school meals for the children of refugee and asylum-seeking families. In these times of his and his family's lives, Wiel took his poem, practised declaiming it with his cousin Shamsun, and together they performed it through a megaphone at a protest meeting against the Bill on the steps of the Sheffield Town Hall, calling out to the city's people, white and black, as they passed – and going beyond, bringing their imaged testimony to all the outcast children of the world. Wiel too had 'added something of his own making', seeking justice and making culture in the municipal heart of his adopted city.

Orphan of war

Yesterday my father was killed.
The day before yesterday, my mother.
Today I am an orphan.
I want to cry but I have no tears.
I am only a child.
I am only a child.
Someone please help me
I want to cry
I want to cry
I want to cry
       but I have no tears.
I want to live
I want to learn
I want a home.
       Where is my love?
       Where is my family?
This is my life
This is my future.
I am alone
       I want to cry.[8]

Changing Literacies has brought all this back to my mind. And it has shown me also how forces and modes of the new technology can change literacy positively, but how they can leave it immobile too – or even drag it backwards for the millions who need it most and who could grow and liberate their lives through its benefits. How, in Lankshear's own words to me in a letter, 'new means can maintain old inequalities', and how some 'new' work orders further entrench the exclusion of the already downtrodden. Hence the challenge to its readers, people like you and me.

Notes

1 Anonymous poem published in C. Searle (ed.) (1971) *Stepney Words*. London: Reality Press.
2 'Firvale', by Haneef Ur-Rehman, in C. Searle (ed.) (1995) *Heart of Sheffield*. Sheffield: Earl Marshal School.
3 'School of the World', by Amber Pearce, in C. Searle (ed.) (1994) *School of the World*. Sheffield: Earl Marshal School.
4 From 'Community of Understanding', by Ghulam Farooq, in *Heart of Sheffield* (op. cit.).
5 From 'Know', by Shahid Khan, in *School of the World* (op. cit.).
6 Freire, P. (1974) *Education for Critical Consciousness*. London: Sheed and Ward, 4–5.
7 'The Syringe', by Sarah Weatherall, in *Heart of Sheffield* (op. cit.).
8 Unpublished poem by Wiel Mohammed, Sheffield 1995.

REFERENCES

Abercrombie, N., Hill, S. and Turner, B. (1988) *The Penguin Dictionary of Sociology*, 2nd edn. Harmondsworth: Penguin Books.

Anderson, G. and Irvine, P. (1993) Informing critical literacy with ethnography, in C. Lankshear and P. McLaren (eds) *Critical Literacy: Politics, Praxis and the Postmodern*. Albany, NY: State University of New York Press, 81–104.

Angus, E. (1981) The awakening of a people: Nicaragua's literacy campaign, *Two Thirds*, 2(3): 6–32.

Apple, M. (1993) *Official Knowledge: Democratic Education in a Conservative Age*. New York: Routledge.

Apple, M. (1995) *Education and Power*, 2nd edn. New York: Routledge.

Apple, M. (1996) *Cultural Politics and Education*. New York: Teachers College Press.

Arnove, R. (1986) *Education and Revolution in Nicaragua*. New York: Praeger Press.

Atkinson, J. (1988) Recent changes in the internal labour market structure in the UK, in W. Buitelaar (ed.) *Technology at Work: Labour Studies in England, Germany and the Netherlands*. Aldershot: Avebury, 133–49.

The Australian (1996) The world's youngest web builder, 6 February.

Australian Reading Association (1993) *The Australian Journal of Language and Literacy*, 16, 4.

Baker, C. and Freebody, P. (1989) *Children's First Schoolbooks*. Oxford: Blackwell.

Baker, C. and Luke, A. (eds) (1991) *Towards a Critical Sociology of Reading Pedagogy*. Amsterdam: John Benjamins.

Balson, A. and Balson, S. (1996) Alex's Scribbles – Koala Trouble, http://www.peg.apc.org/˜balson/story

Balson, S./Global Web Builders (1996) Definitive Lifestyle Guide to Australian Webs, http://www.gwb.com.au/gwb/guide.html

Barndt, D. (1985) Popular education, in T. Walker (ed.) *Nicaragua: the First Five Years*. New York: Praeger Press, 317–46.

Bee, B. (1993) Critical literacy and gender, in C. Lankshear and P. McLaren (eds) *Critical Literacy: Politics, Praxis and the Postmodern*. Albany, NY: State University of New York Press, 105–32.

Bennett, T., Martin, G., Mercer, C. and Woollacott, J. (eds) (1981) *Culture, Ideology and Social Process*. London: Oxford University Press.

Bereiter, C. and Scardamalia, M. (1993) *Surpassing Ourselves: an Inquiry into the Nature and Implications of Expertise*. Chicago: Open Court.

Berlin, I. (1969) *Four Essays on Liberty*. London: Oxford University Press.

Best, M. (1990) *The New Competition: Institutions of Industrial Restructuring*. Cambridge, MA: Harvard University Press.

Bigum, C. and Green, B. (1992) Technologizing literacy: the dark side of the dream, *Discourse: the Australian Journal of Educational Studies*, 12(2): 4–28.

Booth, J. (1982) *The End and the Beginning: the Nicaraguan Revolution*. Boulder, CO: Westview Press.

Bourdieu, P. (1991) *Language and Symbolic Power*. Oxford: Oxford University Press.

Boyett, J. H. and Conn, H. P. (1992) *Workplace 2000: the Revolution Shaping American Business*. New York: Plume.

Branwyn, G. (1994) *Mosaic Quick Tour for Windows: Accessing and Navigating the Internet's World Wide Web*. Chapel Hill, NC: Ventana Press.

Braverman, H. (1974) *Labour and Monopoly Capitalism: the Degradation of Work in the Twentieth Century*. New York: Monthly Review Press.

Brookfield, S. (1986) *Understanding and Facilitating Adult Learning*. Milton Keynes: Open University Press.

Cardenal, F. and Miller, V. (1981) Nicaragua 1980: the battle of the ABCs, *Harvard Educational Review*, 51(1): 1–26.

Cardoso, F. H. (1993) North–South relations in the present context: a new dependency? in M. Carnoy, M. Castells, S. Cohen and F. H. Cardoso, *The New Global Economy in the Information Age: Reflections on Our Changing World*. University Park, PA: Pennsylvania State University Press, 149–59.

Carnoy, M., Castells, M., Cohen, S. and Cardoso, F. H. (1993) *The New Global Economy in the Information Age: Reflections on Our Changing World*. University Park, PA: Pennsylvania State University Press.

Carton, B. (1994) Students facing difficult job search, *Boston Globe*, 246(108) special supplement, 16 October: 1.

Castellino, R. (1992) Drought in Africa – again, *Red Cross Red Crescent*, September–December: 8–10.

Castells, M. (1993) The informational economy and the new international division of labour, in M. Carnoy, M. Castells, S. Cohen and F. H. Cardoso, *The New Global Economy in the Information Age: Reflections on Our Changing World*. University Park, PA: Pennsylvania State University Press, 15–43.

Cazden, C. (1979) Peekaboo as an instructional model: discourse development at home and at school, *Papers and Reports in Child Language Development*, 17: 1–29.

Chambers, J. (ed.) (1983) *Black English: Educational Equity and the Law*. Ann Arbor, MI: Karoma.

Chmiel, E. (1993) *HSC Digital Morph 1.1*. Palo Alto, CA: Pacific Coast Software.

Christopherson, S. and Storper, M. (1989) The effects of flexible specialization on industrial politics, *Industrial and Labor Relations Review*, 42(3): 331–47.

Clarke, J., Hall, S., Jefferson, T. and Roberts, B. (1981) Sub cultures, cultures and class, in T. Bennett, G. Martin, C. Mercer and J. Woollacott (eds) *Culture, Ideology and Social Process*. London: Oxford University Press, 53–79.

Cohen, D. (1987) Educational technology, policy, and practice, *Educational Evaluation and Policy Analysis*, 9(Summer): 153–70.

Cranston, M. (1953) *Freedom: a New Analysis*. London: Longmans Green.

Cuban, L. (1986) *Teachers and Machines: the Classroom Use of Technology since 1920*. New York: Teachers College Press.

Curriculum Corporation (1994) *A Statement on English for Australian Schools*. Carlton, Victoria: Curriculum Corporation.

Dale, R. (1991) Review of Andy Green, *Education and State Formation*, *Journal of Education Policy*, 6(4): 417–18.

Davis, R. (1980) Education for awareness: a talk with Paulo Freire, in R. Mackie (ed.) *Literacy and Revolution: the Pedagogy of Paulo Freire*. London: Writers and Readers, 57–69.

Delgado-Gaitan, C. (1990) *Literacy for Empowerment: the Role of Parents in Children's Education*. London: Falmer Press.

Delgado-Gaitan, C. and Trueba, H. (1991) *Crossing Cultural Borders: Education for Immigrant Families in America*. London: Falmer Press.

Department of Education, Queensland (1994) *English in Years 1 to 10 Syllabus Materials: Syllabus for Years 1 to 10*. Brisbane: Department of Education, Queensland.

Department of Education, Queensland (1995) *The Year 2 Diagnostic Net: Literacy Validation*, trial version. Brisbane: Studies Directorate, Department of Education, Queensland.

Department of Employment, Education and Training, Australia (DEET 1991a) *Australia's Language: the Australian Language and Literacy Policy*. Canberra: The Australian Government Publishing Service.

Department of Employment, Education and Training, Australia (DEET 1991b) *Australia's Language: the Australian Language and Literacy Policy – a Companion Volume to the Policy Paper*. Canberra: The Australian Government Publishing Service.

Dery, M. (ed.) (1994) *Flame Wars: the Discourse of Cyberculture*. Durham and London: Duke University Press.

Dibbell, J. (1994) A rape in cyberspace; or, how an evil clown, a Haitian trickster spirit, two wizards, and a cast of dozens turned a database into a society, in M. Dery (ed.) *Flame Wars: the Discourse of Cyberculture*. Durham and London: Duke University Press, 237–61.

Dorward, D. (1991) Famine: the economics and politics of the food crisis in Africa, *Current Affairs Bulletin*, December: 5–11.

Drucker, P. (1985) *Innovation and Entrepreneurship: Practice and Principles*. London: Heinemann.

Drucker, P. (1993) *Post-Capitalist Society*. New York: Harper.

Dyer, W. (1991) *Pulling Your Own Strings*. New York: Harper Collins.

Eades, D. (1993) Aboriginal English, *Pen 93*. Newtown, NSW: Primary English Teaching Association.

Edelsky, C. (1991) *With Literacy and Social Justice for All*. London: Falmer Press.

Ellsworth, E. (1989) Why doesn't this feel empowering? Working through the repressive myths of critical pedagogy, *Harvard Educational Review*, 59(3): 297–324.

Emmitt, M. and Pollock, J. (1991) *Language and Learning*. Melbourne: Oxford University Press.

Fairclough, N. (1989) *Language and Power*. London: Longman.

Fairclough, N. (ed.) (1992) *Critical Language Awareness*. Harlow: Longman.

Feinberg, J. (1973) *Social Philosophy*. Englewood Cliffs, NJ: Prentice Hall.

Feldman, L. (1993) *The American Encyclopedia (Electronic Version)*, compact disk. Danbury, CT: Grolier.

Fiske, J. (1989a) *Understanding Popular Culture*. London: Unwin Hyman.

Fiske, J. (1989b) *Reading the Popular*. London: Unwin Hyman.

Fiske, J., Hodge, B. and Turner, G. (1987) *Myths of Oz*. Sydney: Allen and Unwin.

Frasse, M. (1994) *The Windows Internet Tour Guide: Cruising the Internet the Easy Way*. Berkeley, CA: Ventana Press.

Freebody, P., Luke, A. and Gilbert, P. (1991) Reading positions and practices in the classroom, *Curriculum Inquiry*, 21: 435–58.

Freire, P. (1972) *Pedagogy of the Oppressed*. Harmondsworth: Penguin.

Freire, P. (1973) *Cultural Action for Freedom*. Harmondsworth: Penguin.

Freire, P. (1974) *Education for Critical Consciousness*. London: Sheed and Ward.

Freire, P. (1976) *Education: the Practice of Freedom*. London: Writers and Readers.

Freire, P. (1985) *The Politics of Education*. London: Macmillan.

Freire, P. and Macedo, D. (1987) *Literacy: Reading the Word and the World*. South Hadley, MA: Bergin and Garvey.

FSLN (1969, 1982) The historic program of the FSLN, in T. Borge *et al.* (eds) *Sandinistas Speak*. New York: Pathfinder Press, 13–22.

Galeano, E. (1973) *The Open Veins of Latin America*. New York: Monthly Review Press.

Gardner, H. (1991) *The Unschooled Mind: How Children Think and How Schools Should Teach*. New York: Basic Books.

Gee, J. P. (1990) *Social Linguistics and Literacies: Ideology in Discourses*. London: Falmer Press.

Gee, J. P. (1991) What is literacy? in C. Mitchell and K. Weiler (eds) *Rewriting Literacy: Culture and the Discourse of the Other*. New York: Bergin and Garvey, 1–11.

Gee, J. P. (1992) *The Social Mind: Language, Ideology, and Social Practice*. New York: Bergin and Garvey.

Gee, J. P. (1993a) Quality, science and the lifeworld: the alignment of business and education, *Critical Forum*, 2(3): 3–14.

Gee, J. P. (1993b) Postmodernism and literacies, in C. Lankshear and P. McLaren (eds) *Critical Literacy: Politics, Praxis and the Postmodern*. Albany, NY: State University of New York Press, 271–96.

Gee, J. P. (1993c) Literacies: tuning into forms of life, *Education Australia*, 19: 13–14.

Gee, J. P. (1994a) New alignments and old literacies: critical literacy, postmodernism and fast capitalism, in P. O'Connor (ed.) *Thinking Work*, vol. 1. Sydney: ALBSAC, 82–104.

Gee, J. P. (1994b) New alignments and old literacies: from fast capitalism to the canon, in B. Shortland-Jones, B. Bosich and J. Rivalland (eds) *Living Literacy:*

1994 Australian Reading Association Twentieth National Conference. Carlton South, Victoria: Australian Reading Association, 1–35.

Gee, J. P. (1996) *Social Linguistics and Literacies: Ideology in Discourses*, 2nd edn. London: Taylor and Francis.

Gee, J. P., Hull, G. and Lankshear, C. (1996) *The New Work Order: Behind the Language of the New Capitalism*. Sydney and Boulder, CO: Allen and Unwin and Westview Press.

Gilbert, P. (1989) *Writing, Schooling and Deconstruction: from Voice to Text in the Classroom*. London: Routledge.

Gilbert, P. (1993) (Sub)versions: using sexist language practices to explore critical literacy, *Australian Journal of Language and Literacy*, 16(4): 323–32.

Gilligan, C. (1982) *In a Different Voice*. Cambridge, MA: Harvard University Press.

Giroux, H. (1988) *Schooling and the Struggle for Public Life*. Minneapolis: University of Minnesota Press.

Giroux, H. (1993) Literacy and the politics of difference, in C. Lankshear and P. McLaren (eds) *Critical Literacy: Politics, Praxis and the Postmodern*. Albany, NY: State University of New York Press, 367–78.

Goldstein, C. and Heard, R. (1991) *Getting the Most out of AARNet*. Brisbane: Queensland University of Technology Computing Services.

Gowen, S. (1990) ' "Eyes on a different prize": a critical ethnography of a workplace literacy program', unpublished doctoral dissertation, Atlanta, GA: Georgia State University.

Grayling, A. (1988) *Wittgenstein*. Oxford: Oxford University Press.

Green, B. (1995) On compos(it)ing: writing differently in the post-age. A paper presented at the Annual National Conference of the Australian Association for the Teaching of English, Sydney: AATE.

Green, B. and Bigum, C. (1993) Aliens in the classroom, *Australian Journal of Education*, 37(2): 119–41.

Green, J. (1990) Reading is a social process, *Selected Papers from the 15th Australian Reading Association Conference*. Canberra: ARA, 104–23.

Green, J. and Meyer, L. (1991) The embeddedness of reading in classroom life, in C. Baker and A. Luke (eds) *Towards a Critical Sociology of Reading Pedagogy*. Amsterdam: John Benjamins, 141–60.

Gutiérrez, G. (1973) *A Theology of Liberation: History, Politics and Salvation*. Maryknoll, NY: Orbis Books.

Hahn, H. and Stout, R. (1994) *The Internet Yellow Pages*. Berkeley, CA: Osbourne McGraw-Hill.

Hammer, M. and Champy, J. (1993) *Reengineering the Corporation: a Manifesto for Business Revolution*. New York: Harper Business.

Hamilton, M., Barton, D. and Ivanic, R. (eds) (1994) *Worlds of Literacy*. Clevedon: Multilingual Matters.

Haraway, D. (1991) *Simians, Cyborgs and Women*. New York: Routledge.

Harris, K. (1979) *Education and Knowledge*. London: Routledge and Kegan Paul.

Hay, L. (1991) *The Power is Within You*. Carson, CA: Hay House.

Hayter, T. (1982) *The Creation of World Poverty*. London: Pluto Press.

Heath, S. B. (1982) What no bedtime story means: narrative skills at home and school, *Language and Society*, 11(1): 49–76.

Heath, S. B. (1983) *Ways With Words: Language, Life and Work in Communities and Classrooms.* Cambridge: Cambridge University Press.

Heim, M. (1993) *The Metaphysics of Virtual Reality.* New York: Oxford University Press.

Hirshon, S. (1982) *And Also Teach Them to Read.* Westport, CT: Lawrence Hill.

Hodas, S. (1993) Technology refusal and the organizational culture of schools, *Education Policy Analysis Archives,* 1(10): 1–19.

Howe, N. and Strauss, B. (1993) *13th Gen: Abort, Retry, Ignore, Fail?* New York: Vintage Books.

Hull, G. (1993) Hearing other voices: a critical assessment of popular views on literacy and work, *Harvard Educational Review,* 63(1): 20–49.

Hymes, D. (1972) Models of interactions of language and social life, in J. Gumperz and D. Hymes (eds) *Directions in Sociolinguistics: the Ethnography of Communication.* New York: Holt-Rinehart, 35–71.

Janks, H. (1993a) *Language and Position.* Johannesburg and Randburg: Witwatersrand University Press and Hodder and Stoughton Educational.

Janks, H. (1993b) *Language, Identity and Power.* Johannesburg and Randburg: Witwatersrand University Press and Hodder and Stoughton Educational.

Jones, A. (1986) 'At school I've got a chance: ideology and social reproduction in a secondary school', unpublished Ph.D. thesis, University of Auckland.

Jones, A. (1991) *'At School I've Got a Chance' – Culture/Privilege: Pacific Islands and Pakeha Girls at School.* Palmerston North: Dunmore Press.

Kantor, R., Green, J., Bradley, M. and Lin, L. (1992) The construction of schooled discourse repertoires: an interactional sociolinguistic perspective on learning to talk in preschool, *Linguistics and Education,* 4: 131–72.

Kirp, D. and Rice, D. (1988) Fast forward – styles of California management, *Harvard Business Review,* January–February, 74–83.

Knobel, M. (1993) Simon says 'see what I say': reader response and the teacher as meaning maker, *Australian Journal of Language and Literacy,* 16(4): 295–306.

Knobel, M. and Lankshear, C. (1995) *Learning Genres: Prospects for Empowerment.* Brisbane: National Language and Literacy Institute of Australia Ltd, Child/ESL Literacy Network Node (Queensland).

Knorr Cetina, K. (1992) The couch, the cathedral, and the laboratory: on the relationship between experiment and laboratory, in science, in A. Pickering (ed.) *Science as Practice and Culture.* Chicago: University of Chicago Press, 113–37.

Krashen, S. (1982) *Principles and Practice in Second Language Acquisition.* Hayward, CA: Alemany Press.

Krashen, S. (1985) *Inquiries and Insights.* Hayward, CA: Alemany Press.

Kress, G. (1985) *Linguistic Processes in Sociocultural Practice.* Geelong: Deakin University Press.

Kress, G. (1988a) Language as social practice, in G. Kress (ed.) *Communication and Culture.* Kensington, NSW: University of New South Wales Press, 82–104.

Kress, G. (ed.) (1988b) *Communication and Culture.* Kensington, NSW: University of New South Wales Press.

Kumazawa, M. and Yamada, J. (1989) Jobs and skills under the lifelong Nenko employment practice, in S. Wood (ed.) *The Transformation of Work?* London: Unwin Hyman, 102–26.

Kurland, D. (1996) *The 'Net, the Web, and You.* Belmont: Wadsworth Publishing.

Landow, G. (ed.) (1994) *Hyper/Text/Theory.* Baltimore and London: Johns Hopkins University Press.

Lanham, R. (1993) *The Electronic Word: Democracy, Technology and the Arts.* Chicago and London: University of Chicago Press.

Lankshear, C. (1982) *Freedom and Education.* Auckland: Milton Brookes.

Lankshear, C. (1991) Literacy and running your life: a Nicaraguan example, *Language and Education*, 5(2): 95–112.

Lankshear, C. (1992) Critical literacy and active citizenship. A paper presented to the Working Conference on Critical Literacy, Brisbane: Griffith University, July.

Lankshear, C. (1994a) *Critical Literacy.* Belconnen, ACT: Australian Curriculum Studies Association.

Lankshear, C. (1994b) Afterword, in M. Escobar *et al.* with Paulo Freire, *Paulo Freire on Higher Education.* Albany, NY: State University of New York Press, 161–87.

Lankshear, C. and Knobel, M. (in press) Critical literacy and active citizenship, in P. Freebody, S. Muspratt and A. Luke (eds) *Constructing Critical Literacies.* Norwood, NJ: Hampton Press; Sydney: Allen and Unwin.

Lankshear, C. and Lawler, M. (1989) *Literacy, Schooling and Revolution.* London: Falmer Press.

Lankshear, C. and McLaren, P. (eds) (1993) *Critical Literacy: Politics, Praxis and the Postmodern.* Albany, NY: State University of New York Press.

Lankshear, C., Peters, M. and Knobel, M. (1996) Critical pedagogy and cyberspace, in H. Giroux, C. Lankshear, P. McLaren and M. Peters, *Counternarratives.* New York: Routledge, 149–88.

Latour, B. (1987) *Science in Action.* Cambridge, MA: Harvard University Press.

Latour, B. (1994) On technical mediation – philosophy, sociology, genealogy, *Common Knowledge*, 3(2): 29–64.

Lave, J. (1988) *Cognition in Practice: Mind, Mathematics and Culture in Everyday Life.* Cambridge: Cambridge University Press.

Lave, J. and Wenger, E. (1991) *Situated Learning: Legitimate Peripheral Participation.* New York: Cambridge University Press.

LeCompte, M. and deMarrais, K. B. (1992) The disempowering of empowerment: from social revolution to classroom rhetoric, *Educational Foundations*, 6(3): 5–33.

Lemke, J. (1995) *Textual Politics: Discourse and Social Dynamics.* London: Taylor and Francis.

Levett, A. and Lankshear, C. (1994) Literacies, workplaces and the demands of new times, in M. Brown (ed.) *Literacies and the Workplace: a Collection of Original Essays.* Geelong: Deakin University Press, 25–54.

Lewontin, R. C. (1991) *Biology as Ideology: the Doctrine of DNA.* New York: Harper.

Luke, A. (1988) *Literacy, Textbooks and Ideology: Postwar Literacy Instruction and the Mythology of Dick and Jane.* London: Falmer Press.

Luke, A. (1992) Conference materials. Working Conference on Critical Literacy, Brisbane: Griffith University, July.

Luke, A. (1993a) Shaping literacy in schools: an introduction, in L. Unsworth (ed.)

Literacy Learning and Teaching: Language as Social Practice in the Primary School. Melbourne: Macmillan, 3–53.

Luke, A. (1993b) *The Social Construction of Literacy in the Primary School.* Melbourne: Macmillan Education Australia.

Luke, A. and Walton, C. (1994) Teaching and assessing critical reading, in T. Husén and T. Postlethwaite (eds) *International Encyclopedia of Education*, 2nd edn. Oxford: Pergamon Press, 1194–8.

MacCallum, G. (1967) Negative and positive freedom, *Philosophical Review*, 76: 312–34.

Malcolm, I. (1992) Communicative dysfunction in the Aboriginal classroom, in J. Sherwood (ed.) *Aboriginal Education: Issues and Innovations.* Perth: Creative Research.

Malinowski, B. (1944) *A Scientific Theory of Culture.* Oxford: Oxford University Press.

Mann, M. (ed.) (1983) *The Macmillan Student Encyclopedia of Sociology.* London: Macmillan.

Martin, J. (1985) *Factual Writing: Exploring and Challenging Social Reality.* Geelong: Deakin University Press.

Marx, K. (1970) *Capital*, vol. 1. Moscow: Progress Publishers.

McIntosh, T. (1995) PC ownership up as gap between 'rich' and 'poor' widens, *The Australian*, 21 March: 45.

McLaren, P. (1989) *Life in Schools: an Introduction to Critical Pedagogy in the Foundations of Education.* New York: Longman.

McLaren, P. (1993) Multiculturalism and the postmodern critique, *Cultural Studies*, 7(1): 118–46.

McLaren, P. (1995) *Critical Pedagogy and Predatory Culture.* New York and London: Routledge.

Miller, V. (1985) *Between Struggle and Hope: the Nicaraguan Literacy Crusade.* Boulder, CO: Westview Press.

Mills, C. Wright (1959) *The Sociological Imagination.* New York: Oxford University Press.

Morgan, W. (1992) *A Poststructuralist English Classroom: the Example of Ned Kelly.* Melbourne: Victorian Association for the Teaching of English.

Nash, R. (1993) *Succeeding Generations: Family Resources and Access to Education in New Zealand.* Auckland: Oxford University Press.

New London Group (1996) A pedagogy of multiliteracies: designing social futures, *Harvard Educational Review*, 66(1): 60–92.

Oakley, K. (1954) Skill as a human possession, in C. Singer *et al.* (eds) *A History of Technology*, vol. 1. Oxford: Clarendon Press, 1–31.

O'Connor, P. (1994) Crossing the borders of workers' literacy, *Focus 3.* Sydney: ALBSAC.

Okerson, A. (1994) Oh Lord, won't you buy me a Mercedes Benz, or, is there a there there? in *Surfaces*, 4: 4–13.

Papert, S. (1993) *The Children's Machine: Rethinking School in the Age of the Computer.* New York: Basic Books.

Parker, R. E. (1994) *Flesh Peddlers and Warm Bodies: the Temporary Help Industry and its Workers.* New Brunswick, NJ: Rutgers University Press.

Perelman, L. (1992) *School's Out: the New Technology and the End of Education*. New York: Morrow.

Perkins, D. (1992) *Smart Schools: from Training Memories to Educating Minds*. New York: Free Press.

Peters, M. and Lankshear, C. (1994) Education and hermeneutics: a Freirean interpretation, in P. McLaren and C. Lankshear (eds) *The Politics of Liberation: Paths from Freire*. London: Routledge, 173–92.

Peters, M. and Lankshear, C. (1996) Critical literacy in cyberspace, *Educational Theory*, 46(1): 51–70.

Peters, T. (1992) *Liberation Management: Necessary Disorganization for the Nanosecond Nineties*. New York: Fawcett.

Peters, T. (1994) *The Tom Peters Seminar: Crazy Times Call for Crazy Organizations*. New York: Vintage Books.

Piskurich, G. (1993) *Self-Directed Learning*. San Francisco, CA: Jossey-Bass.

Pollert, A. (1987) The flexible firm: a model in search of reality, *Warwick Papers in Industrial Relations* 19. Coventry: University of Warwick.

Reich, R. (1992) *The Work of Nations*. New York: Vintage Books.

Rockhill, K. (1993) (Dis)connecting literacy and sexuality: speaking the unspeakable in the classroom, in C. Lankshear and P. McLaren (eds) *Critical Literacy: Politics, Praxis and the Postmodern*. Albany, NY: State University of New York Press, 335–66.

Rogoff, B. (1990) *Apprenticeship in Thinking*. New York: Oxford University Press.

Rucker, R., Sirius, R. U. and Queen Mu (1992) *Mondo 2000: a User's Guide to the New Edge*. London: Thames and Hudson.

Rushkoff, D. (ed.) (1994) *The GenX Reader*. New York: Ballantine Books.

Santa Barbara Classroom Discourse Group (1995) Event mapping. Santa Barbara: University of Santa Barbara Graduate School of Education (mimeo).

Searle, C. (1984) *Words Unchained: Language and Revolution in Grenada*. London: Zed Press.

Searle, C. (1993a) Words to a life-land: literacy, the imagination and Palestine, in C. Lankshear and P. McLaren (eds) *Critical Literacy: Politics, Praxis and the Postmodern*. Albany, NY: State University of New York Press, 167–92.

Searle, C. (ed.) (1993b) *Lives of Love and Hope: a Sheffield Herstory*. Sheffield: Earl Marshal School.

Searle, C. (ed.) (1994) *School of the World*. Sheffield: Earl Marshal School.

Searle, C. (ed.) (1995) *Heart of Sheffield*. Sheffield: Earl Marshal School.

Searle, J. (1990) The storm over the university, *New York Review of Books*, 6 December: 34–42.

Senge, P. M. (1991) *The Fifth Discipline: the Art and Practice of the Learning Organization*. New York: Doubleday.

Senge, P. M., Roberts, C., Ross, R. B., Smith, B. J. and Kleiner, A. (1994) *The Fifth-Discipline Fieldbook: Strategies and Tools for Building a Learning Organization*. New York: Doubleday.

Sharples, O. (1988) *Kura Kaupapa Maori: Recommendations for Policy Development*. Auckland: University of Auckland.

Shor, I. (1980) *Critical Teaching and Everyday Life*. Boston, MA: South End Press.

Shor, I. (1992) *Empowering Education: Critical Teaching for Social Change.* Chicago: University of Chicago Press.

Shor, I. (1993) Education is politics: Paulo Freire's critical pedagogy, in P. McLaren and P. Leonard (eds) *Paulo Freire: a Critical Encounter.* London: Routledge, 25–35.

Shor, I. and Freire, P. (1987) *A Pedagogy for Liberation: Dialogues on Transforming Education.* South Hadley, MA: Bergin and Garvey.

Smith, G. (1990) The politics of reforming Maori education: the transforming potential of Kura Kaupapa Maori, in H. Lauder and C. Wylie (eds) *Towards Successful Schooling.* London: Falmer Press, 73–88.

Stein, L. (1988) Famine in Ethiopia, *Quadrant*, 32(3): 8–13.

Stone, A. (1991) Will the real body please stand up? Boundary stories about virtual cultures, in M. Benedikt (ed.) *Cyberspace: First Steps.* Cambridge, MA: MIT Press, 81–119.

Street, B. (1984) *Literacy in Theory and Practice.* Cambridge: Cambridge University Press.

Street, B. (ed.) (1993) *Cross-Cultural Approaches to Literacy.* Cambridge: Cambridge University Press.

Taylor, M. and Saarinen, E. (1994) *Imagologies: Media Philosophy.* London: Routledge.

Thurow, L. (1992) *Head to Head: the Coming Economic Battle Among Japan, Europe and America.* New York: Morrow.

Torres, R.-M. (1983) *La Post Alfabetización en Nicaragua.* Managua: INIES.

Torres, R.-M. (1985) *Nicaragua: Revolución Popular.* Managua: CRIES-INIES.

Torres, R.-M. (1986) *Los CEP: Educación Popular y Democracia Participativa en Nicaragua.* Managua: CRIES-INIES.

Trudgill, P. (1983) *Sociolinguistics.* Harmondsworth: Penguin.

Wallace, C. (1992) Critical language awareness in the EFL classroom, in N. Fairclough (ed.) *Critical Language Awareness.* Harlow: Longman, 59–92.

Wark, M. (1995) Suck on this, planet of noise, in S. Penny (ed.) *Critical Issues in Electronic Media.* Albany, NY: State University of New York Press, 7–25.

Weissberg, A. (1982) *Nicaragua: an Introduction to the Sandinista Revolution.* New York: Pathfinder Press.

Wells, G. (1987) *The Meaning Makers: Children Learning Language and Using Language to Learn.* London: Hodder and Stoughton.

Wertsch, J. (1991) *Voices of the Mind: a Sociocultural Approach to Mediated Action.* Cambridge, MA: Harvard University Press.

White, E. (1994). Glossary, in M. Dery (ed.) *Flame Wars: the Discourse of Cyberculture.* Durham and London: Duke University Press, 321–5.

Wiggenhorn, W. (1990) 'Motorola U': when training becomes an education, *Harvard Business Review*, August: 71–88.

Winters, K. (1996) America's technology literacy challenge, US Department of Education Office of the Under Secretary, kwinters@inet.ed.gov, posted on acw-l@unicorn.acs.ttu.edu 17 February.

Wittgenstein, L. (1953) *Philosophical Investigations.* Oxford: Basil Blackwell.

INDEX

THE TEXTS OF PAULO FREIRE

Paul V. Taylor

Paulo Freire can be numbered among the few, great educators this century. His classroom is the world of the oppressed: his subject is the literacy of liberation.

This volume provides a (re)introduction to Freire. The first part is a fresh, biographical sketch of his life, the context within which he worked and the texts which he has produced. The second part uncovers the genius of his eclecticism and discovers that, contrary to the myth, his revolutionary method is more a radical reinvention of classical pedagogy.

This sets the scene for a review and questioning of Freire's method and of his philosophy of contradiction. There is then a critical examination of his view of literacy through a close reading of the teaching material on which his successful method is based.

The concluding section attempts to reconstruct a practice of literacy, illustrating the importance of Freire's pedagogy of questioning for all those who are working in the field of literacy today.

Contents
Introduction: The textualizing and contextualizing of Freire – A biographical sketch – Backgrounds and borrowings: a review of selected sources and influences – Education and liberation: the means and ends of Dialogue and Conscientization – The 'Método Paulo Freire': generative words and generating literacy – Generating literacy: decoding Freire's ten learning situations – A reconstruction of literacy – Conclusion – Notes – Bibliographies – Index.

176pp   0 335 19019 7 (Paperback)   0 335 19020 0 (Hardback)